The House
of
Dimon

*How JPMorgan's
Jamie Dimon Rose to the Top
of the Financial World*

Patricia Crisafulli

WILEY
John Wiley & Sons, Inc.

Published by John Wiley & Sons, Inc., Hoboken, New Jersey.
Published simultaneously in Canada.

For general information on our other products and services or for technical support, please
contact our Customer Care Department within the United States at (800) 762-2974,
outside the United States at (317) 572-3993 or fax (317) 572-4002.

Wiley also publishes its books in a variety of electronic formats. Some content that appears
in print may not be available in electronic books. For more information about Wiley
products, visit our web site at www.wiley.com.

Library of Congress Cataloging-in-Publication Data:

Crisafulli, Patricia.
    The house of Dimon : how JPMorgan's Jamie Dimon rose to the top of the financial
world / Patricia Crisafulli.
       p. cm.
    Includes bibliographical references and index.
    ISBN 978-0-470-41296-1 (cloth)
       1. Dimon, Jamie.   2. Capitalists and financiers—United States—Biography.
3. J.P. Morgan Chase & Co.   I. Title.
   HG172.D495C75 2009
   332.1092—dc22
[B]   2008052153

Printed in the United States of America

10 9 8 7 6 5 4 3 2 1

In memory of my father, Patrick B. Crisafulli, who taught me the difference between "the fast nickel and the slow dime"
1918–2006

From everyone who has been given much, much will be demanded; and from the one who has been entrusted with much, much more will be asked.
—LUKE 12:47-49 (NEW INTERNATIONAL VERSION)

I tell people there is a book on every single one of you. If I want to know you, all I have to do is talk to people who work with you and for you, clients, counterparts at other firms, friends, and relatives. . . . I will know you . . . much better than you think; in fact, maybe even better than if I spent an hour with you or two. . . . There is a book on everybody, and part of it is to try to make sure you figure out that book.
—JAMIE DIMON, OCTOBER 2002 SPEECH
NORTHWESTERN UNIVERSITY, KELLOGG SCHOOL OF MANAGEMENT
EXECUTIVE MASTER'S PROGRAM

Contents

Part Two: The Making of a Wall Street Leader

Part Three: Weathering the Storm

Preface

We would not seek a battle as we are, Nor, as we are, we say we will not shun it.

—WILLIAM SHAKESPEARE, *HENRY V*, ACT III.6

The stock market was an outrageous place in 2008: a plunge that wiped out years of gains in market capitalization and trillions of dollars of stock market wealth for investors and professionals alike. Amid the wreckage, the deadliest toll has been in the financial sector, with the demise of the weakest companies and body blows suffered by even the strongest. As a recession—at first feared and then declared a certainty—gripped the United States and started to spread globally, Wall Street became a dire place: profits dwindling, losses mounting, and thousands of jobs slashed.

This is not a typical backdrop for a business book, in what is arguably the darkest hour in U.S. financial history since the Great Depression. And yet, these are the times that face us. No one gets to choose when or how such times will occur; certainly if there were any choice in the matter it would be to avoid them altogether. The only way to survive the assault is by facing it head-on, embracing the reality of just how bad it is and how much worse it could possibly get.

To paraphrase Thomas Paine, these are the times that try one's soul. Yet these are the very same times that define one's leadership: not in the midst of all that goes well, but in the worst of all possible scenarios. Here is the real proving ground for those who will survive.

The market is rife with dramatic themes: of bloody battles, agonizing losses, crushing defeats, and, for some, the potential for victory. No one will emerge unscarred from the Shakespearean tragedy that is the financial crisis of 2007–2008. Yet some players stand to gain more (or at least to lose less) than others in an industry that has suffered at its own hands: the aftermath of taking on risks that proved to be not only unwise but untenable.

As with most good stories, this one continues to unfold. Indeed, the challenge of writing this book has been to find the place where it at least pauses for a moment. With no clear end in sight, nor the ability to pronounce with even the slightest certainty how it will turn out, the story of the rise of Jamie Dimon to the top of Wall Street (albeit a beleaguered place these days) provides lessons for today and as we head into an uncertain tomorrow.

Within the financial crisis drama, Dimon has been a central character as he has taken on not one, but two, acquisitions of failed or failing firms. He and his team have managed to do this—although not without significant difficulties and challenges—because of his leadership style that focuses on preparedness above all. Thus in *The House of Dimon* we look at not only the current tumultuous events, but the developments that have brought Dimon—and JPMorgan Chase—to this moment in time.

Act I of Dimon's career begins with a man born to the financial industry: the son and grandson of stockbrokers, and the protégé of Sandy Weill, with whom Dimon helped to build what eventually became Citigroup. Act I comes to a dramatic climax with Dimon's firing from Citigroup, a move that stunned him as well as the marketplace. Act II opens with Dimon's reemergence from an 18-month hiatus as the CEO of Bank One, which was in need of strong leadership and a turnaround. Then came the sale of Bank One to JPMorgan Chase and Dimon's ascent to the top executive spot at the financial institution named for legendary financier J. Pierpont Morgan. The real drama of Act II still rages with a credit crisis that has spared no one, not even the strongest. If Dimon's past is at all predictive of his future, however, he will emerge from this stronger perhaps and, as a student of history, undoubtedly wiser from the lessons learned.

James Dimon, known the world over as Jamie, has made his mark on JPMorgan, itself a legendary firm. For that reason the company he leads as a hands-on, full-accountability executive is the House of Dimon, reflective of his leadership style and management vision. The success of the firm is intertwined with his own and is largely dependent upon the ability of Dimon and his team to navigate through the worst of this storm and make it, one expects, to the other side.

—TRICIA CRISAFULLI

Author's Note: The company name appears through much of the manuscript as JPMorgan Chase, in keeping with the firm's own style, or shortened to JPMorgan. When referring to the firm in the past, particularly prior to its merger with Chase, the name J.P. Morgan & Company is used. In addition, some news organizations, which are quoted herein, refer to the company as J.P. Morgan Chase. The author has attempted to use the company name consistently while respecting these preferences, and apologizes for any inadvertent confusion.

Acknowledgments

Special thanks to my husband, Joe Tulacz, for your love, support, and understanding. Being married to a writer—especially one on deadline—is not easy.

To my son, Pat, for your sense of humor and for making me laugh (especially at myself). Watching you grow up is pure joy.

To Susan and Steve Dolan; thank you for your enthusiasm and feedback. What a joy to have neighbors who are not just good friends, but also good readers!

To my sisters, Bernadette Crisafulli and Jeannie Zastawny, and my brother-in-law, Ben Zastawny; thank you for your love and prayers. And for my niece, Stephanie Crisafulli, who is an inspiration.

To supportive friends too numerous to mention, especially Janie Gabbett, Margaret McSweeney, Leslie Levine, and Debi Spellman; to Rich Green, my UBS stockbroker and friend; and Fari Hamzei of Hamzei Analytics, dear friend and wise adviser. Thank you all for cheering me on.

To my editor at John Wiley & Sons, Kevin Commins, who championed this book from the first conversation, and coached and encouraged me at every step. Thank you for your faith in me. Thanks to

Meg Freeborn, development editor, for the time and care taken with this manuscript. And thanks to Mary Daniello, senior production editor, and the entire Wiley team.

To my agent, Doris S. Michaels, at DSM Literary Agency, and Delia Berrigan Fakis, director of development at DSM. A huge thank-you for so many, many things. What a journey we're having together!

Thanks to Joseph Evangelisti of JPMorgan Chase for arranging interviews and fielding questions. And to the many people who agreed to be interviewed and graciously gave of their time, thank you; without you, this book would not have been possible.

Part One

IN THE EYE OF
THE STORM

I think you're going to be writing and learning from this for years: cases and books about different things from SIVs to accounting to the business purpose of CDO-squareds to regulatory rules to globalization to the balkanization of regulation. . . . Honestly, I think if you made a list today, you probably wouldn't get half of them. We're in the thick of it.

—Jamie Dimon

Chapter 1

The Dimon Way

When you are running an institution . . . you are only one piece of it. I feel like I'm riding a bronco and hanging on for dear life.
— JAMIE DIMON, SPEECH BEFORE THE YALE CEO SUMMIT

On yet another bloody day on Wall Street in early October 2008, the carnage glowed red on financial news screens as the Dow Jones Industrial Average plunged to even lower levels in one of the worst weeks in its history. With an hour and a half to go before the market closed, when it would achieve the dubious distinction of the Dow settling below 9,000 for the first time in five years, Jamie Dimon stepped out of his office on the executive floor of the JPMorgan Chase building on Park Avenue in the heart of Manhattan and led the way to a conference room. In his shirtsleeves, but his blue tie still on, Dimon had worked up to the minute of a scheduled interview. The once-crisp white shirt he wore looked a bit rumpled from an already long day that had started very early.

Sitting at the far end of the table, Dimon spread out two pieces of paper in front of him: one a memo with a list of topics to be discussed, and the other his trademark 8½ × 11 sheet on which he keeps track of any number of things—especially information that people owe him. His intense blue eyes focused, Dimon glanced at the two pages and then turned to the business at hand: a discussion in the midst of one of Wall Street's most tumultuous times.

"I used to make a joke that my daughter called up and she asked, 'Dad, what is this crisis about?'" Dimon commented, repeating a story that appears in his letter to shareholders in the 2007 JPMorgan Chase annual report, which is dated March 2008.

As the story in the chairman's letter goes, Dimon answered her by saying, "It's something that happens every five to ten years." Dimon's daughter—one of three, who range in age from late teens to midtwenties—replied, "So why is everyone so surprised?"

Repeating the story seven months after the chairman's letter appeared Dimon had a different punch line. "I used to say, 'It's normal. Why are people surprised?' I can't say that any more, because it's gone beyond the normal every six- or seven-year convulsion."

The credit crisis of 2007 turned into the cataclysm of 2008, creating mounting worries over the stability of the entire financial system. Question marks have hovered over names that were once sacrosanct as Merrill Lynch was sold, Lehman Brothers went bankrupt, and other players such as Goldman Sachs and Morgan Stanley sought capital infusions from strategic investors. An economy in recession raised the specter of increasing unemployment, which would lead to further losses in bank loan portfolios and charge-offs for credit card delinquencies. For Wall Street executives such challenges have become the daily reality.

Dimon shuffled the two pages in front of him, revealing a glimpse of the 8½ × 11 sheet that was covered with dozens of little rectangles in blue ink: follow-ups and to-do reminders that had been written down and then thoroughly crossed out. What could be behind all those inked-in boxes on the sheet of white paper, which bore the deep creases of having been folded and carried around in a shirt pocket? Perhaps calls made to or from Henry Paulson, who was Treasury Secretary at the time, or Federal Reserve Chairman Ben Bernanke to discuss the latest developments in the financial crisis that had engulfed Wall Street firms, creating risk and uncertainty for even the strongest players. Maybe progress reports on the integration of two major acquisitions that JPMorgan had undertaken in the past six months: first, the stunning $1.2 billion rescue/takeover of beleaguered investment bank

Bear Stearns in March 2008, and then, in late September, the $1.9 billion purchase of failed thrift institution Washington Mutual (WaMu), which had been JPMorgan's number one acquisition target. Or maybe the status of markdowns on mortgage trading positions and leveraged loans, and higher credit costs in home lending—which, as the bank would announce a week later, had resulted in a precipitous drop in profits for the third quarter of 2008.

No doubt there was much on Dimon's 8½ × 11 paper and on his mind. What had started out as a decline in housing prices and mounting losses in subprime loans had spread like a pandemic flu outbreak throughout the global financial services industry. By October 2008, worries about the credit risks posed by other players were causing banks to balk at lending overnight to each other. As the credit market froze, liquidity needed by businesses slowed to a trickle. A controversial $700 billion rescue package sold hard by Secretary Paulson and passed by a white-knuckled Congress that feared catastrophe if no action was taken had done little in its early days to ease the crisis and stop the bleeding in the stock market.

While not unscathed from subprime and loan issues, JPMorgan has fared comparatively well. The bank actually grew during the credit crisis, thanks to the two acquisitions: the Bear Stearns rescue deal that was orchestrated by the federal government and the purchase of Washington Mutual from the Federal Deposit Insurance Corporation (FDIC) after WaMu became the largest U.S. bank failure in history.

JPMorgan is among the industry's leading banks, along with Bank of America, Wells Fargo, and Citigroup. Of the four, Citigroup has been seen as the shakiest, after posting multiple quarters of losses. By January 2009, questions were also raised about the health of Bank of America. In early October 2008, however, the four were among the banks about to get a boost in capital from what was once seen as a highly unlikely source: the U.S. government. Just days after Dimon sat in the JPMorgan conference room, he would be one of several top-level banking executives who gathered around a different table in Washington for a meeting called by Secretary Paulson. At that meeting, the Treasury secretary would unveil a plan for the government to make equity investments in several banks, including JPMorgan, in return for preferred securities as part of the $700 billion plan to bolster the financial services industry. For the banks it was an offer they couldn't refuse.

JPMorgan didn't need the capital injection. After buying WaMu in late September 2008, the bank raised $11 billion in a common stock offering. In a December 2008 interview with CNBC, Dimon said JPMorgan "didn't ask for it, didn't want it, didn't need it," referring to the government's investment. However, the government had asked nine banks to take cash infusions—quite possibly to avoid attaching a stigma to any one player or singling out a party that needed the capital more than the others.[1]

Although JPMorgan hadn't sought the government's cash, when operating in the cyclical banking business in the middle of a maelstrom, there is nothing as comforting as a capital cushion. Additional capital would result in an even greater ability to withstand a recession (which Dimon had been warning about for months) and would provide protection should matters go from bad to worse—and maybe even to severe.

By late 2008, Dimon's warnings appeared to be realized, as the stock market took a pummeling on recession worries and the need for yet another bailout—this time in the U.S. auto industry. JPMorgan shares tumbled as investors got out of the stocks of major banks, falling in late November to a six-year low below $20 a share, far from its recent 52-week high of over $50 a share. JPMorgan stock was also hit by news that it was cutting thousands of jobs in its investment banking division, as other firms were making similar (and in the case of Citigroup far more drastic) staff reductions.

Although JPMorgan Chase continues to face challenges from the financial crisis, it has translated operating strengths into strategy: gathering intelligence and sharing information across separate business lines and drilling deeply to identify risks and uncover potential problems. This management philosophy was probably reflected in a dozen different ways on Dimon's 8½ × 11 sheet of paper.

"The way he walks around with a sheet of paper with 50 bullet points on it in his front pocket," board member David Novak commented. "He writes something down; that gets done; he blocks it out. He's not only capable, he does the strategy and the execution as well as anybody. . . . For example, in the investment banking arena the numbers are so huge it would be very easy to do the chairman thing [of expecting others to know the numbers]. Jamie digs in there deep."

Dimon takes a detailed view of the business from the CEO level, although he sits many layers above the front line of operations. "Three of his greatest characteristics are he's really smart, he has tremendous energy, and he'll get into the details with anybody on anything. Most people who get to the level that he is at are prone to be superficial when it comes to running the business; they don't have enough time or energy to get into the details," observed Harvard Business School professor Paul Marshall.

Dimon admitted to being "a little nerdy" when it comes to getting into the details. "I don't always do it, but I like to do it in some cases. I have to decide when to do it." While he can dig into the minutiae when necessary and quickly discard what isn't worth focusing on, associates say he's not a micromanager. For one thing, JPMorgan Chase is simply too big. Instead, Dimon empowers executives and managers with a high degree of trust and accountability, with expectations that this will be transmitted through the ranks of the organization.

No matter how excellent the team, Dimon still takes the hands-on approach of a real numbers guy who is capable of doing analysis in his head, combined with the intuitive, gut-level sense of someone who grew up in the financial markets going back to the days when he worked summers in a brokerage office with his father and grandfather. The bold lettering in the lobby downstairs may read JPMorgan Chase, but make no mistake: This is the House of Dimon.

Running the House of Dimon

Dimon is at the helm of a financial institution that boasts a legacy dating back more than two centuries and entwined with names like Rockefeller, J. Pierpont Morgan, and Aaron Burr, who founded the first predecessor bank in 1799. Burr, who was vice president under Thomas Jefferson, is well known for the infamous duel in which Alexander Hamilton, the first Treasury secretary, was mortally wounded. Replicas of the famous pistols are displayed in the JPMorgan lobby, while the originals—curious icons of the bank's storied past—are displayed on the executive floor.

The firm may be steeped in history, but today when someone says "JPMorgan Chase," it is Dimon's face that comes to mind. The 52-year-old chairman with the youthful face and gray hair seems to be every-where these days, on magazine covers, in numerous newspaper articles, in testimony before Congress on the financial crisis, and in television interviews. He has emerged as the man of the moment in the financial services industry by completing deals that rescued failed or failing insti-tutions, and has earned respect as a Wall Street statesman. His name was even circulated in the media as being on Barack Obama's short list of potential nominees for Treasury secretary.

Dimon has reached a pinnacle on Wall Street at a time when the quality of leadership is being questioned. Although he is the frequent target of praise and kudos—including a "Legend in Leadership Award" from the Yale School of Management Chief Executive Leadership Institute in December 2008—Dimon does not seek out the spotlight, perhaps fearing that a misstep or mistake in these treacherous times is inevitable for anyone. As he told CNBC, "The pedestal is a terrible place to be. . . . I almost want to get knocked off the pedestal so I don't have to hear this anymore."[2]

Further, as he commented in his remarks at the Yale CEO summit, "If you all knew the truth—how many problems and mistakes we have, and mistakes I've made. . . ."[3]

It is these characteristics—the continual focus on what is or could be wrong, owning up to mistakes, and constantly identifying and managing risks—that make Dimon a leader. He has also demonstrated the willing-ness to be the bearer of bad news, no matter what the impact might be on the bank's stock in the short term, in the interest of full disclosure to all parties—from board members to employees to analysts to investors. In the CNBC interview, he warned about the prospects for "a tough '09," adding, "It's all going to be unemployment driven. . . . Unemployment will drive commercial losses, real estate losses, all consumer product losses. They'll follow the unemployment trend. If we're lucky, it will have two more quarters of this and we'll start to see a recovery. . . . It's possible it's going to get worse and we're in for a tougher time."

In the same breath as the warning came Dimon's assurance. "As a business, we have to be prepared. We can't run that business saying, well, if it doesn't get better, we're in deep trouble. We have to run the busi-ness saying we can handle whatever the environment is going to be out there."[4]

If there is any praise at all, Dimon would rather it be directed toward his team, which is where he gives any credit that's due. "When you are running an institution . . . you are only one piece of it. I feel like I'm riding a bronco and hanging on for dear life," he told the audience at the Yale conference.[5]

Dimon's inner circle includes a close group of executives, many of whom have been with him for years, including back at Citigroup in the 1980s and 1990s. Leadership at JPMorgan Chase consists of about a dozen executives who are members of the operating committee and on the next level below about 45 people on the executive committee. From his office on the 48th floor, Dimon makes the rounds every day to committee members who are in New York, stopping by for conversations lasting three or four minutes. Those outside New York are apt to get a short phone call. Although Dimon uses electronic communication, his preferred mode is personal and when possible face-to-face. He doesn't waste time, but sees these micro-meetings as the most efficient way to following up on issues across the bank's six business units.

Dimon doesn't confine his office visits or phone calls to the person in charge, expecting that executive to follow up with a direct report. Rather, he will reach out to anyone at any level who is involved with a project or task. These short spurts of communication occur throughout the business day, and make for an unusual, yet effective, management style.

In addition, the JPMorgan Chase operating committee meets every week for a half day, and then for a full day and dinner once a month. Dimon also holds monthly meetings with each business unit team for several hours. And in between, Dimon—whom colleagues describe as having a remarkable capacity for remembering questions and details even weeks later—keeps up a steady pace of short, in-person sessions.

When he's traveling to bank offices outside New York, Dimon insists upon speaking to employees, such as in a town hall meeting setting. He'll also schedule visits with senior management, local government officials, regulators, clients, the press, or anyone else deemed important for him to see.

The House of Dimon, however, is not a one-man band. It is an orchestra in which all players must be in tune and synchronized to avoid the kind of cacophony that envelops too many firms, where one division doesn't know or even care what another is doing. At JPMorgan Chase, coordination and cohesion are paramount in order to carry out a global vision, which of late has focused on managing and growing a vast business from retail banking to investment banking in the midst of a financial crisis, and integrating two major acquisitions—all at the same time.

Mention the Bear Stearns deal, and Dimon relates with emotion the hundreds of people who went back to work the night the negotiations began, without being told to do so. Or the daily meetings held at seven o'clock each morning—and sometimes several times a day—in which every conceivable department, business line, and geographic region is represented. "If you saw the teams, it would blow your mind," Dimon said proudly.

But it is clearly Dimon—off-the-charts intelligent, articulate, fast-talking, funny, and a bit profane at times—who leads the way.

The Rise, Fall, and Rise of Jamie Dimon

Dimon has enjoyed two rises to the top and a crash in between. The protégé of former Citigroup chairman and CEO Sanford "Sandy" Weill, Dimon spent nearly 17 years helping to build a financial empire from a Baltimore-based consumer credit company. As Weill's company—known by the successive corporate names of Commercial Credit, Primerica, Travelers, and then Citigroup—made more and more acquisitions, Dimon's influence spread among the various businesses. His many titles while working for Weill included CEO of brokerage firm Smith Barney and co-head of the fabled trading firm Salomon Brothers, as well as president of Travelers and then Citigroup, where he was widely seen as the heir apparent to become CEO one day.

After locking horns one too many times with Weill—including a clash involving Weill's daughter, who had ambitions to be promoted into Citigroup's upper ranks—Dimon was fired in November 1998. He did not emerge from a self-imposed hiatus until the right job came along in March 2000, becoming CEO of Bank One, the ailing Chicago-based bank in desperate need of a turnaround. Dimon assembled a team and worked his magic to restore health and profitability at Bank One, which was sold to JPMorgan Chase in 2004. After serving as president of JPMorgan during an interim period, Dimon ascended to the top job at the end of 2005.

While Dimon quickly established himself as one of the top executives on Wall Street, it was the takeover of Bear Stearns that catapulted his reputation to an entirely new level, followed six months later by the acquisition of Washington Mutual. The bailout of Bear Stearns as it teetered on the brink of bankruptcy was orchestrated by the U.S. Treasury Department and the Federal Reserve to avoid financial catastrophe. The Bear Stearns deal prompted comparisons between Dimon and another Wall Street banker: J. Pierpont Morgan, who 101 years earlier had brokered a deal among his New York banker brethren to save the day in the midst of the Panic of 1907. As the story goes, in order to convince his fellow bankers of the need to take action, Morgan locked them in his library and wouldn't let them out until they came up with an acceptable plan to provide liquidity to troubled banks and trusts that were experiencing waves of runs by panicked depositors.

As for Dimon and Bear Stearns, it was the JPMorgan team that locked themselves into war rooms, as it were, to scour the books and come up with the valuations as the clock ticked against them in order to announce a deal before the Asian markets opened. The takeover of Bear Stearns averted what would have been a catastrophic bankruptcy. And if anyone wonders what would have happened if that had occurred, all they need to do is see the mess of losses and the fear that froze up the credit markets when Lehman Brothers was allowed to fail six months later.

While the Bear Stearns rescue didn't save the day when it came to preventing the overall credit crisis, it earned its place in the column of deals that helped assure the marketplace—at least temporarily. When the federal government looked around to see who could pull off the transaction—essentially buying Bear Stearns over a weekend—JPMorgan Chase was the only candidate.

"The lesson is that financial crises can lead, obviously, to financial trouble, but also to a lot of economic trouble. You can minimize the economic trouble provided that there are people who can step up to the plate and become bold leaders," observed Richard Sylla, professor of economics and New York University's Henry Kaufman Professor of the History of Financial Institutions and Markets. "In doing the Bear

Stearns deal, Jamie Dimon showed that he had some of the old J.P. Morgan pizzazz as the head of JPMorgan Chase."

While the Bear Stearns acquisition stunned the financial world with the speed at which the transaction came together and the initial rock-bottom price of $2 a share, JPMorgan has received its share of criticism and backhanded compliments as a "vulture investor."[6] Observers have also questioned whether the $29 billion in government backing to facilitate the deal was absolutely necessary.

Dimon has said buying Bear Stearns will be good for JPMorgan shareholders in the long term, but it was not an acquisition that the company would have made had it not been for the need to bail out that institution. "The sweat equity, the pain, and the suffering" have been very high—not to mention the Bear Stearns balance sheet that has had to be managed and risks brought into line. "It has cost us quite a bit more money to liquidate those portfolios," Dimon explained. Add to that the escalating cost and sheer effort of integrating a huge investment bank in the middle of an all-out financial crisis.

By comparison, Washington Mutual has been a sweeter deal: more strategic in expanding the Chase retail network, especially to key states such as California and Florida. Although writing down loan losses on the Washington Mutual portfolio has hurt the JPMorgan numbers in the short term, the company sees growth potential in the years to come.

As an aside, Dimon mentioned receiving an e-mail from a JPMorgan employee whose sister works for WaMu. Dimon quoted the e-mail from memory, repeating the woman's unsolicited observations about the JPMorgan team in the midst of the acquisition, saying, " 'Boy, these people move awfully quickly. They already made the management changes. They've announced all these HR programs and stuff like that. . . . They were fair and direct.' And then she did a paragraph on Charlie"— JPMorgan Chase retail banking head Charlie Scharf—"that he stood up in front of the employees; that he took every single question. 'He was honest. He was direct. He was can-do. He's already gotten back to us on a couple of things.' " Smiling, Dimon added, "It just made me feel great."

While Dimon and his team can take a bow for acting swiftly and strategically to build the company for the long term, they're not afraid to take their lumps, either: admitting mistakes, taking write-downs when necessary, and shoring up capital to withstand not only a prolonged credit crisis but a recession. Given the management philosophy that favors disaster preparedness, JPMorgan will likely weather this storm. It has battened down the hatches, as evidenced by its Tier 1 capital ratio, a key indicator of a bank's balance sheet strength. Tier 1 capital functions as the base equity capital of the bank and supports other levels of capital (such as preferred stock and debt). In the third quarter, JPMorgan's Tier 1 capital ratio stood at 8.9 percent, above its target range of 8.0 to 8.5 percent, and rose further to 10.8 percent in the fourth quarter. If things go from bad to worse, with a recession resulting in higher unemployment—and therefore more loan losses and credit card delinquencies—then expect Dimon and his team to do whatever it takes. That's the attitude that Dimon brought to Bank One, where he took $5 billion in charge-offs and write-downs before finally staging a stellar turnaround. His philosophy hasn't changed: to get in front of the problem and tell the truth about what is happening.

"If problems exist, recognize them and take corrective steps immediately." That's how John Hall, a former Bank One board member, described one of the leadership strengths that Dimon exhibited at the Chicago-based bank. Hall, who headed the board committee that recruited Dimon to become CEO, also listed having a strong balance sheet, making sure the right leaders are in place, and keeping costs in line as some of Dimon's other management qualities.

"He'll go back to those principles regardless of what the implications are on the quarterly earnings," added Hall, who said he "thinks the world of Jamie."

"It's the cost of living up to those principles. Even if earnings don't meet the projection, he'll still say, 'That's what we're going to do.'"

For Dimon steps such as taking write-downs when necessary and always preserving the quality of capital are part of "doing the right thing," a phrase he uses a lot, whether to explain the rationale behind a certain action or to communicate the management philosophy. This little phrase carries big implications on everything from customer service to corporate governance to regulatory compliance. "If it's not the right thing to do, don't do it," Dimon said simply. "That goes through the whole company."

What You See Is What You Get

Those who have known Dimon describe him as very direct and straightforward. In fact, two people used the exact same phrase: "With Jamie, what you see is what you get."

And while his first name may be James, people the world over—from employees to shareholders to the guy on the street—call him Jamie. It reflects the kind of familiarity that Dimon cultivates and the accessibility he creates in the company where employees are encouraged to provide feedback, particularly of the critical nature. As Dimon sees it, if a marketing practice, a customer service issue, or anything else is detracting from the company's goals or undermining its drive to be the best it can, he wants to know about it.

Steve Burke, president of Comcast Cable and a JPMorgan Chase board member, is among those who have known Dimon the longest. They met in the early 1980s at Harvard Business School where they were in the same section of students and quickly became friends. "I saw in him then the same things I see in him today. He's very smart, of course. . . . It was very clear very early in the process that he was brilliant in business, and completely fearless and confident. He says exactly what he thinks, not mincing words. He's very honest—with himself and about business issues. He's got great integrity."

Dimon's downside is his impatient and often demanding nature, and a temper that can flare. While he has attracted a loyal team, there have been departures from executive ranks as well. Not everyone could—or should—work for Dimon, an intense, hard-driving executive.

What comes across in an interview, a speech, or a roundtable discussion with business school students is Dimon's willingness to speak his mind—and sometimes venture into politically sensitive topics such as energy policy. He is never at a loss for words, whether telling stories from his career or explaining the state of the financial industry. He doesn't speak cryptically and often uses metaphors and analogies to bring home the point. "If you are going to take a boat across the Atlantic, you don't have to be a brilliant person to know that there are big storms on the Atlantic, and you've got to be able to survive them," Dimon commented in the middle of a discussion on risk management. "And just because it's sunny outside doesn't mean you shouldn't bring your life vest."

Dimon adopts the same clear communication style whether he's addressing employees, shareholders, or Wall Street analysts, and his message has no sugarcoating or spin. Making a presentation at a UBS Securities investment conference in the second quarter of 2008, Dimon talked frankly about the current business challenges even though it was in the middle of the quarter.

"Many CEOs would wait until the end of the quarter, hoping things would get better," said Robert "Bob" Lipp, recently retired as a special adviser to JPMorgan Chase and a member of its board of directors. "They wouldn't want to discuss the bad news yet. But Jamie just got it right. There's credibility in that kind of management. Basically, he thinks it's just the right thing to do: to be very visible and quick with news that's not moving in the right direction—for example, when he disclosed losses on credit cards and upping reserves for loan foreclosures."

The same goes when Dimon speaks with employees, whom he enjoys meeting in town hall presentations, which energizes him as much as they motivate others. Rather than engage in "buck up the troops" sessions, Dimon tells it like it is as he answers questions frankly and listens to marketplace intelligence from those who are nearest to the customers.

"Jamie likes to talk to people. He wants to know them and what they think. He believes that accurate information is essential for everyone: investors, employees, newspaper reporters. And it won't be doctored up," Lipp continued.

Dimon makes no bones about his dislikes, especially the corporate speak that falls under the category heading of "b's" (including needless bureaucracy and cover-your-butt and blame-someone-else attitudes). His manner is refreshing to the point of being disarming. But when those blue eyes narrow a millimeter or so and suddenly he's asking the questions, it's best to have an answer—and preferably *the* answer.

Straight Talk about a Credit Crisis

On that brutal day in the stock market in early October, which was fast becoming one of many with significant downdrafts, Dimon spoke with his usual frankness about the current financial crisis. All the various components and contributing factors—the proliferation of bad mortgages to borrowers with questionable credit histories, the securitization of loans that escalated into complex derivatives that carried far too much risk, and much more—will be debated for decades.

"Some of the things are fundamental truths; they never change," Dimon commented. "Too much leverage. Too much short-term borrowing."

In his chairman's letter summarizing 2007, Dimon listed several issues and insights from the financial crisis thus far—among them that structured investment vehicles (SIVs) served no business purpose and that subprime mortgages and subprime collateralized debt obligations (CDOs) were more dangerous than originally thought.

Previously obscure in the minds of many investors, SIVs and CDOs suddenly erupted into full-blown awareness. While they are not the only problems in the credit crisis, the proliferation of these types of investments showed just how far the financial world had gone in its insatiable quest for return—unfortunately at the expense of taking on far too much risk. Created as separate entities, SIVs shouldered off-balance-sheet exposure. The objective was to make money on arbitrage, meaning the difference between two assets. In this case, the SIV sold shorter-term debt such as commercial paper, medium-term notes, or subordinated capital notes. It then used that money to buy longer-term assets, such as asset-backed or mortgage-backed securities, which presumably would pay a much higher return than what the SIV would pay out on the shorter-term notes that it sold.

That worked fine until the market for the short-term debt suddenly dried up, and the income generated by longer-term asset-backed securities declined because of defaults. The riskier the longer-term assets held by the SIV were, the more imbalanced the equation became. When losses swamped the SIVs, the banks that had created these entities suddenly had to put the assets onto their balance sheets.

JPMorgan avoided SIVs. The only one it ever had, dating back several years to when it bought Bank One in 2004, was sold long before the credit crisis. Rival Citigroup was the lead issuer in what was estimated to be a $500 billion market. According to a September 2008 *Fortune* article, the SIV meltdown has forced Citigroup to take $58 billion worth of SIVs back on its books. HSBC Bank's SIV exposure on its balance sheet totaled $35 billion. For JPMorgan, the SIV exposure has been zero.[7]

Collateralized debt obligations (CDOs) are fixed-income securities that are linked to underlying debt instruments, including mortgages and other loans. When banks underwrite mortgages, the home loans are pooled together by investment banks. The cash flows generated by the loans are then used to pay off mortgage-backed bonds, which are underwritten by the investment banks. Further, mortgage bonds are often then turned into CDOs and sold off in tranches, or slices, depending on how much return investors want and, of course, how much risk they can handle. Then there was an instrument called a CDO-squared, which, as the name implies, is a CDO that is backed by a portfolio of other CDOs.

In an easy credit market in which home prices were still rising to enable borrowers to refinance their way out of cash flow crunches, these exotic mortgage-based derivatives seemed very attractive. But as soon as the housing market soured and subprime defaults began to rise, CDOs became part of the toxic mess that poisoned the system.

While JPMorgan has had its share of CDO losses, they have been far smaller than those of its peers. As *Fortune* reported, from July 2007 through the second quarter of 2008 JPMorgan took $5 billion in losses on high-risk CDOs and leveraged loans, while Citigroup took $33 billion in losses; Merrill Lynch, $26 billion; and Bank of America, $9 billion. "And in this market, losing less means winning big," *Fortune* added.[8]

Beyond what was happening on Wall Street with SIVs and CDOs, Main Street had undergone a shift that also added to the risk in the marketplace. As Dimon noted in his letter to shareholders, the nature of home equity borrowing had fundamentally changed from a conservative means to get access to cash to taking a leveraged bet that home values would continue to increase.

When subprime default rates rose, the problem was not just a lack of creditworthiness among some borrowers. The escalation of home prices that had allowed refinancing to pay off more debt had stopped. With a decline in housing prices, overleveraged borrowers suddenly faced a mounting debt burden—and in the worst cases owed more than the house was worth.

As Dimon was quick to point out, the problem was not isolated to subprime mortgages alone. Prime mortgages and so-called Alt-A, which is considered the next tier down from prime but still good quality, were also affected.

"Again here is a mistake we made," Dimon said. "We didn't extrapolate that [deterioration in subprime mortgages] really to Alt-A or prime mortgages, and we should have."

The magnitude of the financial crisis of 2008 will yield lessons for decades to come. In the midst of it, we cannot comprehend the implications of all that has happened: the creation of derivatives that carried far more risk than Wall Street realized; the use of trillions of dollars of credit default swaps as a combination insurance and side bet on the creditworthiness of players; and the direct actions taken by the government that hark back to Roosevelt-era policies in the Great Depression. And just as the generations of the past warned that no one should forget the Crash of 1929 and the Great Depression that followed, one hopes the lessons of the current financial crisis don't fade from memory anytime soon.

"Experience and judgment—I don't think they're replaceable. You go to a lot of businesses—they don't remember how bad things can get. It takes someone who has been there," observed Dimon, sounding very much like the avid reader of history that he is. "We will never forget the aftermath of the housing bubble, but 40 years from now, believe me, someone is going to forget again somewhere."

Never, Ever Forget the Downside

Jamie Dimon never forgets the downside. Sharp, witty, and engaged, he does not come across as a pessimist. His mind and his speech patterns crackle with intelligence and vitality. But he is always aware of the cloud—not just the potential for a silver lining. When his management team gathers, the focus is never on what is going well; it's on the handful of problems that need to be addressed. Even in his communiqués to investors—from his first days as CEO of Bank One starting in late March 2000 through the present at JPMorgan Chase—Dimon points out the risks that the businesses face and what could have been done better.

"That's the other thing: I think you have to be self-critical," Dimon said, and then quoted longtime friend and colleague Bob Lipp: "Emphasize the negatives."

"Look where you could be wrong; admit when you're wrong. To me it's important to do that because I want everybody to do that, so that we actually make a better decision the next time," Dimon added.

The perpetual focus on the downside is part of Dimon's overall conservatism when it comes to banking, such as stressing high levels of Tier 1 capital. "With regard to balance sheet management, Jamie is by nature a conservative person. He would always stress the importance of having ample capital and ample liquidity over goals like growing our revenue or market share," commented James Crown, a JPMorgan Chase board member who also served on the Bank One board and helped lead the recruitment team that brought Dimon in as CEO.

Dimon is relatively young to be such a seasoned CEO. He was only 44 when he took the reins at Bank One and 49 when he was handed the top job at JPMorgan Chase following its acquisition of Bank One. Dimon's level of experience and tenets of his management philosophy reflect his many years spent helping to build what eventually became Citigroup. Along the way, he mingled and worked with others who were financial industry leaders in their own right; among them was former Lazard Freres partner Frank Zarb, whom Sandy Weill recruited to become CEO of Smith Barney when it was part of Primerica.

Reflecting on his days at Smith Barney and previous associations with Weill, Zarb, who has also served as chairman and CEO of the NASDAQ stock market, recalled the shared experience of these executives, and in their midst a bright and younger Dimon. "Among all of us there was a leadership philosophy expressed to the entire organization: If there is a problem and you tell me, it's *our* problem. If there is a problem and you don't tell me, it's *your* problem—and you don't want to have a problem!"

That same attitude can be heard in Dimon's discussion on risk management and sharing information. If there's a problem, speak up about it. No one is going to kill the messenger. It's what people don't see or don't say that causes the real problems.

"If a management team gets up there and they always spin the positive, what do you think the person the next [level] down is going to do? They will spin the positive, too—as opposed to saying, 'I'm not sure these mortgages really make sense,'" Dimon said.

The self-criticism discussion extends into a brief postmortem on lending practices and risk that could have been mitigated. No matter that JPMorgan was better at it than others, in Dimon's mind it wasn't enough—and he says so. "We had fairly good controls in that we actually underwrote the mortgages. We still were terrible at the underwriting, but a lot less than some other people because we underwrote everything."

Although JPMorgan did raise its underwriting criteria in 2007, it was too slow and, in hindsight, too conservative in taking these actions. "It was death by a thousand cuts. We should have been—*boom!* By the way, what caused the problem in subprime had to cause the problem in this other stuff [higher-quality loans], too. If we had done that [raised underwriting criteria], we would have saved some extra money because we would have been a little more careful."

A Culture of Transparency

Creating a culture of transparency means talking openly about what went wrong, which strengthens risk management. "Your first reaction is roll up our sleeves and let's figure it out. We have all the right people there," Dimon explained. "Unless there was malfeasance or lying, you don't punish people for that."

He related how even when someone has to be let go, he never makes an example of that person to show the consequences of poor performance. "I would never do that. You never see me embarrass someone publicly—never . . . hang someone high." Instead, Dimon makes sure a party is held for colleagues to acknowledge the person who is leaving.

This is the softer side of Dimon, the demanding boss who sets high expectations, but leads by example. In a business in which stories abound of out-of-touch and hands-off upper management—criticism that dogged former Bear Stearns CEO James Cayne in the months leading up to that once-revered investment firm's near failure—Dimon not only walks the talk, he's at the front of the line leading the way. Since his long hours (Dimon casually mentions working an 80-hour week) are well known, people are more apt to respond with a can-do attitude. "When you say to someone, 'We really need to do this,' they say, 'When do you want me in, seven o'clock Saturday? What do we need to get done?'—not 'Oh, that's so hard to do.' You have to teach people."

When Dimon speaks of teaching people, there is a bit of the professor in him. He enjoys speaking to students, and has been a guest lecturer at Harvard Business School, as well as Northwestern University's Kellogg School of Management and the University of Chicago's Graduate School of Business. (Asked what else he might want to do someday, teaching does cross Dimon's mind.)

In Dimon's school of management, there are high standards and expectations, many of them grounded in basic, commonsense truth. "If you wouldn't treat your mother that way, don't treat the client that way," Dimon says. "If this piece of paper tells the client how much risk they're taking and you don't want to give it to them, they're probably taking on too much risk. Give them the paper."

Those who are new to Dimon's way of doing things are indoctrinated fast. Dimon told of his experiences with some managers who were new to JPMorgan Chase because the company where they had worked was bought or merged into the operation. In the beginning, Dimon will make suggestions: "I say to them, don't you think you should be doing this kind of margin and growing this fast and doing this?" Some managers, perhaps not quite grasping who they're working for, may not get the drift. Instead, they try to explain it all away, saying things such as, "Well, you know it's a little different in my business." Not the right answer.

Instead of defending the way business has been done, managers would be far better off getting with the Dimon program, which is to set higher targets and become self-critical about why they haven't been reached yet. "Eventually I say to them, excuse me, you're the boss. You should be telling me that 'This is what I should be accomplishing. This is what I'm doing well and what I'm doing badly' in a comprehensive kind of way," Dimon explained. "And the standards, by the way, are performance and integrity."

Dimon's style attracts high-performance people who embrace his way of doing things. "If you are going to work with Jamie, do what you say you are going to do. The people he attracts and, more importantly, that he is attracted to are people who clearly get things done,"

Andrea Redmond, one of two executive recruiters who worked with the Bank One board committee during the CEO recruitment, said of Dimon and his team.

"You have to have some strength and conviction and, in that regard, you need to demonstrate and communicate that you have that strength," added Redmond, who today has a consulting relationship with Dimon and JPMorgan Chase and also takes on other select assignments and projects.

For Dimon it's all about the team and accountability to the organization. Although people sometimes profess wanting to work specifically for him, that's not how Dimon defines loyalty. As he told students in a speech at Northwestern's Kellogg School of Management in 2002, "If you walk into my office and say, 'Jamie, I'm loyal to you,' it makes me nervous. I want you to say, 'I'm loyal to the company . . . or the principles . . . what we're trying to build,' not to the individual, and I think it's a very important distinction."[9]

Organization loyalty is a two-way street, meaning mutual support when the going gets tough and the willingness to take on a less-than-desirable assignment for the good of the company. "Let's say we have a big problem and you were running a great division, and you're highly respected. And I say to you, 'I need you to go to Vietnam,'" Dimon explained. "If you trust the company and you trust me, you might say, 'Oh, boy, that's a terrible hardship, but if that's what you need me to do, I'm there.' Most people won't go. You know what they're going to say: 'I got a honeypot here.' If [the move is perceived as] political, they'll say, 'I'll get shot in the back anyway. There's no bridge back.'"

In these situations Dimon counters such resistance first by recognizing it and then by giving assurances that the person will continue to be paid like his or her peers, with no loss of status at the company. "And thank you for doing the toughest, meanest job, and yes, there is a bridge back. And you also know that if you need help, the whole damn team will get on an airplane and fly out there to help you," Dimon concluded.

The moral of this little anecdote is that, in the House of Dimon, people are expected to do what it takes to get the job done, but they don't have to go it alone. Not getting the job done, though, is never an option.

Doing What It Takes to Get the Job Done

When the JPMorgan Chase board was at the corporate headquarters in September 2008, Dimon invited the directors to one of the meetings that are held every day among departments and business lines across the company—partly because he had to be there, but also to show off the team in action. "It's so damn impressive, the knowledge of the people, the sharing of information, the 'I'll get back to you on that,' and 'I'm going to fix that,'" Dimon said proudly.

Perhaps the most impressive have been the integration teams working on Bear Stearns and more recently Washington Mutual. Comprised of technology, operations, and other business support functions, the teams have set up 26 war rooms by product, by system, and by area, and then a master war room. When this group gets together, Dimon said, there is "high-fiving, hugging, and crying."

"They never thought they would accomplish so much in their lives," he added.

The same might be said for Dimon: stepping up to the plate as the banker of last resort to rescue Bear Stearns, buying Washington Mutual the day it was seized by the FDIC without the failed bank's operations missing a beat, and steering a supertanker of a financial institution through very stormy seas.

When the credit crisis began, Dimon won accolades for pulling off a "steal of a deal" with Bear Stearns, but in hindsight that transaction has been put into perspective. It wasn't the defining moment for Dimon, just one of many significant ones.

"Bear Stearns won't represent Jamie's 'last, great deal.' I would fully expect he will add several more accomplishments to his already impressive list of successes as a leader," James Crown observed in early June, just days after the Bear Stearns acquisition formally closed.

After Bear Stearns and Washington Mutual, one can hardly imagine what JPMorgan Chase might do next. No doubt in time there will be more, and not just acquisitions, but also plans for organic growth from its diverse businesses as an ailing economy gets back on its feet.

On that bloody day in early October, with about 15 minutes to go before the stock market closed sharply downward, and the Dow dropped nearly 700 points, Jamie Dimon picked up two pieces of paper from the conference room table. The memo of topics to be discussed could go in the recycling bin now. And if the discussion had made its way to his 8½ × 11 page of reminders and to-dos, it could be crossed off as well, making one more blue-ink block on a well-marked paper.

And then the CEO in shirtsleeves was on to the next thing on his list.

Chapter 2

Taking a Bear-Sized Bite

A Bear Stearns bankruptcy could have been ... a catastrophe for the United States.

—JAMIE DIMON, SPEECH BEFORE THE
FEDERAL DEPOSIT INSURANCE CORPORATION

J amie Dimon's career of more than 25 years has always been highly visible: as the president and presumed heir apparent at Citigroup; the turnaround CEO at Bank One; and then the chairman and CEO of JPMorgan Chase. But the single event that catapulted him to the top of Wall Street and made him a household name in the process was JPMorgan Chase's surprise acquisition of Bear Stearns to rescue the investment bank from bankruptcy.

The initial news on the night of March 16, 2008, that JPMorgan was buying Bear Stearns for an unbelievable $2 a share sent shockwaves through the markets and the media. The reverberations would continue for months. Suddenly Dimon and JPMorgan Chase were everywhere. Congressional hearings on the downfall of Bear Stearns and the rescue deal brokered by the Treasury Department and the Federal Reserve were the subject of Congressional hearings broadcast live a week later. Columnists, politicians, and talking heads opined on all sorts of questions surrounding the deal: Could regulators have opened the discount window to Bear Stearns and preserved Bear's independence? Was the Fed's $29 billion loan guarantee to JPMorgan to facilitate the deal an unwarranted intrusion into the marketplace and an unfair burden to U.S. taxpayers? Was saving Bear Stearns essential to preventing a larger financial crisis?

By any measure, the 11th hour—or perhaps the 11th hour and 59th minute—acquisition of Bear Stearns was a gigantic story. Bear Stearns was the first visible casualty of the credit crisis of 2007–2008, which had been spawned by several years of easy credit, no-documentation and no-money-down mortgages, and the growth of a new class of derivative credit products—many of them backed by subprime mortgages that plummeted in value when housing prices declined and loan defaults rose.

The fall of Bear Stearns gave the credit crisis its first poster children, from employees who had invested most of their life savings in the company stock to a top executive who was painted as hands-off and uninvolved in the day-to-day operations. What started as bewilderment became a full-fledged outcry: How could this have happened? It would not be the last time this refrain was heard.

The near failure of Bear Stearns was the first wake-up call to the severity of the credit crisis. It wasn't just a problem limited to a few bad mortgages that might cause some small bank somewhere to run into trouble. This was Bear Stearns, a once-revered investment bank that was on the brink of bankruptcy. And as serious as the situation was, what looked at the time like a watershed moment was only the first shoe to drop. In the months to come, mortgage giants Fannie Mae and Freddie Mac would be taken over by the government, Lehman Brothers would go bankrupt, Merrill Lynch would be sold, insurer American International Group (AIG) would receive $85 billion in federal government loans to keep from failing and then an additional $40 billion in assistance in return for an ownership stake, and the last two of the big independent investment banks, Goldman Sachs and Morgan Stanley, would file to become bank holding companies in order to gain access to liquidity from deposits.

All this was yet unseen in March 2008 when Bear Stearns suffered a crisis of confidence because of what later appeared to be unfounded rumors about its liquidity. It was a sad downfall for a firm that, for some 85 years, had been a fixture on Wall Street. In the middle of the Bear Stearns rescue was JPMorgan Chase, the only player capable of doing the seemingly impossible: to complete over a weekend what should have taken weeks if not months of negotiations.

In the beginning, buying Bear Stearns added significantly to Dimon's reputation as a deal maker, although challenges in the marketplace that arose later on have diminished the exuberance over the acquisition. JPMorgan Chase, under Dimon's leadership, had taken a comparatively conservative course by eschewing the riskiest of credit derivatives during the boom days of easy money and a market awash in liquidity. The bank had even faced some criticism that its returns during the go-go days of credit derivatives were bland compared to others that had much bigger exposure to structured investment vehicles (SIVs) and collateralized debt obligations (CDOs).

Because of its balance sheet strength, JPMorgan was the only player poised and ready to act when someone had to rescue Bear Stearns. Dimon and his team were prepared to move with the necessary speed required given the urgency of the situation: preventing the meltdown of Bear Stearns.

True, the acquisition, if properly managed, should eventually be a boon to JPMorgan; but that doesn't detract from the general sense that Dimon's decisive actions on that fateful weekend prevented an early casualty in the financial meltdown. With the Bear Stearns "deal of the century," as it was called, Dimon in his own way became a figure of historical importance.

No Ordinary Deal

The Bear Stearns deal was no ordinary acquisition or long-awaited deal that finally comes together and is negotiated by two CEOs at a time of strategic pairings. Bear Stearns was a fire sale in every sense of the phrase: a rock-bottom price for a troubled firm that wouldn't last another business day. Even when JPMorgan agreed to raise its purchase price from $2 a share to $10 a share, the $1.2 billion acquisition was still considered a steal. Its headquarters alone were worth about

$1 billion. Of course, the cost to JPMorgan Chase of merging and inte-grating Bear Stearns has been far greater than the price tag: estimated at about $15 billion, a figure that could rise.

Furthermore, pulling off the Bear Stearns acquisition was no easy feat—and neither has been the gargantuan undertaking of integrating a huge investment bank, particularly in the midst of a full-fledged finan-cial crisis, a stock market crash, and a deteriorating U.S. economy.

When Dimon observed that the JPMorgan integration team has accomplished more than they ever thought possible, it was not just corporate pride speaking. The job has been enormous—and costly. But the long-term reward could be well worth it: the acquisition of a first-class investment bank to complement and expand many of JPMorgan's businesses.

No Bear on the JPMorgan Acquisition Hunt

Seven months after announcing the acquisition of Bear Stearns, Jamie Dimon said Bear Stearns had never been on the JPMorgan radar for a possible deal. "We weren't looking to buy Bear Stearns. We wouldn't have bought it on its own, but we were asked to look at it. We knew the financial system was extremely delicate and Lehman helped prove that."

Indeed, when Lehman Brothers filed for bankruptcy in September 2008, it caused such damage to the credit market—including fear so great about the health of other players that banks were wary of lend-ing to each other—that some said it was the worst move that could have been made. Although it came well after the fact, in some ways the fallout from the Lehman bankruptcy showed the benefits of the Bear Stearns rescue and the $29 billion in federal assistance to take some of the risk off JPMorgan's hands.

Even with the federal guarantees, JPMorgan still had to shoulder most of the burden of buying Bear Stearns, from the sheer effort of integration to controlling risks that were greater than first anticipated in a deteriorating credit environment. As Dimon summed it up: "You know, someone said to me the other night, 'Well, you know you had less risk with Bear Stearns.' I said, 'Are you kidding me? . . . Bear Stearns was being bought because they basically were going to go bankrupt, and you think it's going to be better tomorrow?' It has cost us quite a bit more money to liquidate those portfolios. It takes us a lot of time."

Despite the challenge, Dimon said when the Federal Reserve and Treasury came calling as matchmakers, the prevailing attitude within the JPMorgan ranks was to go for it—as long as there was protection on the downside and the deal ultimately made sense for shareholders. "We were asked by the secretary of the Treasury and the Federal Reserve to 'do whatever you can do,'" Dimon explained. "And we tried."

Tried, yes, and most likely will succeed. "The Bear Stearns deal will go down as a home run," observed Thomas Brown, a former award-winning Wall Street analyst who today runs Second Curve Capital, a hedge fund that focuses on financial services stocks.

Seeds of the deal's eventual success can be found in the very things that Dimon and his team talk about when discussing it: the urgency to identify and manage the risk, the need to put controls in place, and the continual monitoring of firmwide holdings to maintain a strong balance sheet.

Presenting the Deal to Shareholders

Since taking on Bear Stearns, caution has been Dimon's byword. In an interview months later, Dimon would only comment: "Obviously we think we got some value out of it."

Nowhere was Dimon's caution more evident than when he took the podium in May 2008 at the annual JPMorgan Chase shareholders meeting in Lower Manhattan. As he addressed his shareholders, the entire financial world was listening. Notwithstanding the multitude of issues surrounding the rescue, a single question was paramount: Could he make this deal work for JPMorgan shareholders?

Clad in a dark suit, white shirt, and a yellow tie, Dimon played down expectations, as he typically does. Since his days as chairman and CEO of Bank One, he has earned a reputation for underpromising and overdelivering. At the JPMorgan annual meeting, a somber-sounding Dimon told shareholders: "We are very clear to say 'mission not accomplished.' . . . We think our shareholders should judge us on this in a year or two, because it is a very risky and tough proposition and we're in the middle of it right now."

Speaking plainly and concisely, Dimon assured the crowd that despite taking on Bear Stearns' loan portfolio—some of which consisted of subprime mortgages and other risky assets—he was determined to maintain JPMorgan's "fortress balance sheet." He cautioned about the economic environment and the prospects of a recession. Although he was being hailed as the new statesman on Wall Street, Dimon evidenced no hubris or vindication. Nor was there any indication of what *Condé Nast Portfolio* called the "sometimes brash brass-tacks banker."[1]

Dimon was in his best Warren Buffett–inspired investor communication style: full, open disclosure, underscoring the risks involved, but also articulating the philosophy and reasons behind his decisions. And at the annual meeting, there were no objections voiced to the Bear Stearns acquisition. In contrast to Dimon's cautionary tone, many JPMorgan shareholders were overjoyed about the deal and expressed pride in what Dimon had accomplished: buying Bear Stearns—which had traded at a record high of $173 a share in January 2007—for a measly $10 a share in an amended deal announced in March 2008. Of course, the $10 price was five times the original fire-sale terms of $2 a share, but almost everyone in the auditorium seemed to understand that the bid had to be quintupled to placate angry Bear Stearns shareholders and to soothe valuable Bear Stearns employees who were disgruntled at the prospect that their company's stock value had dwindled to almost nothing.

Perhaps JPMorgan shareholders felt smart for being on the winning team. In a few weeks a far different gathering would be held when Bear Stearns shareholders would be charged with voting on the deal. But on this day and appearing before JPMorgan shareholders who addressed him casually and called him by his first name, Dimon was on top of the world.

In the midst of the happy JPMorgan shareholders, Dimon emphasized the risks surrounding the deal. But as he saw it, the transaction was still worth it—for the good of the company that stands to reap the benefits from the Bear Stearns businesses and for the good of the country that avoided the fallout of a probable Bear Stearns bankruptcy.

The New King of Wall Street?

Dimon had earned his stripes as a deal maker for nearly 25 years, starting fresh out of Harvard Business School when he became the right-hand man to Sandy Weill and helped build Citigroup through acquisitions and mergers. In 2003, *Newsweek* called Weill "the king of Wall Street" as he turned over the reins of Citigroup to his hand-picked successor, Charles O. Prince III.[2] Prince's time in the CEO spot at Citigroup would be relatively short. In November 2007, after Citigroup took a $5.9 billion write-down and suffered a sharp drop in profits, Prince surrendered his corporate crown.

After JPMorgan acquired Bear Stearns, Dimon's claim to the myth-ical throne of Wall Street was unquestioned. When things were falling apart in the financial markets, he was the only CEO ready to answer the call for help. He was Wall Street's banker of last resort by virtue of the fact that JPMorgan, while not unscathed from the credit crisis, had not suffered the near-fatal blows that had struck many of its peers.

No matter how opportunistic it might have appeared initially for JPMorgan, the Bear Stearns deal was a bailout, a rescue. Without JPMorgan, Bear Stearns was going down. The situation was so grave that the Federal Reserve and the Treasury had stepped in, at first facili-tating financing and later urging that a deal be done with another Wall Street bank as quickly as possible.

The Federal Reserve and the Treasury would later face some criti-cism for being so intimately involved in a transaction involving an investment bank, which is beyond the Fed's purview over commercial institutions. The harsh spotlight would fall on Timothy Geithner, then the president of the Federal Reserve Bank of New York, who, along with Treasury Secretary Henry Paulson Jr., brokered the deal.

After the JPMorgan–Bear Stearns transaction was announced, Senator Christopher Dodd (D-Connecticut), chairman of the Senate Committee on Banking, Housing, and Urban Affairs, questioned the appropriateness of the government's intervention. Like the nar-rator of an unfolding drama, Dodd painted the picture of the "fate-ful 96 hours [that] have fundamentally altered our financial market landscape and our system of financial market regulation." He then worked his way to center stage by positing that given the "highly unu-sual and unprecedented actions taken by the Federal Reserve Board of Governors, the Federal Reserve Bank of New York, and the support from the Department of Treasury, it is appropriate—indeed, essential—that the Banking Committee exercise its oversight and investigatory functions to examine the authority, economic justification, and public policy implications of these extraordinary recent actions by our nation's federal financial regulators."[3]

And so all the players in the deal of the century—including Dimon, Geithner, Paulson, and Bear Stearns CEO Alan Schwartz—were hauled before Dodd's committee to testify in hearings that were broadcast live. Even the formality of the setting didn't censure the tone of the victor and the defeated. Asked about the adequacy of the price that JPMorgan was paying, Schwartz complained about a lack of negotiating power. "All the leverage went out the window when we were told we had to have a deal done by the end of the weekend," Schwartz said. In his analysis, Dimon, sounding a little cheeky, quipped, "Buying a house is not the same as buying a house on fire."[4]

Long after the completion of the Bear Stearns deal, broader issues will remain. As the credit crisis continues to unfold, and Wall Street examines its own penchant for creating risk that it often cannot measure or manage, there will be more debate over the role of regulators to oversee the market and step in to avert crises. And there will likely be more regulations imposed on the banking industry not only to measure risk, but to consider the impact of risk at one firm on its counterparties and on the industry as a whole.

From March 13 through March 16, however, the urgency of the matter at hand took center stage, overshadowing the longer-term implications. There was little choice in the minds of those most closely involved: Bear Stearns could no longer stand on its own. The Federal Reserve could help only indirectly, provided another party was willing to step in and facilitate the rescue. That party was JPMorgan with its strong balance sheet and capital position.

Step-by-Step Through the Deal That Changed Everything

From the first phone call until the last news release, at the center of the Bear Stearns deal was Dimon: hands-on, directing, asking questions, demanding answers, and leading the teams he has assembled and empowered. He was involved and engaged at a level of detail unusual for most executives, let alone the CEO, and with knowledge of risk man-agement, balance sheets, and transactions that is rare if not unparalleled.

As JPMorgan executives saw it, the Bear Stearns acquisition offered the opportunity to grow its businesses, particularly in key areas such as investment banking, which JPMorgan wanted to expand, and prime brokerage (groups within investment banks that manage stock lending and service hedge fund clients), in which it has had only a small pres-ence. Even with the higher price tag of $10 a share, or $1.2 billion, the prospect of earning $1 billion a year from Bear Stearns' businesses showcased the potential going forward.

As UBS analyst Glenn Schorr observed in a March 2008 report, "Jamie's patience, discipline, and 'fortress balance sheet' mantra are pay-ing off, as JPM gets Bear Stearns."[5]

While the marketplace generally hailed the Bear Stearns deal, if for no other reason than the sheer drama of it, Dimon has focused on the excru-ciating challenges. "The press talks about the price and the great deal—it really wasn't," Dimon told an audience at the Yale CEO summit in December 2008. "We're going to get $1 billion earnings out of it . . . but investment banks implode. We took on $350 billion of assets. It has cost us probably $10 or $15 billion derisking it, which is about five or seven [bil-lion dollars] more than we expected [and] used up the whole margin for error. We didn't know what the environment was going to be."[6]

Beyond the benefits and burdens of making the acquisition, prevent-ing a Bear Stearns bankruptcy was seen as absolutely necessary for the stability of U.S. financial markets. It's widely acknowledged that without JPMorgan, the Federal Reserve would have been hard-pressed to come up with another party to help rescue Bear Stearns. JPMorgan was arguably the only firm that could take on the deal at the whirlwind speed required: from an agreement to provide pass-through financing from the Federal Reserve, which was announced the morning of Friday, March 14, to a shotgun marriage that was broadcast to the world on the night of Sunday, March 16—just as the Asian financial markets were about to open.

A Surprise Phone Call

The saga of the Bear Stearns buyout begins on the night of Thursday, March 13, when Dimon received a phone call that interrupted a dinner celebration with his wife Judy, his parents, and one of his three daughters. (The other two were away at school.) The occasion was Dimon's 52nd birthday. On the line were Bear Stearns CEO Alan Schwartz and Gary Parr, the Lazard Freres investment banker who advised Bear Stearns. The news was grave: Bear Stearns did not have enough capital to meet its obligations in the morning.

"I have known both of them for many, many years, and they were talking about that they had a run," Dimon said in an appearance on the *Charlie Rose* show. "Usually the firms know what they need to finance the next morning. And they didn't. . . . They needed large amounts of financing. I asked how much. What I remember is something like $30 billion, to which I said, 'No, we cannot do that.' And then . . . they had already contacted the government."[7]

Bear Stearns' liquidity troubles were due to a crisis of confidence, fueled by rumors, speculations, and fear. Clients were pulling their money out the firm, which had gone through $15 billion in cash reserves. Lenders refused to replenish its cash coffers, and brokers were flooded with requests from clients who wanted to get out of trades with Bear Stearns.[8]

Later that evening, after speaking with Schwartz and Parr, Dimon spoke with Treasury Secretary Paulson, New York Fed President Geithner, and at one point with Federal Reserve Chairman Ben Bernanke. Throughout the discussion, the burning question was what would happen if Bear Stearns went bankrupt. The picture Dimon painted in retrospect was of a financial implosion. Collateral that had backed certain assets would have been seized and dumped on the market; and people quitting Bear Stearns in droves would have left a gaping hole in the talent needed to handle a dire situation.

After hearing the news, Dimon called Steve Black and Bill Winters, the co-CEOs of the JPMorgan Investment Bank. Black and Winters then began phoning key people in various departments: audit, tax, derivatives and options trading, legal, and real estate around the world.

"The amazing story wasn't the financial engineering. After I got the call from Alan Schwartz, I called Steve Black and Bill Winters, and then we had 50 or 100 people get dressed and come back to work. And by 12 hours later, there were 500 or 1,000 people working on it in every department: bond trading, equity, equity derivatives, all these areas—tax, legal, compliance, system, ops [operations]—everyone doing their job," Dimon said.

As the team assembled in a war room, people scurried back and forth from their departments trying to figure out what could be done, what JPMorgan could handle, what was known, and what was yet unknown. "And that's the amazing kind of thing: people acting that way—just trying to figure it out very quickly. That really enabled us to do [the Bear Stearns deal]. And then the comfort that when we bought the company we could actually manage all that."

A Life Preserver for a Foundering Firm

JPMorgan director James Crown, who chairs the board's risk committee, recalled that on the morning of Friday, March 14, the plan was to extend a 28-day loan to Bear Stearns for a yet-to-be-determined amount of money in exchange for certain collateral. The collateral would be passed to the Federal Reserve Bank of New York, which would then provide the same amount of money to JPMorgan that it was giving to Bear Stearns. This pass-through financing from the Fed put JPMorgan in the middle because of its status as a commercial bank, which gave it access to the Fed's discount window and made it subject to the Fed's supervision.

It was unclear just how big that loan to Bear Stearns was going to be, Crown explained, because Bear Stearns had experienced a run on its capital, which was continuing. "They were uncertain as to what the drawdown would be that day. They wanted to give enough assurance to the marketplace to prevent people from withdrawing even more capital."

On Friday morning, March 14, Bear Stearns put out a news release announcing that an agreement had been reached with JPMorgan to provide a secured loan facility for an initial period of up to 28 days, which would allow the investment bank to access liquidity as needed. Bear Stearns also said it was talking with JPMorgan regarding "permanent financing or other alternatives," but provided no further details at that time.[9]

While the statement was meant to give some assurance, it apparently did little to assuage the concerns of investors, who pummeled Bear Stearns' stock price. After the first hour of trading on Friday,

March 14, Bear shares were down $22.50, or 39 percent, to $34.50 a share.[10]

In the Bear Stearns statement, Schwartz assumed a confident tone as he dismissed concerns about the firm's capital position. "Bear Stearns has been the subject of a multitude of market rumors regarding our liquidity," he said. "We have tried to confront and dispel these rumors and parse fact from fiction. Nevertheless, amidst this market chatter, our liquidity position in the last 24 hours had significantly deteriorated. We took this important step to restore confidence in us in the marketplace, strengthen our liquidity and allow us to continue normal operations."[11]

Reassuring the Market

This was not the first time Bear Stearns had tried to assure the market-place about its capitalization. In October 2007, Schwartz, who was then president of the firm, made a presentation to investors assuring them that Bear Stearns, which had been hit hard by the collapse of the subprime mortgage market, was not looking for a cash infusion. Referring to the Federal Reserve's move to lower rates on September 18, 2007, Schwartz told investors, "Things are getting better. . . . Liquidity has improved." He also pledged that managing risks would take precedence over growth.[12]

Schwartz's comments came after two of Bear Stearns' hedge funds lost $1.6 billion of clients' money. Closing of the funds would later be seen as the beginning of the problems for Bear Stearns. The collapse of the hedge funds also led to a management shake-up at Bear Stearns. In August 2007, Bear Stearns' co-president, Warren J. Spector—whose areas of responsibility included trading, equities, fixed income, energy, and asset management—was asked to step down. After the departure of Spector, who had been viewed by analysts as the likely successor to CEO James Cayne, Schwartz was the sole president. Then in January 2008, amid criticism over the management of the firm and continued deterioration of the stock price, Cayne retired as CEO, although he kept the title of chairman, and was succeeded by Schwartz.

Cayne, who held some 6 percent of Bear Stearns stock, had been hailed when Bear Stearns' stock was trading at well over $100 a share, and his own stake was worth about $1 billion. Discontent with management rose as the share price fell. As problems mounted at Bear

Stearns, Cayne faced increased criticism. Often mentioned was his status as a tournament-level bridge player, a fact that was raised as many questioned how involved he was in day-to-day operations.[13]

As Bear shuffled its management, concerns over its capital position escalated. Still the company tried to calm the marketplace and investors. On March 10, 2008, 80-year-old Alan "Ace" Greenberg, a former chief executive who was serving as chair of Bear Stearns' executive committee, appeared on CNBC, calling liquidity rumors "ridiculous, totally ridiculous."[14]

Industry observers say they believe that Bear Stearns was adequately capitalized; that liquidity should not have been an issue. The problem, however, was that Bear Stearns faced a run on the bank as funds were withdrawn and sources of short-term financing dried up. In testimony before the U.S. Senate Committee on Banking, Housing, and Urban Affairs, Securities and Exchange Commission Chairman Christopher Cox detailed the crisis at Bear Stearns that had been triggered externally. "For the first time, a major investment bank that was well-capitalized and apparently fully liquid experienced a crisis of confidence that denied it not only unsecured financing, but short-term secured financing, even when the collateral consisted of agency securities with a market value in excess of the funds to be borrowed," Cox stated.[15]

Later stories would surface that Bear Stearns had been the victim of rumor-mongering that purposefully pressured the firm to the benefit of certain speculators who had taken short positions in Bear Stearns stock and its credit derivatives. "I would say where there is smoke there's fire. I've heard it. I don't have evidence of it," Dimon said in the *Charlie Rose* interview. "I think the Securities and Exchange Commission should investigate it. I think that if . . . someone knowingly starts a rumor or passes on a rumor, they should go to jail. . . . This is even worse than insider trading. This [is] deliberate and malicious destruction of value and people's lives. . . . Now I don't know if that is true. I really don't know. But I think . . . there has been enough smoke around that I think there should be a full investigation on it."[16]

Compounding Bear Stearns' problems, counterparties would not provide securities lending services and clearing services, and prime brokerage clients moved their cash elsewhere. This prompted other counterparties, clients, and lenders to decide that they, too, would no longer transact business with Bear Stearns. The problems worsened until Bear Stearns faced the hard choices of filing for bankruptcy the morning of March 17 or agreeing to be acquired by another firm.

From Life Preserver to Resuscitation

The short-term loan that was meant to keep Bear Stearns afloat could not keep the firm from sinking. While Bear Stearns executives thought they had more time, it quickly became apparent that the firm needed to be sold immediately to keep from going belly-up, a financial debacle that would have sent a tsunami of fear and losses through the markets. Schwartz received a call from Treasury Secretary Paulson and Federal Reserve Bank of New York President Geithner, telling him a deal needed to be struck by Sunday night.[17]

All through the talks, Dimon and his team kept the board of directors well informed, and over the weekend, there were numerous conference calls. "Jamie and others at the bank were very conscientious about keeping the board informed as to the milestones of what was going on, what the nature of the conversation was, and where things were headed," Crown stated. Coincidentally, the board already had meetings scheduled for Monday and Tuesday, March 17 and 18, which would prove to be fortuitous timing to discuss the deal that was about to be announced.

A Deal Is Unveiled

On Sunday evening, March 16, an agreement was approved by the boards of both companies: an all-stock deal equivalent to $2 a share for Bear Stearns stock. Also part of the transaction was a special, nonrecourse financing facility put in place with the Federal Reserve that provided a safety net for up to $30 billion (later reduced to $29 billion) of illiquid assets in Bear Stearns' holdings, most of them mortgage-related.

In a statement that evening, Dimon's message was one of assurance for both the marketplace and his shareholders. "JPMorgan Chase stands behind Bear Stearns," he stated. "Bear Stearns' clients and counterparties should feel secure that JPMorgan is guaranteeing Bear Stearns' counterparty risk. We welcome their clients, counterparties and employees to our firm, and we are glad to be their partner."

He also emphasized that the transaction would provide "good long-term value" for JPMorgan shareholders, while meeting its key criteria. "We are taking reasonable risk, we have built in an appropriate margin for error, it strengthens our business, and we have a clear ability to execute."[18]

In a Sunday night conference call with analysts on March 16, JPMorgan Chase Chief Financial Officer Mike Cavanagh called the deal "a good economic transaction for JPMorgan Chase shareholders," adding: "Obviously the price that's being paid here . . . gives us flexibility and margin for error that was appropriate given the speed at which the transaction came together."

Cavanagh—who had worked with Dimon back in the Citigroup days and later joined him at Bank One—highlighted the expectation of a $1 billion after-tax boost to JPMorgan's earnings from Bear Stearns. The main profit contributor would be the prime brokerage and clearing business, which, he said, "is fully additive to what we do here at JPMorgan Chase."[19]

JPMorgan Investment Bank co-CEO Steve Black stressed the strategic fit of Bear Stearns, furthering JPMorgan's goals to build its presence in several key areas. Black—another long-time Dimon colleague from the Citigroup days—told analysts to "go back and look at . . . the things that we outlined [in a recent investor presentation] as potential growth areas in things that we still wanted to invest in and add, whether it was continuing to grow in scale in the equity business, the strong desire to find some way to get a prime brokerage capability, continuing to build out in our securitized product and mortgage business, continuing to add in our commodity space particularly around energy, the fact that we have been building a prime brokerage fixed income business but wanted to continue to build out that in that scope."

Further, although JPMorgan had a leading investment banking franchise with its merger and acquisition equity capital and debt capital market share, Black said, "We still thought there was great opportunity to expand the wallet with the number of clients that we don't happen to do business with."

Black's optimism about the deal was clear: "The Bear Stearns platform across every single one of those areas fits exactly the bill that we outlined. . . . So it's a terrific fit from a very well established franchise."[20]

While JPMorgan did see opportunity from the businesses it was acquiring, it was well aware of the risks that posed a danger. As Dimon described later on: "Remember that day, when we signed that piece of paper, we bought someone else's $350 billion of assets, you know."[21]

Raising the Price

JPMorgan executives had made the case that the $2-a-share price was reflective of the risk on the Bear Stearns balance sheet and the potential for even more risks that had not yet been uncovered, since the deal was put together over a weekend. However, the terms were perceived to be too much of a steal for JPMorgan in the eyes of some Bear Stearns executives and shareholders. Billionaire investor Joseph Lewis, who held more than 8 percent of Bear Stearns stock, had stated that he would take action to protect his investment.

Concerned that a deal might not be approved, JPMorgan agreed to sweeten the terms to $10 a share, or about a $1.2 billion purchase price. "We believe the amended terms are fair to all sides and reflect the value and risks of the Bear Stearns franchise, and bring more certainty for our respective shareholders, clients, and the marketplace," Dimon said in a statement.[22]

The word *certainty* was key for several reasons. First, JPMorgan's agreement to back Bear Stearns trades was expanded and clarified, giving assurance to the marketplace. Further, after the amended purchase agreement was approved, members of the Bear Stearns' board announced their intention to vote their shares in favor of the merger, which provided key support for the transaction. Additionally, both sides entered into a share purchase agreement, allowing JPMorgan to buy 95 million newly issued shares of Bear Stearns stock, or 39.5 percent of outstanding stock.

Schwartz said the Bear Stearns board believed the terms reflected "significantly greater value to our shareholders, many of whom are Bear Stearns employees, and enhanced coverage and certainty for our customers, counterparties, and lenders." Referring to the sale of the 39.5 percent stake to JPMorgan, Schwartz said it was necessary in order to obtain the "full set of amended terms, which in turn were essential to maintaining Bear Stearns' financial stability."[23]

In an interview a few months after the deal was struck, Dimon brushed off the difference between the price at $2 and at $10 a share, noting that either figure is a very low price, which he felt was absolutely necessary, given the amount of risk that JPMorgan was assuming through the acquisition. "The issue wasn't the price at $2 or $10. In any event, that was a very low price. The issue is was there enough margin for error such that I can go to my shareholders a week later and a year later? . . . We think we got a lot of great things, but we have to . . . downsize enormously a complex company, and so a little bit remains to be seen. We just needed a margin for error. Without that, we simply couldn't do it."[24]

Reining In the Risks

Although the deal did not officially close until June 1, in the two months after the acquisition was announced significant efforts to reduce the Bear Stearns risk were undertaken. As the *Wall Street Journal* reported, just days after an agreement was reached, fiber-optic cables were run under the streets, connecting computers at Bear Stearns' headquarters on Madison Avenue with JPMorgan's offices nearby on Park Avenue. This allowed JPMorgan to see everything on the Bear Stearns systems, especially the massive mortgage portfolio. Although, legally, JPMorgan couldn't make trading decisions for Bear Stearns while the two companies were separate entities, it was allowed to unwind some of the riskiest positions.[25]

As of May 20, 2008, the day of the annual shareholders meeting, Dimon reported that Bear Stearns' overall risk had been reduced by about 50 percent; personnel decisions had resulted in the retention of nearly half of the investment bank's staff, or 7,000 out of about 14,000 employees. Dimon, who in his own career had been fired as president of Citigroup, told JPMorgan shareholders of making a "special effort" to try to get jobs for the Bear Stearns staff who were being let go. To help place these employees, more than 1,300 other companies in the New York area had been contacted.

Decisions had been made about infrastructure, real estate, and data centers—all part of a swiftly executed plan by a team that had stepped up to Dimon's demands and example: identify the risks and deal with them.

"You really try to evaluate the risks and provide for them. Whether it's going to be a pleasant or unpleasant surprise, you try to evaluate the risk. That's the attitude that Jamie exhibits," explained Bob Lipp, a longtime associate of Dimon's and a member of the JPMorgan board. "Jamie never would have done anything that would not have made sense for JPMorgan shareholders—even though it was done in a very short period of time because it had to be, which increases the risk."

Several times in his comments to shareholders, Dimon circled around back to the risks—not only those posed by the Bear Stearns deal, but also uncertainties in the banking industry because of the state of the U.S. economy. In May 2008, Dimon saw another threat looming. The new worry on his mind was an economic slowdown, and whether or not the United States would slip into recession, which would worsen credit troubles for consumers and businesses and force banks to bolster their reserves against losses even further.

"What we are more worried about is whether or not there will be a recession. We think it's very complex to determine that. There are a lot of forces at work, and we do think that we see continuous erosion of commercial wholesale credit in the United States: it's in credit card, it's in auto, it's in mortgages, it's in subprime, it's in home equity . . . ," Dimon told shareholders. "There could be a second round of financial effects on commercial banks if in fact they are underreserved . . . then you have not only higher losses but you have to add to reserves over time. We remain extremely cautious and prepared."

On Dimon's Shoulders

The Bear Stearns deal could be one of the crowning achievements in Dimon's career to date—that is, if it turns out as planned: providing long-term value and new business opportunities. If Dimon accomplishes what he set out to do, he will confirm the accolades being heaped on him as a premier Wall Street statesman, the one who stepped in when no one else could to keep Bear Stearns from failing.

"He has all the skills, the brain power, the experience, and the judgment," longtime Wall Street executive Frank Zarb said of Dimon and his ability to steer the Bear Stearns acquisition to a successful conclusion.

Publicly, Dimon deflects credit onto his team, including the hundreds, even thousands, of JPMorgan people who worked through the night and over the weekend to hammer out a deal. He lauds the talent and capability of the team that scoured the books and crunched numbers while the clock ticked against them. "Without the talent and the capability of those people it simply would not have been possible," Dimon told shareholders at the annual meeting.

He also credited his team for what they did "both for the country and for JPMorgan," a sentiment he would repeat in a July 2008 speech to the Federal Deposit Insurance Corporation's Forum on Mortgage Lending, when he noted: "A Bear Stearns bankruptcy could have been . . . a catastrophe for the United States."[26]

In apparent response to criticism over the Federal Reserve's $29 billion safety net in the JPMorgan–Bear Stearns transaction to reduce some of the risk involved, Dimon reflected on what the cost could have been to American taxpayers had a deal not been struck and Bear Stearns was forced to file for bankruptcy. "It would have been enormous," he said. "I'm not sure that number would be $10 or $50 or $100 billion. You just don't know. And so, to me, there was no question that the right thing was done."[27]

One can only imagine what might have happened had the last-minute deal not been reached: collateral that backed assets seized and sold at fire-sale prices, and derivatives dumped on a shaky market; Bear Stearns' stock dropping to pennies as investors bailed out, and causing a steep plunge in the equities market over the coming days that might have made the crash of 1987 look like a hiccup. The contagion, as Ben Bernanke called it, would have spread throughout the broader markets, which are interconnected today to an unprecedented degree, hitting everything from an already-pressured U.S. dollar to commercial real estate. In fact, that was exactly the outcome when Lehman Brothers filed for bankruptcy.

As much as Dimon deflects the accolades, the deal rests on his shoulders, not only because he holds the CEO title, but also because of his intensely involved management style. One could easily make the argument that JPMorgan's board approved the deal because of Dimon's sureness that it was the right move, that it added value to the company, and that his team was capable of such a bold and ambitious undertaking.

As JPMorgan board member Crown stated, "You had to trust the people and their high level of competence to be willing to accept their reassurance that, 'Yes, we can do this and make this work.' A deal of this magnitude would normally take months and months to investigate and analyze. This was collapsed into a weekend."

As he observed, the board had already witnessed how the technology team merged systems and created an integrated technology platform. Financial managers had demonstrated that they knew how to manage balance sheets, value assets, and reserve against them accordingly. Bank managers had shown they could communicate with customers and reassure them that their money was safe.

"If you had not seen people over the past three or four years do that so effectively, you would not have enough confidence as a board member to say, 'Yes, we can act this quickly and take this risk; we can handle this,'" added Crown.

Past accomplishments across all JPMorgan businesses and departments provided the board with the necessary assurance to move forward with the transaction. Given the uncertainty in the economy and the financial markets, the success of the Bear Stearns acquisition is not assured. Yet Dimon's role as CEO and as the one who is ultimately in charge of the integration and operation of the combined business is perceived as a stabilizing force.

"The depth and knowledge that Jamie has, and that the team he built has, are extremely comforting in any time, but especially in precarious times," said David Novak, a JPMorgan director who also served on the Bank One board. "It's hard to imagine how we can have a better CEO in terms of making this work."

The Right Place, the Right Time

Taking Dimon's advice to shareholders, one cannot pass judgment on the Bear Stearns acquisition now. Time will tell whether the right thing was done in terms of JPMorgan Chase, its shareholders, employees, customers, and management. The good news is that for Dimon, who orchestrated the Bank One turnaround as part of the renaissance of his career in 2000, this is what he does best: take an acquisition and make it work. Yet there is no doubt, as the Bear Stearns integration continues in rocky and uncertain times in the market and in the economy, Dimon is facing a defining moment in his career—but certainly not the last one.

Over the past 25 years or so, Dimon has created his own legacy as a builder of companies. He's skilled at acquisitions and particularly gifted in bringing them together. (Some observers say the Bear Stearns acquisition will work out simply because Dimon will make it work.) And looking at where he started, Dimon appears to have positioned himself into exactly the right place and at the most opportune time.

Part Two

THE MAKING OF
A WALL STREET
LEADER

I went to work for Sandy because my goal in life was not to be a partner in an investment bank, and frankly it wasn't money. It was to build something, whatever that meant. . . . The reason I went to work for Sandy is because I liked him. . . . You can pick your partners, your spouses, your friends, your business partners—and pick them wisely. That will make a very big difference in your life.

— JAMIE DIMON, KELLOGG SCHOOL OF MANAGEMENT
PRESENTATION, 2002

Chapter 3

The Weill Years:
In the Trenches

*It was a crummy little company in Baltimore. We didn't care. . . . We called
it "combat." We were having the time of our lives.*
—Jamie Dimon, describing his early days
with Sandy Weill at Commercial Credit

J amie Dimon defined his career very early on by avoiding the
conventional path out of business school and into investment banking at a prestigious firm. Instead he took a corporate job for less
money because of the experience it would provide. Then he walked out
the door literally on that opportunity to follow his boss into temporary
obscurity and from there to a small firm off the beaten path, which
would eventually become the platform for success. That success would
be followed by a sharp and painful downfall, and then a second rise to
even greater accomplishment.

Dimon rose to early prominence on his intelligence and drive and
a good dose of boldness. His true defining moment, however, came
after his fall from grace at Citigroup when his mentor and boss Sanford
"Sandy" Weill suddenly fired him. The one-time heir apparent to the
financial empire he helped to build was suddenly without a job.

At 23 years Weill's junior, Dimon had been widely seen as the successor to the throne at Citigroup no matter how many times Weill would say he wasn't going anywhere. And then it was Dimon who did the leaving: fired as president of Citigroup. As the reasons were sifted through and weighed, often cited is Dimon's clash with Weill's daughter, Jessica Bibliowicz, who had been a friend since childhood and whom Dimon refused to promote further into the power echelon at the firm. But a single event cannot completely explain the rupture in a nearly 17-year working relationship between two men who were mentor and protégé, and then architect and builder of a financial powerhouse. As the company they created grew and expanded in gargantuan proportions, tensions mounted between Dimon and Weill. Although their dynamic had always been to debate ideas and counterpoints to the brink of arguments, the shouting matches became more frequent. A close-knit relationship had unraveled long before it disintegrated completely.

"The rupture happened for a long time before it really happened, because I'm not too courageous in facing up to problems at times," Weill reflected.

Asked once if the conflict with Weill could have been averted, Dimon observed, "Perhaps I should have said quietly to Sandy that we need to meet every Sunday for a couple of hours to talk about the week and what we were both trying to accomplish. It might not have worked, but perhaps it could have."[1]

Reconciled a year after Dimon's firing, the relationship became strained again with the publication of Weill's memoir. Weill's account is favorable to Dimon during the early days, but later speaks of rivalries between Dimon and others in the inner circle. "I think he probably sees some things differently than I saw them, but I wrote in the book what I saw and what I felt at the time to the best of my recollection," Weill explained.

Although the two do not see each other much anymore, Weill is quick to praise Dimon. "I am very proud of what Jamie has done. I think the deal that he did with JPMorgan [the 2004 acquisition of Bank One] was brilliant. I think that the way he has managed the company since he went into JPMorgan—first as president and then as CEO—has so far been executed very, very well."

Those who have known Jamie Dimon for years remember a brilliant, energetic, and ambitious young man, with a dedicated work ethic and a strong character. These are the makings of a leader, with abilities and skills that became polished over time with his rise through the ranks of what eventually became Citigroup. Yet the real story of the making of Jamie Dimon is what happened afterward—on his own. He left Wall Street for Chicago to take charge at Bank One, which was then a financially troubled regional bank undercut by divisiveness and burdened by inefficiencies. From there, Dimon staged the spectacular turnaround at Bank One and its acquisition by JPMorgan Chase, which put him back on Wall Street and in close proximity and comparison to Citigroup.

"He has certainly experienced as many spectacular reversals of fortune as any Shakespearean hero," New York Mayor Michael Bloomberg wrote in his essay on Dimon for *Time* magazine's 2007 feature on the world's most influential people.[2]

Now in his early fifties, the whiz kid of Wall Street is a wiser statesman, having proved his mettle by surviving the credit crisis, with JPMorgan faring so much better than others. He has proved himself to be even more than a skilled acquirer who seeks value at the best price, and the integrator who can slash and burn inefficiencies better than most. He is a leader, setting the example of diligence and discipline, especially where risks are concerned. And with experience, Dimon's rougher edges have been smoothed. As Frank Zarb, who worked closely with Dimon a decade ago, observed, "The Jamie Dimon I know today is a very thoughtful, balanced, good executive."

In the early days of Dimon's career—the opening scenes of Act I in this Wall Street drama—he first went to work for Sandy Weill in early 1982. Such a close connection was forged between them that some observers compared it to a father-son dynamic, especially given the 23-year age difference. (Years later, when asked about his "father and son" relationship with Weill, Dimon would reply, "I've got my own father, thank you."[3])

Yet Dimon is no shadow of the man who helped to mold him. His attributes are all his own: from a Harvard MBA to the ability to wrap his mind around any problem and work toward a solution. From technology platforms to balance sheets, Dimon digs down to the details and owns them. The man we see at the helm of JPMorgan today, rolling up his sleeves to complete two acquisitions in six months, is still as involved in day-to-day operations as he was back in 1986 when he helped to take over a financial services company in Baltimore—the humble start of what became Citigroup.

Detailed, demanding, driven, Dimon asks nothing of his team that he doesn't do himself. He is a talent magnet, especially now that he has emerged as one of the strongest players in the financial industry. While any rising star will attract those who want to jump on the proverbial bandwagon, Dimon has built and maintained a team that shares his vision and his commitment. Accountability to each other and the organization is paramount, and Dimon rewards those who have earned his trust with his confidence and loyalty.

Before the statesman, however, there was the young man who knew what he wanted and, more important, what he was capable of achieving. And from the beginning Jamie Dimon seemed destined to be exactly where he is today.

The Making of Jamie Dimon

Given his background, his education, and the opportunities afforded him early on in his career, Dimon was groomed from the beginning to make his mark and fortune on Wall Street.

Although he was formally schooled at Tufts University and Harvard Business School, working closely with his long-time boss Sandy Weill gave him an invaluable education. Dimon developed and honed his talent while working beside Weill for nearly two decades, but there comes a point when the student must distance himself from the teacher, perhaps even surpassing him, in order to become a master on his own. Whatever the dynamic with Weill—father and son, teacher and student, master and apprentice—Dimon forged his career with the decision early on not to join the ranks of firms such as Goldman Sachs or Merrill Lynch. Courted by any number of Wall Street houses early in his career, no doubt Dimon would have achieved success anywhere he landed. But Wall Street in the 1980s was all about doing deals—not building something from the ground up. In a backwater of a company in Baltimore, Dimon learned the management of a firm from the bottom up, and inside out. Arguably had Dimon made any other choice in his life, he would not have the breadth of experience in acquiring companies and making deals work that allows him to take on something as bold as buying Bear Stearns over a weekend before the noble investment house crumbled into bankruptcy, and then taking on the strategic acquisition of Washington Mutual six months later.

As he undertakes the integration of these two firms while steering JPMorgan Chase through the rocks and shoals of the credit crisis and a faltering U.S. economy, the skills that Dimon calls upon now were honed years ago when he cast his lot with Weill.

The Market in His Blood

As formative as Dimon's experiences with Weill were, one cannot forget that he has the market in his blood. He grew up, literally, in and around the brokerage business, which he understands not only strategically but also intuitively. His family story begins with his grandfather, who emigrated from Greece to New York City in 1919 and worked his way up from dishwasher to stockbroker, and later taught Jamie's father the business. Along the way, the family name, Papademetriou, was changed to Dimon. This legacy makes Dimon part of the all-American success story. Dimon's grandfather and father not only provided for the family financially, but also opened doors of opportunity.

New York City born and bred, young Jamie moved with his family from Queens to Manhattan, settling into a Park Avenue apartment. No matter where he would go in life, the minute he opened his mouth he proved himself to be a New Yorker. Even from his earliest days, there were glimpses of the man in the making. When he was nine years old, his father asked him and his two brothers what they wanted to be when they grew up. Older brother Peter said a physician. Twin brother Ted said he didn't know. Jamie, however, piped up, "I want to be rich." As his father later recalled in a magazine interview, "He wanted to run something and have power."[4]

As he got older, Jamie spent summers learning the brokerage business from his father and grandfather. His father, Theodore "Ted" Dimon, worked for Weill for 30 years. (In August 2006—just a few months after Weill retired as chairman of Citigroup—Ted Dimon was part of a team of brokers hired away from Citigroup by Merrill Lynch. At the time, Ted Dimon was 75 years old and had been a stockbroker for 52 years.[5])

It was through his parents that Dimon first met Weill. The Dimons were close friends with Weill and his wife, Joan, and bought a country house in Greenwich, Connecticut, not far from the Weill home. Ted and Themis Dimon and their three boys often socialized with Sandy and Joan Weill and their two children, Marc and Jessica.

At school, Dimon distinguished himself at Tufts University, from which he graduated summa cum laude. In 1976, after his sophomore year at Tufts, Weill offered him a summer job at his company, Shearson Hayden Stone, working on the budgets for the retail brokerage operation. Dimon's handling of the project impressed his future boss.

In his memoir, Weill recalled sitting in the backyard and proudly pointing out that the analyses showed all the branches to be profitable. "'No they're not,' he [Dimon] piped up. 'The analysis is flawed. Portland doesn't make any money; neither does Seattle.' I don't know whether he was right or wrong, but I sure liked the way he confidently spoke his mind even if he had the nerve to question the professionals for whom he worked."[6]

For Dimon, speaking up and speaking his mind would never be a problem. His outspoken confidence would lead some to label him as brash. Frank Zarb, who would later appoint Dimon as second-in-command at Smith Barney when it was part of Weill's conglomerate then known as Primerica, downplayed any abundance of hubris in the Dimon-in-the-rough. "Brashness is a characteristic that is hung on a young person who is succeeding quickly," he observed.

The Harvard Scholar in Jeans and a Leather Jacket

After Tufts, Dimon took a job with Management Analysis Center, a consulting firm in Boston, in 1978. Following a two-year stint as a consultant, Dimon enrolled in Harvard Business School, where he would distinguish himself—and not just for the academic performance that earned him a Baker Scholar designation, which is given to Harvard students who receive their MBAs with distinction.

Steve Burke, president of Comcast Cable and a JPMorgan Chase board member, recalled the day he first saw Dimon when they were section-mates at Harvard Business School. It was the early 1980s and the typical Harvard dress was standard-issue preppy: button-down shirt, blazer, and briefcase. Then there was this one guy wearing blue jeans, a T-shirt, and a leather jacket who carried his books in a gym bag.

"He didn't look like anybody else, and when he opened his mouth he had total confidence," Burke recalled. "He really stood out. Out of 90 people in the section, it was clear that he was special. A lot of people looked at him like, 'Who is this guy?' because he was so blunt. I always thought it was terrific and an appealing trait."

One of Burke's favorite "Jamie stories" from their days at Harvard was an episode that occurred about a month into their first year. Presenting a case study to the class, the professor wrote a formula and other information on the board to describe how to analyze a specific business situation. "Now, we're in the first month of school. There are 90 people in the class and 89 of them are thinking that they are there only because the admissions department made a mistake. So they are all sitting there, nodding as the professor writes," Burke recalled. "Then Jamie raises his hand and says, 'I don't think you did that right.' You could have heard a pin drop. Eighty-nine heads whipped around in his direction, and half of them were eager to see what would happen to Jamie next."

When Dimon asked if he could come up to the board to explain his point, the professor stepped aside. Dimon wrote for about five minutes on the board and then explained how he would assess the case. While the professor did not agree with every aspect of Dimon's approach, he conceded that it was a very good way of looking at the situation, Burke remembered. "It was like there had been a glass wall between the teacher and the students and Jamie ran through the glass wall. Everybody could see that this guy was one of a kind."

While at Harvard, Dimon arranged for Weill, who was a family friend at this point and not yet his boss, to speak to his classmates. According to Weill, the young man he saw had matured. Weill was also introduced to Dimon's classmate and fiancée, Judy Kent, who was working on a special project commissioned by financial services firm Shearson. Coincidentally, her team would make the recommendation to Shearson that it should merge with American Express, a conclusion that the company would also reach, and a deal would come together soon thereafter.[7]

Hardwick "Wick" Simmons, former chairman and CEO of the NASDAQ Stock Market and retired CEO of Prudential Securities, recalled meeting the former Judy Kent when she was among three or four Harvard Business School students who were hired to spend a year at Shearson and gain a broad overview of the business. "To this day, I have a very soft spot for her," Simmons said. "I've always felt that Jamie, as smart as he is, has an intellectual superior at home."

Going to Work for Weill

After Harvard Business School, Dimon was courted by several Wall Street firms, including Goldman Sachs where he had been an intern in 1978, Morgan Stanley, and Lehman Brothers. Even though a job at Goldman Sachs would have paid him more money, Dimon said he "turned them all down to go to work for a guy called Sandy Weill who had just sold his company, Shearson, to American Express and he wasn't the president yet. He was chairman of the executive committee. I liked him because he was down-to-earth, no BS; [he] called it the way it was."[8]

Knowing Dimon and his family for so many years, there was no risk for Weill in hiring this young man. Dimon's character and the "very good value system that he inherited from his parents" was all the assurance that Weill needed. "I saw somebody who was very smart and whom I had watched grow up and knew very well. I was not taking a risk on an unknown person. I was making a decision in the comfort zone of mine with a lot of knowledge about the person and his mother and father," Weill added.

Weill did not recruit Dimon per se. Rather the opportunity for the two of them to work together was the outgrowth of a conversation that started when Dimon sought Weill's advice about the next stage of his career. Weill listened to the various job offers that Dimon was considering and then asked him a question: "I said to Jamie, 'How important is money to you, because I think whether you take a job at Goldman Sachs or Morgan Stanley or Lehman, or whatever, it could be terrific, and they certainly would pay you a decent amount of money. Or you could come to work for me in a very good company and learn a lot. It would be like an extension of what you learned at business school, but I couldn't pay you as much."

In saying yes to Sandy Weill, Jamie Dimon forever defined his career as a builder of companies.

Dimon was a natural to work for Weill. As Wick Simmons, who had also been an associate of Weill's over the years, observed, Dimon was the kind of protégé who would thrive with Weill, given his "great head for numbers and intuitive understanding of the brokerage business and investment banking."

"Sandy took to him as he took to all people who had those capabilities," Simmons added. "Plus, if you had an idea and told it to Sandy, he'd listen and then put it down for a day or two. Then, if he liked it, he'd come back to you as if he had come up with it. Jamie understood that."

Dimon also possessed two key factors that made him both valuable to Weill and successful in the business. One was grounding in the brokerage business, thanks to his father and grandfather, which allowed him to understand the business from an insider's point of view. The other was his fast mind that grasped details, sorted through what was important, and made decisive analyses. The fact that as a young man Dimon didn't hesitate when it came to voicing his opinions confidently also impressed his boss. "Jamie didn't mind coming up with ideas. Sandy liked to be challenged, and Jamie challenged him," Simmons remarked. "Jamie always came up with the questions that Sandy didn't want to hear. He had grown up in the business. He was young and hadn't had all the specific training that he would later get in the various disciplines, but he understood how the business worked."

From the earliest days in his career, Dimon displayed the ability to get up to speed quickly if a topic was beyond his element or experience. "Jamie did his homework; he didn't blow much smoke," Simmons said. "He knew what he was talking about because he prepared himself beforehand."

They were a well-matched team: the older, more experienced executive who had already built a financial empire of sorts even before he got to American Express, and the bright, eager, and ambitious younger man.

The Rise of Sandy Weill

To appreciate Dimon's years with Weill, one must look at the development of Weill's career and his drive to build what eventually became Citigroup, which included Smith Barney, Shearson, and Salomon Brothers.

Weill's career in the business started in 1960 when, at the age of 27, he and three partners formed a securities brokerage. It was a bold move for a young man from Flatbush, Brooklyn, who after graduating in 1955 from Cornell University became a runner for Bear Stearns, making $50 a week.[9] (Years later, Weill would remember his alma mater as chairman and benefactor of the Weill Medical College of Cornell University.)

The brokerage firm that Weill and his friends started was called Carter, Berlind, Potoma, & Weill. After steady growth through the 1960s and with a few changes in partners, the firm was known as Cogan, Berlind, Weill & Levitt (nicknamed CBWL, or corned beef with lettuce). Then came an important acquisition in 1971: buying the much larger brokerage firm, Hayden Stone. With the Hayden Stone acquisition, Weill noted, "a minnow had swallowed a whale."[10] By 1970, Weill's firm employed more than 1,500 people and brought in nearly $12 million in revenue—a virtual explosion from the $400,000 generated in 1960.

After Hayden Stone came several other acquisitions to expand the retail brokerage. Then, in 1974, Weill acquired Shearson Hammill. The combined firm, Shearson Hayden Stone, was the tenth largest brokerage firm on Wall Street. More acquisitions followed in the 1970s, and in 1979 Weill's company bought Loeb, Rhoades, creating a combined firm known as Shearson Loeb Rhoades, which was second only to Merrill Lynch.[11]

Selling to American Express

Then came the deal of deals, not an acquisition, but a sale: American Express bought Shearson Loeb Rhoades in 1981 in a $1 billion deal. As part of the transaction, Weill became president of American Express, in the number two position behind James Robinson III, the chairman and CEO. Jamie Dimon became Weill's executive assistant.

The American Express culture was not a good fit for Weill. In 1985, four years after American Express bought Shearson, he resigned as president. In a show of loyalty and in pursuit of opportunity, Dimon decided to throw his lot in with his boss and follow him to a then-unknown future, even though his first daughter had been born just a few weeks earlier.

Weill urged Dimon to stay at American Express, which would have welcomed the opportunity to keep the young executive. Weill was headed toward an uncertainty. "I didn't know what I would be able to get or how long it could take. I was in a different stage of my life than he was. If I never did anything again, it would be possibly okay. I didn't have that pressure that I had to go back to work. Jamie was just starting his career. But he decided to leave with me and basically hang his hat with an unemployed person."

Such loyalty by Dimon did not go unnoticed or, later on, unrewarded.

In July 1985, Weill and Dimon went to work. For Weill, that meant devoting himself to raising money for the renovation of Carnegie Hall and working in an office suite in the Seagram Building at Park Avenue and 53rd Street. Mostly, he and Dimon monitored the stock market, plotted their next move, and waited to see what would happen next.

One possibility that Weill and Dimon pursued was providing a $1 billion infusion to BankAmerica Corporation, a proposal that was rejected outright. While they were stung by the rebuff, it generated a fortuitous bit of publicity. An article ran in *Fortune* magazine with a headline worded like a want ad: "Sanford Weill, 53, Exp'd Mgr, Gd Refs." The article summarized Weill's latest campaign and also chronicled his ambitions. "His audacious try to become chief of BankAmerica flopped, so the former president of American Express is looking for another company to run. He might settle for something small. What he probably wants most is something big and in trouble."[12]

The Phone Call That Changed It All

What Weill got was a phone call from Robert Volland, vice president of finance at Commercial Credit Company, a consumer loan company owned by Control Data Corporation, which needed cash. Control Data had bought Commercial Credit in 1968, hoping to use it to finance the sale and leasing of computer systems, but competition from Japanese companies and the rise of personal computers that outmoded mainframes crimped that opportunity. When Volland and Paul Burner, Commercial Credit's assistant treasurer, saw the *Fortune* article about Weill looking for an opportunity with a company that needed a turn-around, they figured a call wouldn't hurt.

Weill was familiar with Commercial Credit, having looked at it before in 1984, but concluded that it was "a piece of crap." This time, however, it appeared that restructuring had improved the compa-ny's financial condition, making it ripe for a turnaround. He assigned Dimon the task of looking up the latest Securities and Exchange Commission (SEC) filings and other documents on Commercial Credit and Control Data.

Weill and Dimon surveyed the company, which had offices in 28 states, annual revenues of $1.1 billion, and assets totaling $5.5 billion. Dimon charted the 10-year financial performance of similar finance companies, discovering that companies in decent shape had a return on equity of 15 percent or more and an annual growth rate of 10 percent or more. Commercial Credit had a measly 4 percent return on equity. The two men quickly became convinced that if they could turn it around and get it up to a par performance for the industry, Commercial Credit's earnings would rise. Once Commercial Credit was spun off from its parent, its stock price would follow.[13]

The proposal to Control Data was an interesting one: make Weill CEO of Commercial Credit and he would help the company spin off the consumer loan operation. After rounds of negotiation, on September 12, 1986, Control Data officially named Weill chairman and CEO of Commercial Credit and agreed to reduce its ownership stake to 20 percent through an initial public offering (IPO). Weill and his new management team would own 10 percent of the firm via stock purchases and option grants.

Weill was back in business, with Dimon at his side.

In the Trenches at Commercial Credit

Hunkered down in an ailing consumer loan company in Baltimore, they called it "combat," as Dimon recalled in a speech he gave in 2002. And in the trenches were Weill, Dimon, and a handpicked team. From the beginning, the belief was they could build the then 75-year-old firm into a much bigger company. "It was a crummy little company in Baltimore. We didn't care. . . . We were having the time of our lives," Dimon reflected.[14]

The "crummy little company," as Dimon affectionately called it, would indeed grow into something that seems almost unimaginable, given where it started. It would eventually turn into Citigroup. Such a transformation seems impossible, or at least improbable, until one considers the brainpower and sheer willpower of those involved.

The Molehill That Became a Mountain

1986—Control Data spins off Commercial Credit; Sandy Weill becomes CEO of Commercial Credit.

1988—Commercial Credit agrees to acquire Primerica Corporation, which includes brokerage Smith Barney, for $1.7 billion. Name is changed to Primerica.

1992—Primerica agrees to invest $722.5 million for a 27 percent equity stake in Travelers Insurance.

1993—Shearson operations are acquired from American Express and merged into Smith Barney.

December 1993—Remaining 73 percent of Travelers is purchased for $3.4 billion. Primerica and Travelers operations are combined, and company name is changed to Travelers Inc.

1995—Name is changed to Travelers Group.

1997—Travelers acquires Salomon Brothers in $9 billion pooling of assets.

1998—Travelers Group and Citicorp announce largest merger to date, creating financial services colossus, Citigroup.

Refugees from Bureaucracy

Long before Citigroup was a gleam in anybody's eye, Weill and his team shucked off the layers of bureaucracy from which they had come, and set up their own shop, their own way. For Dimon, working at Commercial Credit would be full indoctrination into the Weill school of acquisitions: find the prospect, make the deal, reap the synergies, pare the costs, and integrate. Dimon would bring to the team full appreciation for what Weill was trying to accomplish.

After completing the Commercial Credit deal, Weill began assembling a new management team, seeking out those who were experienced in financial services as they built a new kind of company. The offer was to take a cut in salary, join a risky venture, but earn a portion of the ownership in a company and a share of the profits based on performance. Among Weill's newest team members was Robert I. Lipp, a former Chemical Bank operating president.

The team spirit of the early days of Commercial Credit was evident as Lipp recalled when he headed consumer finance at the company. "We all had our interest in the stock price. We took cuts in salary to have an interest in the company," explained Lipp, who after holding several executive positions at Citigroup and Travelers, retired as chairman of Travelers in September 2005.

Looking back on the 22 years since the Commercial Credit days, Lipp spoke fondly and with good humor about those times when, as he put it, "We were refugees—refugees from bureaucracy." His fondness deepened as he talked about Dimon, whom he first met at Commercial Credit, and who impressed him with his hard work and intensity. "The same things I see in him now, I saw in him then," said Lipp, who calls Dimon, some 18 years his junior, "a great role model."

"He's as smart as can be. He's a quick learner," Lipp continued. "He did a great amount of study and analysis on his own. If we were signing a lease, Jamie would end up reading the lease himself that night."

From the beginning, Dimon distinguished himself with a total grasp of the details. The hands-on management style he exhibits today can be linked back to the days when he was accountable because it was Weill who was asking him for the analysis. At Commercial Credit, when risk analysis needed to be conducted, Dimon ran the numbers. Since then, he has not distanced himself from the discipline. When the JPMorgan board asks for a risk analysis, Dimon is fully capable of giving the report himself, even though his team supplies the numbers. Responsibility and accountability begin and end with him.

Dimon's total-immersion education in acquisitions and integrating businesses spanned every aspect of operations. When the company needed a chief financial officer, Dimon, then aged 30, stepped up to the job, even though it had a steep learning curve. He embarked on his balance sheet training by spending time with CFOs of other firms, shadowing them and asking questions. "I said, 'My name is Jamie Dimon. Will you spend a couple of days with me?' and they said, 'Sure.' I went through each one: their taxes, their books, their products, their credit, their research, their tax returns. . . . You can learn a tremendous amount from other people," Dimon recalled.[15]

What was so unique about the Commercial Credit experience was the intensity and camaraderie that brought together a group of highly intelligent, ambitious people out of Wall Street and transplanted them to Baltimore. "We would take Piedmont Airlines out of La Guardia for Baltimore around seven on Monday mornings. Then we'd come back on Thursdays. Our families were all here in New York. And on Friday, we were crammed into a conference room in the Seagram Building," Lipp remembered. "It gave us a great feeling, and it was great fun."

In his memoir, Weill spoke of the first 18 months in Baltimore as "one of the most simulating and enjoyable times in our professional lives. We were a bunch of vagabonds in an unfamiliar city, working exceptionally hard with a shared purpose. I looked at it almost like going to a sleepaway camp for boys—there was that same intensity of spirit and camaraderie. We were all learning a new business from scratch, and no one was afraid to speak out for fear of appearing foolish."[16]

Lipp said Commercial Credit had the feeling of being a real partnership, in which they were all engaged, operating from their separate strengths, but also dependent upon and supportive of each other. "It was new and exciting. . . . It was very different. We were throwing ourselves into an organization and trying to make it significantly better. It was none of the bureaucracy that Sandy and Jamie had through the American Express experience, and that I had through a large company experience, although Chemical Bank was a great organization."

A Culture of Their Own

Far from the corporate hierarchies they'd left behind, the Commercial Credit team created their own culture, which Lipp called "the antithesis of the traditional bureaucracy."

"You wanted to do a great job on your piece of the organization so that the whole thing would work better. It wasn't that you were trying to advance in title or get more responsibility," explained Lipp, who today is a JPMorgan board member. "I could be full-out on consumer finance with my team. Then on a monthly basis we'd get together to review the results and dive deep into the numbers. There was no political stuff. It was factual: straightforward and sharing [information]."

With their families back in New York, the Commercial Credit team in Baltimore worked and practically lived together. "There was nothing to do but live, breathe, and work," Weill recalled. "Jamie and I shared a two-bedroom suite at the hotel. Here's how I'd wake him up: The first thing in the morning I'd have a cup of coffee, read the paper, and then light up a cigar, and that awful cigar smoke would go right under his bedroom door."

Lipp recalled with a laugh how "we all left Jamie to deal with the cigar smoke. We stayed at a different hotel. That was our excuse, anyway. But we were together morning, noon, and night. It was all about business, but also a lot of laughs. Everybody was enthusiastic. The creative intelligence within that group, with Sandy and Jamie especially, was really good."

Commercial Credit was a no-frills organization, but the team thrived on it. Turning around the company and building it into something bigger was far more important than the perks and titles of corporate life. And when the hard work and risks paid off, they'd all be handsomely rewarded.

"We had a board, of course. And you know how with board meetings today there are all these fancy presentations with slides and PowerPoints. Well, we used acetate sheets and an overhead projector," Lipp recounted. "That was enough! If you did slides in those days the reaction was, 'Why are you wasting time on that? Just put the numbers up.'"

Commercial Credit wasn't all fun and games. It was a serious business managed for growth. A year and a half later, Commercial Credit had been transformed into an aggressive, entrepreneurial, and results-oriented organization. The company was ready, and so was its executive team, to take on a major acquisition. It was the deal for which they'd all been waiting and preparing.

Buying Primerica—A New Second Chance

Weill had his eye on Primerica. The company had been American Can until it was changed by CEO Gerald Tsai into Primerica, which had several financial and retail operations, while shedding its manufacturing businesses. By the late 1980s, Primerica owned Smith Barney, several insurance companies, a large mutual fund complex, a mortgage company, hotels, and retail ventures. After the October 1987 stock market crash, Primerica was saddled with serious losses at Smith Barney and a hefty debt burden.

Weill was captivated by the opportunity presented by Primerica, and especially liked becoming the CEO of a broad-based company. Smith Barney was also a plus, as it would allow Weill to return to his roots in the securities business. Ironically, he had tried back in the 1970s to buy Smith Barney, but had not been successful in doing so. Now, with the Primerica deal, he had a second chance.

The $1.7 billion acquisition of Primerica in August 1988 gave Commercial Credit a new name: Primerica. For Weill, Dimon, and the other principals, it was also the end of the exile to Baltimore, as the company was moving back to New York—a triumphant return for Weill in a deal that was trumpeted in the media. "Life is sweet again for Sanford I. Weill. Three years after resigning the presidency of American Express, a job where he said he had the status of Deputy Dog, he is back in the big time," *Fortune* magazine declared.

Now, with the merger between Primerica and Commercial Credit, "Weill will be top dog of the combined entity. . . . Like Iacocca after Ford, Sandy Weill, 55, now has his big chance to do it all over again. The challenge: to build a motley collection of businesses into something greater than the sum of its parts."[17]

Observers at the time mused about whether Weill, Dimon, and the rest of the team were trying to make their own "mini-American Express," a mountain that appeared too steep to scale. The combination of Commercial Credit and Primerica would rank No. 17 on *Fortune's* 1988 list of largest diversified financial services companies, the magazine noted. American Express was firmly in the top spot with assets at the time of $116.4 billion—seven times the assets of Primerica, it added. But noting as an example the growth of Weill's old firm from humble beginnings until Shearson ranked No. 2 to Merrill Lynch, *Fortune* added, "You haven't heard the last of Sandy Weill."[18]

The world would soon hear more from Dimon as the up-and-coming rising star. Joseph A. Califano Jr., who was on the board at Primerica when it was acquired, recalled the first board meeting after the deal was completed and the presentation made by Dimon on the integration of Commercial Credit and Primerica and what could be done with each of the businesses. "I have been on a lot of boards and probably 10 or 15 boards by that time. Jamie's presentation was unquestionably the most brilliant, perceptive presentation I'd ever seen. Afterwards I said to one of the other board members, 'This guy is going to be one of America's business leaders.'"

Dimon's ability to impress came from his attention to detail as well as his ability to convey a vision of what was possible. "It wasn't just the numbers, but what those numbers meant in terms of building the businesses, building a corporation, and the potential for the future," Califano said.

As Primerica grew and changed through transactions, Dimon was the one who made the financial presentations at board meetings. "He was the guy who laid out the pros and cons of the acquisitions, the numbers and the potential, and then became critical in implementing it," Califano added. "Jamie was clearly the number one guy for Sandy Weill in all those businesses."

Rebuilding Primerica

Now at the helm of Primerica, Weill put together top talent, including Frank Zarb, a Lazard Freres partner, who became the CEO of Smith Barney. Zarb requested that Dimon be made Smith Barney's senior executive vice president and chief administrative officer, while still serving as Primerica's chief financial officer. For Dimon, it was a first step into a wider recognition of his skill as a manager on Wall Street— and inching out of the shadow of his mentor, Weill.

"At that moment in time, Smith Barney was a turnaround—losing money with administrative and financial inefficiencies in terms of processes and people. A lot of work needed to be done," recalled Zarb, who today is managing director of Hellman & Friedman, a leading private equity group.

In Zarb's view, Dimon had the right knowledge, skills, and abilities to help orchestrate the turnaround of Smith Barney. "Jamie had a very incisive mind to focus and concentrate on the mission at hand, at any given moment, and execute it with good people," Zarb said. "At Smith Barney, we needed a chief administrative/chief financial guy, and someone to help look at the capital markets. Jamie jumped in with both feet and did a fantastic job. Smith Barney was turned around in a little less than two years. That took a lot of people, but if I had to pick the top three people who were the most instrumental, Jamie was one of them."

The emphasis at Primerica was to cut costs, eliminate losing operations, restaff key jobs, and gain control over the operations. Specific improvements (which sound incredibly similar to issues Dimon would later face at Bank One) were the combination of back office activities, consolidation of data centers from nine down to four, and tighter expense controls. Primerica's major businesses were Commercial Credit, headquartered in Baltimore; Smith Barney in New York; and Primerica Financial Services in Atlanta; they all reported to Primerica's corporate office in Manhattan.

As a 1992 Harvard Business School case study on Primerica noted, Dimon functioned as the chief aide to Weill in managing resources—especially cash, which was yet another sign of the close working relationship between the two and Dimon's likely position even then to succeed his mentor someday in the top spot at the company.[19]

Weill was a hands-on, involved manager, which set the tone of the Primerica culture. Weill called managers on the phone, paid impromptu visits to other executives' offices, and made it a habit to visit employees and customers in the field. Status and reporting relationships made no difference to him; he spoke to whomever he wanted, when he wanted, and about whatever subject was on his mind. As Dimon later described, Weill "dealt with the secretaries, the drivers, and the clerks the same way that he dealt with anybody else."[20]

Smith Barney Shines

Changes were afoot at Primerica. Assets that were considered to be non-strategic were divested and proceeds invested in the core business, including the acquisition of two units to strengthen the consumer finance operation. The star of the show, as far as profits are concerned in the early 1990s, was Smith Barney—thanks to increased demand for stocks by individuals and institutions, as well as demand from corporations for debt financing. The numbers said it all: For the third quarter of 1991, Smith Barney posted profits that more than tripled to $35.9 million, helping to boost Primerica's results by 31.4 percent to $123.5 million.[21]

And so at the midpoint of Act I of Dimon's Wall Street career, a milestone of accomplishment in the turnaround of Smith Barney was reached. In the next scene would come Dimon's reward for his job well done.

The synergies at Primerica reflected the strong connection within the management team, especially between Weill and Dimon. They worked in tandem not only through the consolidating phase, but also into the expansion mode, as Weill would put together the acquisition deals and Dimon would figure out how to make them work by improving operations. "I had a lot of faith in Jamie. Jamie is very smart and driven. We worked well together: analyzing these various opportunities that came out of the long-term relationships that existed with the sellers, which allowed us to have the opportunity to do a lot of these things," Weill reflected.

Lipp recalled the "great relationship" between Weill and Dimon and the complementary abilities of the two. "Sandy was a genius at finding deals, and Jamie was the one who, personally, did all the due diligence: going over the taxes and the accounting and the complexities. . . . Jamie had everybody's confidence that he was so good at understanding everything."

Looking at the early days of Dimon's career, the strong influence of his former boss and mentor is clearly seen. The long association with Weill that defined his career, however, was possible only because Dimon made a key choice himself: He walked away from the more likely path from Harvard Business School to Wall Street and any one of the prestigious firms that would have been glad to hire him. That decision was key to the making of Jamie Dimon as the acquirer of companies, integrator of operations, hands-on executive—and the Wall Street statesman he is today.

As Dimon grew in experience and influence, he was widely seen as the obvious choice to take over when Weill retired one day. By the close of Act I of Dimon's Wall Street career, however, tensions would arise and the close-knit connections between Weill and Dimon would come undone for several reasons. Rivalries, battles, a company that expanded so far so fast, and a host of other reasons could be cited. And perhaps as Dimon stepped into the limelight the shadow he cast was larger than Weill liked. Whatever the reason, Dimon would soon face professional devastation, but would not lose his sense of self as a strong and capable leader.

Chapter 4

A Force on Wall Street

I was the president of Citigroup. I walked in and [Weill] said, "I want you to resign," and believe me, it was like I was shocked. I didn't expect it in any way, shape, or form.

—JAMIE DIMON

Jamie Dimon has been delivered a complete surprise twice in his career. The first came when, in an unexpected move, Sandy Weill named him president of Primerica in 1991. "When Sandy told me, I almost fell off my chair," Dimon, who was then 35 years old, said in an interview at the time.[1]

For Dimon, being named president of Primerica elicited the superlatives that stressed his age and accomplishments: He was one of the youngest presidents of a major financial services firm, one of the youngest to hold that post in a Fortune 500 company, and, as the *New York Times* noted, "one of the most powerful members of his generation on Wall Street."[2]

For Weill, promoting Dimon was a fitting reward for a job well done. The Smith Barney brokerage unit he helped manage had seen an explosion in profitability, which boosted the results for parent company Primerica. "It seemed appropriate to promote Jamie, who has done a fantastic job in understanding and relating to every part of our business, and give him the opportunity to grow and do a lot more," Weill said.[3]

Along with Dimon's promotion, other management changes were made at Primerica. Named to the new positions of vice chairmen were Bob Lipp, who was also chair of Primerica's consumer service division, and Frank Zarb, who headed Smith Barney as its chairman and chief executive officer. The changes reflected the expansion at Primerica, which in time would prove to be only the beginning as the firm would undertake more acquisitions and change its name two more times until it became Citigroup.

Seven years after the first surprise of being named president of Primerica, Dimon was delivered the second. By then Dimon was president of Citigroup and co-head of the combined investment bank and brokerage unit known as Salomon Smith Barney. When Weill called Dimon into a meeting in early November 1998, he had a far different message for the man who had been with him nearly 17 years, from protégé to right-hand man to the co-creator of the merger and acquisition deals made over the years. Weill wanted Dimon to resign.

Today, Dimon pulls no punches when he says he was fired—no corporate euphemisms for him of stepping down or parting ways. "I was the president of Citigroup. I walked in and [Weill] said, 'I want you to resign,' and believe me, it was like I was shocked. I didn't expect it in any way, shape, or form," Dimon said in a 2002 speech.

He even jokes about it: "I always tell people when they get advice from me, I'm not sure you're going to get ahead using it, because remember I did get fired once."[4]

Such transparency and self-disclosure reflect Dimon's philosophy of openness and his habit of directness. But one also has to wonder what his refrain, "I was fired, folks," might also mean. Perhaps owning up to the difficult truth each and every time disarms anyone who would whisper, "He was fired, you know," because Dimon has already said it first. Or maybe it's simply the truth, and Dimon, who places a high value on being a truth teller, is compelled to say exactly what happened.

The two surprises—being named president of Primerica and then seven years later being fired as president of Citigroup—mark the second half of Act I of Dimon's career on Wall Street. In between were the dramas that come with the territory of big egos, huge rewards, and cataclysmic losses. Rivalries, clashes, and conflicts introduced increasing uncertainty into what had seemed assured: that sometime in the future he would take over Citigroup as Weill's successor, and a new king of Wall Street would reign.

As Dimon's job grew, so did his power, influence, and independence. Becoming head of Smith Barney, the result of a management shake-up in which he emerged victorious, Dimon was his own man and was recognized as such. Young, bright, and ambitious, Dimon's path to the CEO post appeared unobstructed. But it was not to be. By the end of Act I, Dimon had won a battle with Weill's daughter, Jessica Bibliowicz, whose ambitions were to rise further into the power circle, but he would lose the war.

Dimon's exile was swift and painful. But this was only one of several rifts that had developed between Weill and Dimon, who as the "refugees from bureaucracy" had taken over Commercial Credit and then formed an unwieldy behemoth that was the largest financial services firm in the world.

At the midpoint of Act I of Dimon's Wall Street career, he and Weill were still a matched set of minds. As Monica Langley described in her book on the building of Citigroup, *Tearing Down the Walls*, "By far the most important relationship within Primerica was between Sandy and Jamie Dimon. Over the years Dimon had gone from being Sandy's understudy to his full-fledged alter ego. Had the pair been painting a mural instead of building a company, Sandy would be making the broad brushstrokes to set the theme; Dimon would fill in the details with perceptive and precise specifics."

When Weill had an idea, it was Dimon he turned to for the specifics. "Dimon, capable of calculating several transactions in his head simultaneously, would quickly give Sandy the exact answer he wanted. In their rapid-fire banter, the two executives frequently would complete each other's sentences. They even developed their own unconscious forms of verbal shorthand. One needed to speak only a few words of a sentence for the other to understand completely what was left unsaid."[5]

When they clashed, Dimon had no difficulty standing up to Weill, shouting him down if necessary; it was all part of their dynamic. But as Dimon grew to become a Wall Street power in his own right, it was inevitable that there would be mounting tensions between the two.

As one insider noted in 1996, by the time Dimon became CEO of Smith Barney, "there have been a few confrontations" between Dimon and Weill. "Jamie's riding high on Smith Barney's success. He can hold stronger views than ever before."[6]

But as the curtain rises on the next scene in Act I of Dimon's Wall Street career, it was a time of possibility; Primerica had room to grow, and the young president was poised for much bigger things.

Primerica Grows

Soon after the acquisition that turned Commercial Credit into Primerica, the company looked to build its business through more deals. In 1989, it had bought 16 of 43 retail offices owned by Drexel Burnham Lambert in return for assuming the office leases and paying about $4 million for the furniture and equipment. For Drexel, the sale of its retail business followed a settlement reached with the Securities and Exchange Commission on charges of securities fraud in a case that eventually brought down the firm and its junk-bond king, Michael Milken. The Drexel offices grew Smith Barney's retail sales force to about 2,600 and added about 250,000 new accounts. Primerica had cherry-picked among the Drexel offices, choosing some of the largest and taking on 500 brokers who were among the biggest producers. "Their productivity is high, like ours," Zarb said of the acquisition at the time.[7]

Also in 1989, Primerica bought the consumer finance business of BarclaysAmerican Corporation for $1.35 billion in cash, in a deal that would add 220 offices to the 490 it already operated in 29 states. The Barclays unit added strength in real estate lending to Primerica's Commercial Credit business.

While strategic, and in the case of the Drexel offices a real bargain for the value, neither deal brought Primerica up a rung on Wall Street's ladder. To do that, Primerica would need to make a sizable acquisition. On Weill's radar was Shearson, his old firm, which he had sold to American Express back in 1981. In early 1990, Weill was at the negotiating table with James Robinson III, chairman and CEO of American Express. In the words of Yogi Berra, it must have felt like "déjà vu all over again": Weill in talks with American Express over Shearson. But unlike a decade earlier when Weill was selling Shearson to American Express, this time he was trying to buy it back and meld it into his Smith Barney unit at Primerica. Those talks ended without agreement.[8]

It was also no-go for another round of talks, this time with General Electric's Jack Welch for GE's Kidder Peabody unit. Weill and Welch looked like they had a done deal until they hit a snag over retiree health and pensions benefits. Welch and Weill shook hands and walked away from the table.[9]

In 1992, Primerica made its next strategic move, not in investment banking and brokerage, but this time in insurance. Travelers Insurance, a household name, was looking for strategic investors. Although Weill did not find it particularly appealing to become a minority investor, an initial offer was put together: $500 million in return for slightly more than 20 percent of Travelers. Travelers' CEO rebuffed the offer at first, but Hurricane Andrew changed everything. The devastation in Florida cost Travelers more than $400 million in claims. Then a deal between Primerica and Travelers went from possibility to necessity. Rather than offering $500 million, which would go out of Travelers in the form of claims from Hurricane Andrew, Primerica raised its bid to $700 million in return for a 27 percent stake.[10]

The Travelers stake was seen as a surprising move since property-casualty insurance was not one of Primerica's core interests, which at the time included Smith Barney brokerage, Commercial Credit consumer finance, and Primerica Financial Services, which sold term insurance and mutual funds.[11] In time, however, Travelers would become an even larger part of the business, while providing a new corporate identity.

Bringing Home Shearson

With Bob Lipp, who headed Primerica's consumer finance division, dispatched to watch over the company's investment in Travelers, attention turned to the brokerage side once again. In early 1993, Robinson was ousted as CEO of American Express and replaced by Harvey Golub, a longtime friend of Weill's. All Weill needed to start negotiations was to pick up the phone and call Golub. What Weill wanted was Shearson's retail brokerage business—not the investment bank

Lehman Brothers, which American Express would later spin off in a public offering. After Golub and Weill roughed out terms of the deal, they sent in their teams to close it. On the Primerica side were Dimon and Charles "Chuck" Prince, a brilliant lawyer whom Weill would later name as his successor as CEO of Citigroup. Thus began the late-night talks, from 6:00 P.M. to 6:00 A.M., after a full day of work at Primerica.[12]

The late-night talks call to mind a more recent transaction in Dimon's career: the acquisition of Bear Stearns, which was completed over a weekend to keep the investment bank from bankruptcy. But as Dimon himself has observed, there is a difference between buying a house and buying a house on fire. With Shearson there was no smoke (not even from Weill's cigar, since he had finally given up chain-smoking them). All Primerica saw was a chance to grow its retail brokerage larger and stronger, especially now that Smith Barney was on better financial footing.

Zarb credits Dimon for completing the Shearson deal, noting, "Jamie did 90 percent of the negotiations for getting that transaction done." Splitting apart Shearson and Lehman was difficult, but necessary. "We were never keen on managing balance sheets with large capital markets exposure," Zarb recalled. "We were very good at running retail systems and with a thin balance sheet. What we saw [in Shearson] was the ability to get the distribution and not take on the balance sheet exposure."

The transaction had the kind of synergies that Weill and Dimon liked: not only growth, but also a chance to improve efficiencies and reap cost savings. Specifically, Smith Barney needed to find a new headquarters, and Shearson had excess space in its building on Greenwich Street, just north of the World Trade Center. That would save nearly all of the $300 million cost of a new headquarters, and Smith Barney would also gain a modern computer and communication system that would have taken an estimated seven years to establish.[13]

"We were very much stronger at Smith Barney—a stronger team at the top. It was easier to run things [at Shearson] after they were acquired," Zarb added.

One might think that the Primerica team would have had its hands full with the minority stake in Travelers and now buying Shearson.

Instead, Weill was convinced it was time to buy all of Travelers and complete a merger. In September 1993, both companies announced a \$4 billion merger offer, creating one of the largest and most diverse financial services companies in the country. The deal brought Primerica not only a profitable insurance company, but also a new name—Travelers—which was one of the most identifiable brands in the financial markets.

The deal promised numerous synergies (a trademark of success for Weill and his team), such as selling Travelers' insurance products, including annuities and variable life policies, through Smith Barney Shearson. Wall Street saw the combined company as less vulnerable to profit fluctuations that are common in both financial services and insurance, allowing the firm to share customers and products.

The "crummy little company" in Baltimore, as Dimon had once affectionately described Commercial Credit, was realizing the potential that the core team had seen in those early days. Solid, but in need of a turnaround, Commercial Credit had proved be so much more than a consumer lending business. For those who had taken the risk back then—including Weill, Dimon, and Lipp, whom *BusinessWeek* would later name one of the top managers in business—it was a sweet payoff and affirmation combined.

A New Team for a New Corporate Entity

With the Travelers' deal about to close, Primerica announced a management reorganization, which presaged far bigger and more tumultuous changes to come. Primerica, which was changing its name to Travelers, would be managed by four executives, three of whom had long associations working day-to-day with Weill, who remained chairman and CEO. Also on the team was a relative newcomer, whose management style put him on a collision course with Dimon.

Dimon, who was then 37, gained the additional title of chief operating officer of Primerica, while continuing as president. Lipp was made chief executive of the Travelers insurance business. Zarb, a long-time associate of Weill's who had originally been brought in to run Smith Barney, headed Primerica Financial Services, an insurance company that sold term life policies to middle-income consumers, and also

American Capital Management and Research, a mutual fund company with $16.6 billion in assets.

Zarb's latest titles reflected the fact he had been brought into the ranks of the parent company. He had been replaced at Smith Barney Shearson by Robert F. Greenhill, a former Morgan Stanley investment banker who joined Primerica in June 1993 in a move to strengthen the investment banking capability at the firm, adding to its position as a retail brokerage. It was a tough undertaking to combine investment banking for corporate clients and retail services for individuals. Up until that point, only Merrill Lynch had succeeded in both businesses. American Express, which had sold Shearson and planned to shed Lehman as soon as its financial condition improved, had not been successful at it.

Like so many who were part of the corporate ranks, Greenhill had history with Weill. He was a friend and the banker who had advised Weill during his rise at American Express, his departure from that company, and the building of Primerica—including handling the purchase of Commercial Credit in 1986.

Greenhill's arrival was also seen as adding to some overcrowding in the executive suite under Weill, which included Zarb, Lipp, and, of course, Dimon. Although Dimon was still seen as the most likely to become CEO one day, Weill rejected any thought of retirement and shrugged off such speculation. No one could claim to be No. 2, Weill said: "We don't have that kind of stuff."[14]

Smith Barney Shake-Up

Greenhill's arrival coincided with the beginning of a tumultuous time for Dimon, when his drive to keep expenses in line and reduce risk would run afoul of the largesse of the investment banking environment of the time. Greenhill, a legendary deal maker, came onboard Smith Barney Shearson with a compensation package said to be worth $36 million. Recruits who followed were given contracts and generous guarantees, in some cases a minimum of $3 million a year for three years.

By early 1995, Smith Barney was besieged by infighting between Greenhill and his deal makers on one side and Smith Barney veterans on the other. Things were okay in 1993 when Greenhill and company arrived and Wall Street was enjoying a highly profitable year. But in 1994, Smith Barney's earnings from operations were nearly flat at $368.2 million, while its fourth-quarter 1994 operating profit was down 50 percent. Negotiating bonuses at year-end, Dimon, who was then chief operating officer for Smith Barney, asked the bankers to take five-year notes in lieu of cash. But there was a caveat: If the bankers left Smith Barney before the notes came due, the principal was forfeited. In the end, the new investment bankers received a combination of cash and notes, and some quietly began job searches.[15]

The clashes between Dimon and Greenhill went beyond salaries and bonuses for Greenhill's team, showing the divisions between their management styles and philosophies. Greenhill pushed to globalize, with offices in Hong Kong and Beijing, and looked for acquisitions. Dimon wanted to rein in costs and control Greenhill's spending. A temporary peace settlement was arranged: By the summer of 1995, Dimon was given complete control over running Smith Barney Shearson, although Greenhill still had his title and focused on doing deals.

Evidence of Dimon's firm grip on Smith Barney was seen in the dismissal of the managing director of bond trading after Dimon learned that the department had not reduced risks as he had ordered and was still trading large positions. Plus, returns were lacking. When the bond department head left in May 1995, three others followed him out the door.[16]

Dimon's plate was full, given the tremendous task of integrating Smith Barney and Shearson, as well as the Morgan Stanley investment bankers. As he observed at the time, just melding computer systems was a huge undertaking, and separating Shearson from Lehman Brothers, its sister operation at American Express, "was like splitting apart Siamese twins."[17]

In October 1995, Dimon made more changes at Smith Barney, this time reassigning the head of its research department, which the brokerage firm was trying to beef up as support for its retail brokerage and investment banking groups. The change followed a drop in Smith Barney's ranking on the *Institutional Investor* list of top securities firms' research departments to eighth, down from fifth a year before.[18]

Years later, reflecting on his time running Smith Barney Shearson, Dimon spoke of demoting people who were well-liked but who needed to be moved to different jobs. He never mentioned specifically who the people were or the titles that they held. In his comments made in a 2002 presentation, he only referred to someone supposedly named "John." Dimon told of meeting with a group of people at Smith Barney who praised his abilities as a leader, but complained that "it's hard to be loyal to a place that just demoted and embarrassed John publicly." When asked what he had to say about that, Dimon recalled he "babbled; I didn't know what to say."

The next day, however, Dimon had a better answer for the person who had asked the question, and called him to explain that "John" was in the wrong job. "People had said to me, 'It's not working; you've got to make a change.' I tried to make it respectfully. It's hard to demote someone."

As if he were still defending his decision, Dimon pointed out that loyalty cannot be to one person, regardless of position or title. Loyalty, he said, is always to the organization, for the good of all. "If I had been loyal to that person . . . who would I have been disloyal to? Everybody else."[19]

As the head of Smith Barney, Dimon showed his commitment to the organization by making the tough decisions. Although he had helped to bring Greenhill on board, the arrangement was clearly not working out. Weill then moved to make official what had been happening all along: Dimon would be CEO of Smith Barney and Greenhill could stay on as chairman and do deals. But Greenhill would not hear of it, and resigned.[20]

In January 1996, Smith Barney announced that Dimon had been named chairman and CEO of Smith Barney, officially in charge of the operation he had been running.

After Greenhill left, many bankers also departed, blaming Dimon for mismanagement and poor treatment. An ex-Smith Barney banker was quoted as calling Dimon "charming and smart," but lacking in the knowledge of investment banking. In an interview at the time, Dimon said the problem was trying to do too much too fast, and publicly took all the responsibility for the failure, saying, "blame it on me, not Bob [Greenhill]."[21]

Growing Tensions

Dimon's struggle over Smith Barney that pitted him against Greenhill was nothing compared to the battle that would soon rage. One of the bitterest conflicts Dimon would face was with Weill's daughter, Jessica Bibliowicz, then aged 36, ambitious and close to her father. She had also been friends with Dimon since they were teenagers.

The father-son dynamic between Weill and Dimon had been batted about in the news columns for years, and the former protégé was still seen as the odds-on favorite to step into Weill's shoes when he finally retired. But the dynamic between them was changing as Dimon came more into his own at Smith Barney. Then Bibliowicz joined Travelers as executive vice president in charge of Smith Barney's mutual funds.

Weill had wanted both of his children to work at Travelers. His son, Marc, had joined Smith Barney and was later made vice president of investments. His daughter, however, had rebuffed Weill's first offer to join the firm, instead going to work for Prudential. But when she was passed over for a promotion at Prudential, Bibliowicz decided to come to work for Travelers.

Dimon's recommendation was that Bibliowicz report to him at Smith Barney, where she oversaw sales and marketing and managed $58 billion in mutual fund assets, rather than go to work at the parent company with her father. Less than a year into the job, Bibliowicz began pushing for more responsibility and authority, including wanting to run the mutual fund operation. A management move was orchestrated, reassigning another executive to allow Bibliowicz to take over as head of mutual fund operations. Despite that move, which had been largely arranged by Dimon, tensions between the two sparked. One issue was Dimon's decision, based on his market analysis, of offering no-load funds, which were growing popular with retail investors, instead of continuing to offer load funds that charged fees to investors. Bibliowicz was against no-loads because the fees had traditionally been a high source of profits for the firm. Weill intervened, casting doubts on the plan, although Dimon would eventually win out and Smith Barney would introduce new no-load products in July 1996—becoming the first major Wall Street broker to do so.[22]

Bibliowicz and Dimon also clashed because of their respective strengths: hers in marketing and his in analysis and financial details. When Dimon grilled her for numbers, Bibliowicz felt attacked. Tensions between the two of them mounted further when Bibliowicz wanted to be promoted and Weill agreed; Dimon opposed the move, saying she wasn't ready.

Had Dimon given in, as some had advised him to do, one wonders what the outcome would have been. Would there have been peace in the kingdom with Bibliowicz occupying a higher position closer to her father? Would Dimon have been able to concede and focus on his enormous task of running Smith Barney Shearson, which was about to grow even larger with the acquisition of Salomon Brothers? And would Dimon have stayed at Citigroup, where he would have remained a top contender for the top job? One can only speculate on the outcome that could have been. But contention over Bibliowicz's role caused a further split in what was a fractured relationship between Weill and Dimon. Some have said that Dimon sealed his fate the day Bibliowicz left, even though he would stay on at company for another year.

In his memoir, Weill recounts talking to Dimon about Bibliowicz, expressing his fears that she would leave the firm. "Jamie seemed responsive, saying, 'I *do* think she's good, and we *should* keep her.' Assuming Jamie would speak to Jessica and straighten things out, Joanie and I headed off for our annual two-week vacation in France. To my dismay, however, I returned to learn that Jamie never approached Jessica and that my daughter had now firmly made up her mind to resign. Jamie's lack of follow-up infuriated me—Jessica might have ended up staying if only Jamie had demonstrated his support for her."[23]

Another account suggested that Dimon offered Bibliowicz part of the West Coast branch network to manage, but not the entire state of California, saying the job was too big. Although Bibliowicz had looked favorably on moving west with her husband and two young sons, she decided it was best to leave the company. When she departed, Weill blamed Dimon.[24]

In June 1997, Bibliowicz joined John A. Levin & Company, a New York investment advisory firm, as president, chief operating officer, and a director. The move came as a shock to fund industry analysts, because Levin was so much smaller than Smith Barney, and Bibliowicz was seen as having an inside track to run Smith Barney one day.

In the press, everyone appeared to be one big happy family. Bibliowicz said in an interview her decision was prompted by the desire to do something more entrepreneurial, to build something on her own.

Dimon denied there had been any contentiousness between him and Bibliowicz, stating, "There was no strain on our relationship." Weill, for his part, said there were no disagreements at Smith Barney that caused his daughter to leave, adding that while he was unhappy that she was leaving because she had done a "terrific job," he was happy that she had an entrepreneurial opportunity.[25]

Fourteen months later, the news headlines would be filled with a different departure: this time Dimon's ouster from Citigroup. Although the announcements would portray it at first as a resignation, there was no doubt that Dimon had been fired. Through all the speculation as to the cause, many people would see a direct link to Dimon's refusal to promote Bibliowicz as a major cause of the downfall.

Just a few months after Bibliowicz's decision to leave the firm, however, it appeared that Dimon had survived yet another battle and that his relationship with Weill, although strained, was still intact. The two men were about to embark on yet another adventure in the drive to expand Smith Barney: this time the acquisition of Salomon Brothers.

The Salomon Deal

Of all the names on Wall Street, Salomon Brothers had a distinct cachet: elite, edgy, and a tough trading firm. It also had something of a past, having paid $290 million in fines in a Treasury bond scandal in 1991. Salomon had allegedly violated rules related to its status as a primary dealer of bonds and other securities purchased directly from the federal government. Salomon was charged with buying more than the legal limit of the securities and altering records to cover it up. After the Treasury bond mess was put behind Salomon, it had lost much of its swagger, but was still a trading force on the Street.

By 1997, as Travelers continued its acquisition prowl, Salomon was more than just a consolation prize after losing out on several potential deals, including an attempt to buy J.P. Morgan & Company. (And in the irony that is Wall Street, it would be Dimon, in his next iteration as chairman and CEO of Bank One, who would pull off a deal with J.P. Morgan.) There was also speculation that Travelers was looking at Bankers Trust, and Weill had been in talks about acquiring Goldman, Sachs & Company but nothing materialized.

Salomon filled an important gap for Travelers, providing a bigger presence in investment banking and in overseas operations. Salomon also had brains and talent, which it applied to key areas such as arbitrage. In short, Salomon was a *name* and its top traders, dubbed "masters of the universe," took big risks and reaped huge rewards.

Salomon weathered the storm of the Treasury bond scandal under the leadership of none other than Warren Buffett, the billionaire investor, whose firm, Berkshire Hathaway, had bought a $700 million stake in Salomon Brothers in 1987. As the interim chairman, Buffett put Salomon on a straight-and-narrow path, and surprised insiders and outsiders alike by naming as his chief operating officer Deryck C. Maughan. An Englishman and described as a professional manager, as opposed to being a trader, Maughan had been chairman of Salomon Brothers Asia Ltd., running the firm's "crown jewel" in Tokyo.[26] In May 1992, Maughan was named chairman and CEO of Salomon Brothers.

In 1997, with a consolidation wave swallowing up firms on Wall Street, Salomon was for sale, and Weill was at the top of Maughan's list of possible suitors. In September 1997, Wall Street hailed the announcement that Travelers was buying Salomon in a $9 billion stock transaction. As the *New York Times* crowed about the deal, "After combining with Salomon . . . Travelers will rival the likes of Merrill Lynch & Company, the American Express Company and Citicorp, as well as the biggest financial companies in Europe and Japan." It was also hailed as "a crowning achievement for Sanford I. Weill, the Travelers chairman who, despite occasional setbacks, has impatiently sought for years to climb to the very top of the greased pole of Wall Street."[27]

As the deal was dissected, questions were raised about the culture fit between Salomon, with its large bond trading operation in which star traders earned tens of millions of dollars, and the retail brokerage operation of Smith Barney. Another issue was the big premium paid for Salomon. The purchase price of more than $9 billion was nearly twice the book value of $4.6 billion.

As the combined firm of Salomon Smith Barney was created, Dimon, who had been chairman and CEO of Smith Barney (as well as being chief operating officer and president of Travelers) was made co-CEO of the merged operation along with Maughan. If the combination irked either executive at first, it was not evident in their words.

"We want to operate as a team. The idea of partnership is not foreign to us," the 49-year-old Maughan said at the time. "There's plenty of work for us both to do here," added Dimon. To demonstrate their cohesion, Dimon noted that by the time the Salomon acquisition was announced, he and Maughan had already assembled a management committee with top people from both firms.[28]

In time, the Salomon Smith Barney quarters would prove to be too close for two CEOs to work together. Then mounting headaches and trading losses would overcome even the best of intentions.

As for the creation of Salomon Smith Barney, however, Dimon later called the deal a "no-brainer" for the strategic advantage of combining the two investment banks. While Smith Barney's research department was rated somewhat higher than Salomon's, the sum total of the two created the No. 1 research department, as rated by *Institutional Investor*. Salomon's fixed income operation was dominant, but when combined with Smith Barney's retail capability in that area, the whole fixed income department improved. Moreover, Salomon's fixed income business complemented Smith Barney's strength in equity. Then, combining Salomon's 800 investment bankers with 800 from Smith Barney, the result was a force of 1,600 who had a full array of products to offer in the marketplace. "The investment bank now had a full equity product [and] a full fixed income product. The investment bank before at Smith Barney had the equity, but not the fixed income. The investment bank at Salomon had the fixed income, but not the equity. And now we had the whole thing and the best research department in the country," Dimon commented in a 2006 speech.[29]

The Deal of Deals

If Sandy Weill was happy with pulling off the Salomon transaction, he was ecstatic over what came next: the creation of the world's largest financial services company with a $70 billion merger—the largest to date—between Travelers and Citicorp. For Weill, the deal was the ultimate glory in a long career.

The possibility of a deal with Citicorp had surfaced in late 1997 when Travelers' Planning Group comprised of top executives began tossing out a wish list of names for a possible deal: Merrill Lynch,

Goldman Sachs, American Express, J.P. Morgan. . . . Then the name
Citicorp, the largest bank in the United States and the leader in financial services globally, was suggested.[30] At first dismissed as a preposter-
ous idea and then seen as an intriguing proposition, Citicorp stirred
imaginations and whetted appetites.

In order to pull off the "mother of all deals," Weill, 65, would have
to share the top spot with Citicorp CEO John S. Reed, 59, a polished,
conservative, and cerebral banker. But being co-chairmen and co-
CEOs was the only way the deal would work. In fact, as Weill had first
proposed it, equality would be showcased from the chairman's office
to the boardroom to shareholders themselves. When Reed, who was
surprised by Weill's overture at first, agreed to pursue a possible merger,
Weill immediately called Dimon.

Their enthusiasm over the opportunity was mutual and contagious.
It seemed like the old days when the two pursued opportunities, con-
gratulated each other when they were victorious, and then eagerly
set about the hard work to make the deal happen. For the Travelers-
Citicorp transaction to proceed, it would take more orchestrating than
either had experienced before.

The Travelers-Citicorp combination made headlines for many
reasons beyond the size and boldness of the move. There were serious regulatory restrictions, including the Glass-Steagall Act of 1933
that separated commercial and investment banking and put regulatory
limits on the financial products that banks could offer. The Travelers-
Citicorp deal would corner regulators and lawmakers in a tough spot:
They would have to either end the restrictions on banks and insurance
companies joining forces, prevent the merger from happening, or force
the new company to cut back on what it could offer its customers.[31]

The call to end Glass-Steagall, however, predated Citigroup.
More than 10 years previously, policy makers had debated the mer-
its of repealing Glass-Steagall, at least under certain circumstances. The
Travelers-Citicorp deal would force the issue to resolution.

Glass-Steagall came to an end when the Gramm-Leach-Bliley bill
was signed into law in November 1999. Senator Phil Gramm, who was
the lead bill sponsor, said that repealing Glass-Steagall was acknowledgment that "government is not the answer . . . that freedom and competition are the answers."[32]

The Travelers-Citicorp merger to create the combined company known as Citigroup was widely credited with helping to shatter Glass-Steagall. Nearly a decade later, with Wall Street awash in losses due to the credit crisis and the Federal Reserve stepping in to help rescue firms and facilitate takeovers, questions would be raised as to how financial services regulation should operate in the post-Glass-Steagall era. The debate would resurface as to the merits of allowing retail banking, investment banking, and insurance and investment products to mingle under one corporate roof—and just how far the Fed's purview should be stretched to also cover investment banks.

Managing Salomon

With the Travelers-Citicorp deal, Weill realized his dream of creating the biggest force on Wall Street and a rival to any financial services power in the world. Dimon, however, was managing a nightmare of risks at Salomon Smith Barney. Perhaps the worries at Salomon kept him from thinking about the other upset he had endured: Weill had not offered to put him on the Citigroup board. Weill's reasons were that the board would get too large; that if Dimon were to serve as a director, then someone from Citicorp would need to be added as well. Looking back, however, it appears that being passed over for a board seat was a glaring sign that Dimon was being edged out from the inner circle of Citigroup management.

By the summer of 1998, Dimon was up to his eyeballs in risk management. The risks taken on routinely by Salomon, including by its famed arbitrage unit, would prove too much for Dimon's tolerance. The magnitude of those risks was captured by Richard Bookstaber, who has held risk management positions at several prestigious Wall Street firms and was a member of Salomon's risk management committee. In his book, *A Demon of Our Own Design: Markets, Hedge Funds, and the Perils of Financial Innovation*, Bookstaber described an end-of-quarter analysis of the arbitrage unit's performance prepared for Dimon after June 1998 showing that "since March, they had an interest rate exposure that would lose $3 million for each basis point drop in rates. Over that time, the 10-year Treasury bond had dropped by 35 basis points," accounting for "about $100 million of their losses, more than half of their total of $170 million."[33]

Losses at Salomon had to be reined in, even if it meant disbanding the bond arbitrage group. Right after the July 4th holiday, a memo was put out to employees announcing the U.S. arbitrage group was being shut down after posting $15 million in losses in the second quarter. Citing a memo entitled "Reorganization of Global Arbitrage," authored by Dimon and Maughan, the *New York Times* reported that the firm's global arbitrage group was expected to post a small loss for the third quarter of 1998, compared with about $100 million in profits in the prior quarter—"in large part driven by the reduced performance of the U.S. arbitrage unit."[34]Although such losses were considered small for firms that trade billions of dollars, the bigger issue was the sea change that had occurred since Salomon had been taken over by Travelers, where, particularly under Dimon's watchful eye, anything less than strict risk management would not be tolerated.

Closing the arbitrage unit reflected the conservative and risk-averse culture that dominated Salomon Smith Barney, compared with the more freewheeling days of Salomon's past. Citing several people at Salomon Smith Barney, the *Times* reported that "less risk, and particularly less big risk-taking with the firm's own money, is now the order of the day. . . . The business of trading for customers is now, some executives said, prized over proprietary trading with the firm's own money."[35]

When it came to risk management, it seemed everywhere Dimon turned at Salomon he was faced with a new problem. The marketplace was rocked when the hedge fund Long-Term Capital Management blew apart after its investment portfolio, which had been thought to be perfectly hedged, came unglued when Russia defaulted on its domestic debt. Long-Term Capital wasn't the only one suffering from Russia exposure, as Dimon was painfully aware.

Dimon had already put out the word to the Salomon Smith Barney arbitrage group: reduce the Russia exposure to next to nothing. Or as Bookstaber recalled, describing Dimon holding his thumb and forefinger in the air nearly touching, the exposure was to be reduced "down to this."

"Everybody at Salomon wanted to hate Dimon for interjecting himself into our culture, but over time he won widespread respect, even admiration," Bookstaber wrote. "The fact is that he could have done almost everyone's job better than they could. His dogged pressure to get out of the Russia position would have earned him a Salomon Trader of the Year award in an earlier era."[36]

No one was handing out prizes when, despite Dimon's warnings, Salomon posted huge losses. In late August 1998, Salomon reported that, in the past two months alone, it had lost an estimated $360 million after taxes in its arbitrage and Russian-related credit businesses. Not that it was much consolation, but Salomon was hardly alone as other firms were reporting hundreds of millions in losses.

Tallying up the damages, Salomon said that, for July and August 1998, it would have $60 million in Russian-related credit losses, $120 million in losses from its U.S. bond arbitrage portfolio, and $180 million in losses from its international arbitrage business. Helping to offset the losses were profits from the firm's private client and fund management businesses, which totaled $210 million for the previous two months.

As the co-CEO of Salomon Smith Barney, Dimon was in the hot seat. The integration of the two firms was not going as well as expected, and he locked horns with Maughan over management of the business. The timing couldn't have been worse, with Travelers in the midst of making history by joining forces with Citicorp to form Citigroup.

The Firing of Jamie Dimon

Challenges with the Citigroup integration, from differing management styles to culture clashes, spilled over to ignite long-simmering tensions between Dimon and Weill. In the well-publicized accounts, the final showdown came in the fall of 1998. The scene was an outing for Citigroup corporate executives and their spouses, four days of golf, planning, and bonding at the Greenbrier resort in West Virginia. Just days before, Citigroup had posted a dramatic drop in its third-quarter 1998 profits. Those who had gone to Greenbrier were soon complaining loudly about how to manage the colossus that had been created.

At one point Steve Black, a senior Citigroup executive who today is co-CEO of the JPMorgan Chase investment bank and a close associate of Dimon's, quarreled loudly with Maughan over how to manage the corporate and investment banking businesses. Dimon stepped in between them, as he had been charged with smoothing out differences.

A week later, on Sunday, November 1, 1998, Dimon received a call at home: Weill asked him to come up to a company conference center in Armonk, New York. Dimon wasn't sure what to expect when he got there—and certainly not for Weill to ask for his resignation.

Dimon's dismissal stunned Wall Street and the company. "I found it shocking," one top Citigroup executive told the *New York Times*. "He was basically fired, and a lot of it had to do with corporate politics. Jamie had a lot of fans here."[37]

As reasons for Dimon's departure became grist for the rumor mill, the conflict with Jessica Bibliowicz was often mentioned. Another factor cited was the mounting losses at Salomon Smith Barney, which Dimon co-managed with Maughan. The *Times* also mused whether Weill, aged 65, had grown resentful of Dimon's "spot in the limelight and generally stellar reputation on Wall Street."[38]

Most likely it was not due to any one reason: not Bibliowicz, or Salomon, or the difficulty of the Citigroup deal. Just as with any long-term friendship or even a marriage, there is rarely one event that brings it all to an end. The relationship between Weill and Dimon had been crumbling for years, perhaps longer than either would want to admit or address. What was clear, however, was that Dimon had changed over the nearly two decades of working for and with Weill. The right-hand man had become a Wall Street executive in his own right.

Chapter 5

The Recruitment of Jamie Dimon

I think the [Bank One] board made a very tough decision, by the way.
I was much harder to hire: a young guy, out of New York.

—Jamie Dimon

I n the creation and re-creation of careers, the theme of second chances runs through the story of Jamie Dimon. New York Mayor Michael Bloomberg, in a salute to Dimon and reflecting on the end of his own 15-year career at Salomon Brothers "with a surprise boot out the door," wrote: ". . . life has given better second and third acts to us both—in Jamie's case, a lead role in ending our winter of financial discontent."[1]

In Dimon's Wall Street drama, Act I encompassed his years with Sandy Weill: following his deposed boss out the door of American Express into the obscurity of Commercial Credit; becoming president of Primerica, and then the clashes and battles that led to him being fired from Citigroup. Now, at the start of Act II, Dimon's career renaissance begins, from a self-imposed 18-month hiatus to becoming CEO of Bank One. As chairman and CEO of the Chicago-based regional bank, Dimon would use his full range of leadership skills to catalyze a dramatic turnaround, from delving into the details of every business line to strategizing the big picture of what would come next. In the process, he would take Bank One to such a level of excellence that it became attractive to none other than JPMorgan Chase, in a move that would eventually put him back on Wall Street, where he would emerge as a statesman and one of the most recognized leaders of his generation.

Although he had been fired from Citigroup, it's important to understand that, for Dimon, becoming Bank One CEO was not a staging ground. He wasn't trying to make a comeback by first testing the waters elsewhere. From the beginning, Bank One was no dress rehearsal; this was it—the opportunity that Dimon hungered for. Here was a solid organization that needed a turnaround, a place where he could apply his talent and experience from the Citigroup days to make a real difference. In that, Jamie Dimon and Bank One were made for each other.

With his high visibility at Citigroup and the very public way in which he was fired, Dimon would attract attention wherever he would go next. Act II of Dimon's career would be just as public as his rise to the No. 2 spot at Citigroup and his precipitous fall from grace. Everyone would be watching, evaluating, and chiming in regarding Dimon's choices, challenges, and chances for success.

Life after Citigroup

"It hurt," Jamie Dimon admitted, recalling his sudden dismissal from Citigroup nearly 10 years after the fact. "But as I tell people . . . it was my net worth, not my self-worth, involved in the company. I didn't feel less of a person, but all of a sudden you do feel kind of naked out there. You don't do this thing; you aren't president of Travelers or Citigroup."

In the midst of such a life-changing event as being fired from a top executive position, there were bound to be lessons to learn. For Dimon, one of them was finding out who his friends were. "Every single person I would call my friend was still my friend afterwards. There was none of this 'they disappeared.' It was the other way around: They were calling me up and taking me to lunch."

After negotiating a severance package (reportedly worth $30 million) and extracting himself from Citigroup, there was never any doubt that Dimon would land in a CEO position somewhere. His only concern was "I wanted my kids to be fine." Rather than rushing back to the executive suite, first he took time for relaxation.

"I made a list of all the stuff I wanted to do. I love history, I love reading, I love biographies. I went to the bookstore the next day and bought 30 or 40 books. . . . I love reading the paper, so instead of reading for an hour and a half in the morning I read the paper for three hours," he recalled. "But I couldn't read 12 to 15 hours a day."

Dimon also took up boxing at the urging of a friend to stay physically active. "He said come on downtown [to the gym] and I started."

During his time off work he planned a family trip to Europe— "five or six weeks with the kids . . . totally leisure, which we had never done before. Before that it was RV trips or Alaska, the Grand Canyon. We went to visit my brother in Denmark."

Dimon also devoted extensive time to discerning what he would do next. He spoke to everyone who contacted him, even if he wasn't that interested in the position: Internet companies, investment banks, Dun & Bradstreet, Home Depot. "I don't even remember them all," Dimon said. He considered joining a private equity firm, and even entertained becoming national finance chair for Al Gore's presidential campaign, but didn't want to travel every Saturday and Sunday and ask people for money. Recognizing that this interim period was a chance to rethink what he wanted to do with his life, Dimon followed the wise advice he had been given of not rejecting anything out of hand, but rather to sit with it for a few days, to see how it would feel.

As Dimon decided what he would do next, one of the projects he took on was serving on the board of Yum! Brands, a former PepsiCo spin-off that today includes brand-name restaurant chains A&W, KFC, Long John Silver's, Pizza Hut, and Taco Bell. The late Andrall "Andy" Pearson, a former PepsiCo president and a professor of management at Harvard Business School (and also co-author of a case study on Primerica) had suggested that Dimon be invited to sit on the board. Yum! Brands jumped at the chance to have a well-known executive of Dimon's caliber as a director.

"Any time you bring on a new board member, you want the stature to reflect the standards you have set for your company. When Jamie

Dimon was on our board—this was shortly after he parted ways with Citigroup—he had a tremendous reputation for being one of the top financial people on Wall Street," recalled David Novak, who is chairman and CEO of Yum! Brands and was among the first new directors brought on the Bank One board by Dimon.

Novak described Dimon as "hard-driving," and yet also "a lot more humble than his reputation might be in the industry because he's such a rock star." As a director, Dimon showed his usual level of attention to detail: always taking notes, asking questions, and giving guidance. Dimon also demonstrated his commitment as a board member in a move that presaged what he would do later on a bigger scale at Bank One. "He bought a lot of stock," Novak recalled. "He has said to our people that we were one of the five stocks that he owned. That gave people a lot of confidence. Here you have this guru on Wall Street putting a lot of skin in the game. That's one of the things he did for us."

Dimon also held himself accountable for being a highly effective board member, even criticizing himself when he felt he could have done a better job. Novak recalled an incident early on when Yum! Brands fired its CFO and, in response, the company's stock dropped. "Jamie came to me and said, 'When you fire a CFO it creates some angst in the Wall Street community that something is wrong. I knew that and should have told you.' He took accountability, saying, 'That's our fault. We really let you down.'"

Taking responsibility for actions and decisions also led him to mend fences with Sandy Weill after a year had passed. "I called him up. I told him, 'I never would have done what you did . . . but I'd like to tell you what I did wrong,' because in any of these things it takes two people," Dimon recalled in a 2002 presentation.

Dimon's list of his own offenses included being "really obnoxious to him," avoiding certain meetings, and staying in the downtown office at Smith Barney while Weill and Citigroup co-CEO John Reed were uptown. "I did all these things which, I think, were not in the best interest of the company. They were rather immature."[2]

While Dimon stayed busy, he could stay on the sidelines only so long. One day the call came from Russell Reynolds, the executive recruitment firm that had been hired by Bank One to help manage its CEO search. An interim leader had been put in place at the Chicago-based bank after the chairman and CEO stepped down. Although the job meant relocating his family, including three school-age daughters, Dimon was intrigued. For one thing, this was a return to financial services, an industry that was more than familiar; it was home.

"You know, I really missed the camaraderie. I missed the action. It was that plain and simple," Dimon reflected. "It could have been another business. I tell people, you spend your whole life playing golf or tennis; it's hard to go play another sport. Finance was my craft. I learned that. But honestly I could have . . . enjoyed other businesses, but this I know something about: I can walk through a trading floor . . . and actually have an opinion about it."

The opportunity at Bank One was an interesting one. Here was a bank in need of a turnaround and a culture overhaul to put an end to divisiveness in its ranks. But first, Dimon would have to undergo a rigorous interview process with a six-member search committee in order to convince a sharply divided 22-member board of directors that he was the right person for the job.

Bank One's Search for a CEO

Recruiting the next chairman and CEO was not only a search process, but also the culmination of a shake-up at Bank One. In December 1999, Chairman and CEO John B. McCoy, aged 56, whose family had started the predecessor bank to the holding company Bank One, stepped down. His departure was announced as a retirement, effective immediately, with his duties assumed by Verne G. Istock, then aged 59, who had been president of Bank One. John R. Hall, retired chairman and CEO of oil refining company Ashland Inc. and a member of the Bank One board, was named interim chairman as the search for a permanent replacement began.

It was a tumultuous time for a bank with a long history in the Midwest and an appetite for growing by acquisitions. But the acquisitions the bank had made were never fully integrated in terms of operations and culture. With a new millennium to come, Bank One had to leave behind its history and strike out on a different course with a leadership change.

Bank One History

Bank One's roots go back to 1870 and City National Bank (CNB) in Columbus, Ohio, which was run as a family business. Upon the death of his father in 1958, John G. McCoy took over as president of CNB and set out on a mission to provide financial services to people who he believed chose a bank solely because of convenience. CNB was innovative: becoming the first bank to offer credit cards outside of California with the introduction in 1966 of City National BankAmericard (which later became Visa). In 1969, the bank introduced the forerunner of the automated teller machine (ATM).

From the late 1960s through the 1970s, CNB grew through acquisitions: 22 small banks in Ohio within a holding company that eventually became Banc (with a "c") One Corporation. In 1984 John G. McCoy retired, and his son, John B. McCoy, took over as CEO and president. Ascending to the position, John B. was soon pursuing more acquisitions to expand the bank's territory. State laws were changing, allowing bank holding companies to acquire banks in other states. For Banc One, this opened the door to acquisitions in Indiana, Kentucky, Wisconsin, Texas, Arizona, and Louisiana. In June 1997, Banc One acquired credit card issuer First USA Inc., and began to grow its credit card portfolio through acquisitions.

Then in October 1998 came the largest transaction in Banc One's history: the $29 billion deal (which later declined in value to just over $20 billion due to a drop in share prices) to join forces with First Chicago NBD. First Chicago NBD was comprised of the two Midwest banking firms: First Chicago and NBD Bancorp of Detroit. The result was a new bank holding company: Chicago-based Bank (with a "k") One.

The creation of Bank One came only a week after the Citicorp-Travelers deal to form Citigroup was announced. Citigroup put more pressure on other financial companies to merge to remain competitive, including the smaller, regional players. Thus while Dimon was an integral part of the creation of Citigroup, which changed the competitive landscape of the financial industry, the company he would lead two years later was scrambling to keep up.

The formation of Bank One was a merger of equals when it came to size: Banc One with its approximately $116 billion in assets and First

Chicago NBD with assets of $114 billion. By mid-1999, with $260 billion in assets, Bank One assumed the fifth-place position among the largest U.S. banks, behind Citigroup, Bank of America, Chase, and J.P. Morgan.[3]

Such a combination looked good on paper; however, each bank had distinctly different cultures that would not blend easily. First Chicago NBD had a reputation for being conservative, while Banc One was seen as more entrepreneurial. "Banc One had been very acquisition and deal oriented, with very rapid movement that led to incredible growth. Also, Banc One had been decentralized in its operations," explained John R. Hall, who chaired the search committee for the new CEO. "First Chicago was very centralized, and very careful and very analytical. I don't say which one was right. But Banc One would say, 'First Chicago never does anything; they analyze it to death.' And First Chicago would say, 'The Banc One people are making quick deals when they don't have all the information.' That's why we had to have a strong leader."

In their diametrically opposed views of each other, Banc One and First Chicago were probably both right to some degree. The problem, however, was that neither one culture nor the other ever infused the new Bank One organization. People, divisions, operations, systems, information technology (IT) platforms, and all the rest bore the marks of a fractured organization.

Bank One "was a company that had been put together by mergers without a Jamie Dimon–like person in charge, and all the disparate information systems and reporting systems never got standardized," commented Harvard Business School Professor Paul W. Marshall, who was also lead author of a Harvard case study on Bank One.

New leadership was needed at Bank One, which was suffering not only from a lack of cohesion in its ranks, but also from a dramatic drop in profitability. As the problems surfaced, Bank One's board had to take decisive action.

Profit Disappointments Call for Leadership Change

Profitability problems began surfacing at Bank One after its First USA credit card unit began facing competitive pressures and customer defections. In August 1999, Bank One announced that First USA, the consumer lending and credit card unit, which was the second largest credit card issuer in the country behind Citigroup, was likely to earn $500 million less than anticipated. In response to the news, Bank One share prices dropped 23 percent.

A second earnings warning came out a few months later, in November 1999: this time that fourth-quarter 1999 earnings forecasts would have to be reduced by as much as 16 percent. The profit disappointment was blamed on First USA, which had more than 64 million credit card holders and a portfolio of about $70 billion in consumer loans. After the latest round of disappointing earnings news from Bank One, share prices declined again—and were 50 percent lower than where they had been six months previously.[4]

The escalating problems at Bank One called into question the credibility of management, which, as one analyst noted at the time, "cannot be restored in the near term."[5]

When McCoy stepped down, Bank One's board set about the task of recruiting a new CEO. Bank One President Verne Istock was put in place as the acting CEO and would continue to be a contender to take on the job permanently, given his experience as CEO of two predecessor banks that had become part of Bank One.

Hall, as interim chairman, had the respect of directors from both the First Chicago and Banc One sides on what was a divided board. Hall had risen through the ranks of Ashland Inc., where he started as a chemical engineer in 1957, to become vice chairman and chief operating officer in 1979, and then chairman and CEO of the oil refining company in 1981. A former Academic All-American who played football on scholarship at Vanderbilt University, Hall was a natural to lead an oversized team of 22 directors through the process of picking a new leader.

As a board member from the Banc One side, Hall partnered with James Crown, a legacy director from First Chicago, who today serves on the board of JPMorgan Chase. Crown is president of Henry Crown and Company, a diversified investment firm that has holdings ranging from sports teams (with stakes in the Chicago Bulls and the New York Yankees) to manufacturing, banking, and real estate.

Hall and Crown forged a partnership as the anchors of a six-member search committee composed of outside directors, which selected executive search firm Russell Reynolds to help identify and evaluate candidates. With the help of Russell Reynolds, the search committee pared its list of candidates from 150 names initially to 25 finalists, and then 15 who were interviewed extensively.

Andrea Redmond, who was one of the Russell Reynolds recruiters working closely with Bank One, recalled the diligence of the search committee to evaluate the candidates. "It was one of the most thorough jobs on the part of any search committee. They interviewed a lot of people, not because they weren't finding the right candidates, but because John Hall and Jim Crown wanted to make sure that they met and touched anybody who was in the running."

On a short list of five candidates, Dimon was a favorite, particularly among directors who had worked for Bank One before the merger with First Chicago. Istock still had supporters from the First Chicago side who saw him as an experienced bank executive, having served as CEO of First Chicago NBD from 1996 until the 1998 merger that created Bank One, and who previously had been CEO of NBD Bancorp from 1994 through 1995.

All five candidates on the short list had similar qualifications. Dimon was the only one who was not actively employed as either a CEO or chairman of a major financial institution. This made it imperative that the search committee find out more information about the candidates than was apparent on their resumes.[6]

Checking Out the CEO Candidates

Hall and Crown tapped into their corporate networks to learn more about the external candidates. Crown had previously in his career spent five years at Salomon Brothers and still had some friends from that firm with whom he could speak about Dimon, who had served as co-CEO of Salomon Smith Barney.

For Crown, interviewing Dimon as part of the recruitment process at Bank One was a second chance to meet him. In the late 1990s, Crown and some associates had visited Dimon while he was working at Citigroup to ask his opinion about the equity markets and some international investment exposure. "What was interesting and impressive about Jamie then was if you asked him a question, he thought about it for just a little bit and then he gave you a direct and directional answer. There was not a lot of 'Well, you might do this and you might do that,'" Crown recalled.

Dimon impressed Crown in that earlier conversation with his "absolute confidence and clarity." Rather than giving both sides of the argument in a couched answer, Dimon gave an informed opinion and his reasons behind it. As Crown described it, "There was no word-mincing and no circumlocution around the question. Jamie was very direct."

The decisiveness and discernment that Crown saw in Dimon in 1990 also came through in the Bank One CEO candidate interviews. "Jamie came out of this process as just a white-hot, superior level of intelligence, very knowledgeable about financial services, the securities industry, and banking, and as a tireless worker," Crown said.

Topping the list of desired qualifications for the CEO candidate was excellent knowledge of financial services. While there were many contenders who could claim that criterion, Dimon's background and experience with Citigroup made him tough to beat. "We had lots of good candidates with lots of good knowledge of financial services, but we felt Jamie had the strongest background of any and the strongest knowledge of the financial services industry," Hall said. "We also thought he was a natural leader and a very articulate person. We were very impressed with him in our initial interviews and in our second and third interviews."

Dimon wowed the board not only with his knowledge but with his take-charge attitude that he displayed from the first moment he met the search committee directors. Even on his first interview, Dimon laid out plans to turn the bank around. "Basically, at his first interview he came in and said, 'If you give me this job, this is what I would do. This is what I think your problems are, and these are the things I would be working on.' He laid it out for us," Hall continued. "We knew from his experiences at Citigroup and other financial institutions that he had a thorough knowledge of where we had balance sheet problems, and where our costs were too high."

While Dimon was not the unanimous choice in the interview process—and Istock would remain a strong contender for the job—he had certainly impressed everyone on the search committee. Tom Brown of Second Curve Capital, LLC, recalled the recruitment process at Bank One, during which he was an adviser to board member John Hall. While there were many talented contenders, "Jamie was the sort of leader that Bank One—a company divided by different cultures— needed," Brown said.

Breaking Too Much China

Although Dimon had stellar qualifications in financial services, he also had a reputation for being demanding, impatient, and brash. The Bank One search committee was aware that Dimon's personality could rub some people the wrong way, although there was no doubt about his ability to devise a plan and execute it brilliantly. Perhaps the fast-talking, hard-driving New Yorker—the kind who could corral the super-traders of Salomon Brothers into seeing risk management his way—would be too much for the Midwest sensibilities of a regional bank set in its own ways.

"There was from the start some concern that a person from New York, with a New York financial community background, would not fit the Chicago culture. And that Jamie would 'break too much china,'" Hall explained. "We talked to Jamie about it. He said he would work hard to do the right thing. He recognized that maybe some of them were used to a different style. There were a lot of concerns that we had to overcome on that particular issue."

Dimon, himself, pointed out the fact that hiring him to become CEO of Bank One required some discernment about the fit factor on the part of the board. "I think the board made a very tough decision, by the way. I was much harder to hire: a young guy, out of New York."[7]

If there were any questions at all about Dimon's abilities, they may have centered around whether this seasoned deal maker was the best executive to lead Bank One through a turnaround. Bank One was in no position to do another deal. If anything, its biggest need was to complete the acquisitions it had made over the years, in terms of integrating systems and unifying people. The job called for strong management skills—someone who could unite and lead a fragmented team, and who could shore up a balance sheet that was in worse shape than the board had realized. In time, the Bank One search committee became convinced that Dimon—even though he did not have in-depth experience in retail banking—was the right person for the job.

"Jamie brought to the table a wealth of merger and acquisition experience because of all the work he had done with Sandy Weill. We felt we had a good leader who would be able to finish the merger work of the prior decade. While those deals had *legally* been completed, they weren't *functionally* complete. There was no unified or unifying leadership working to create a stable, consistent platform for the bank," Crown summarized.

By the March 2000 board meeting to vote on a permanent chairman and CEO, the search committee was ready to make its recommendation. Then it was time to call Dimon, to have him at the ready should the full board agree to bring him on as the next leader of Bank One.

The New Bank One CEO

Jamie Dimon was in Vail, Colorado, with his family when he received a phone call summoning him to Chicago. Thus far Dimon had only met with the members of the search committee. If all went well, he would be addressing the entire Bank One board for the first time. For Dimon, becoming CEO of Bank One meant moving his family out of New York. This was probably the hardest part of the transition, but it would have been an absolute deal breaker if Dimon and his wife, Judy, had not decided to move to Chicago with their three school-age daughters.

Looking back on the relocation to Chicago, Dimon said it meant "ripping [the] family out of a whole life and support system. [In New York] I had dinner with my parents every Sunday night. . . . My wife was on 10 boards in New York. All your friends are there, your restaurants, all the things you like to do. That was the hardest part."[8]

Dimon arrived in Chicago on Sunday, March 26, 2000, accompanied at the last minute by one of his daughters. That evening he had dinner with Russell Reynolds recruiters Andrea Redmond and Charles A. Tribbett III, and also asked to be taken to the Bank One offices to see them for the first time. Until then, Dimon had not set foot in the Bank One headquarters, because all the search committee meetings had been held off-site to preserve confidentiality.

The following day, Dimon was back at Bank One, waiting in another room while the board deliberated. The issue came down to Istock versus Dimon. With Istock serving as acting CEO, the board could have asked him to keep the job on a permanent basis and to assume the additional title of chairman. Or it could go in a new direction with a leader from the outside.

On Monday, March 27, 2000—about two weeks after Dimon's 44th birthday (and nearly eight years to the day before JPMorgan would revise its offer to acquire Bear Stearns)—Bank One announced Dimon's appointment as the new chairman and CEO. "I think part of this decision was the context of the matter," commented Harvard professor Rakesh Khurana, who has studied and written extensively about the CEO recruitment process. "Bank One wasn't doing well. Moreover, having an insider candidate in the form of Verne Istock wasn't fully appealing to the board, which had been split as a consequence of the merger of Banc One and First Chicago NBD. Also, the types of problems that Bank One was facing were deeply operational: dealing with the credit card business, and the lack of integration of companies that had been run as stand-alones. That necessity aligned well with the perception of what Jamie Dimon could bring to the table. . . . His strong experience, recognition of the importance of integrated information technology, and being very performance-oriented made Dimon a strong candidate."

In the end, the board decided on Dimon in what Hall recalled was "very nearly a unanimous vote." The Bank One board then welcomed its new CEO.

That moment in the Bank One boardroom, recruiter Andrea Redmond came full circle in her career. "The last time I had been in that boardroom was when I was an intern at First Chicago," she recalled. Placing the next CEO of the bank was a proud moment for Redmond who felt the company where she had "grown up" was in good hands with Dimon. Even though the Bank One ranks were in for a shake-up, Dimon was exactly what the organization needed if it was to survive and thrive in an increasingly competitive environment.

For Dimon, meeting the full board for the first time on the day he was elected CEO enabled him to declare his intentions that he could orchestrate a turnaround. "I walked in that morning and shook all their hands. I said, 'I really appreciate the opportunity, and I'm going to make you proud of the place.' And I went to work. I went downstairs and I said, 'Where's the office and can I have a secretary?'"[9]

Dimon was ready to get to work.

Outside Captain for the Home Team

If anyone doubted Dimon's commitment from day one at Bank One, he put his money where his mouth was. Proving that he was "all in"—or as Dimon liked to say, that he was willing to eat his own cooking—he invested nearly $60 million of his own money, estimated to be half his net worth at the time, in Bank One stock. It was symbolic and substantive, and greatly impressed the board. It also energized Bank One employees, who recognized that the new CEO had committed personally as well as professionally to the company's success. "There was a real buzz among the people at Bank One when he made the stock purchase. It showed he meant business," recalled Kathy Schroeder, who was a first vice president of National Learning, the employee development and training department at Bank One.

Many of those who had known Dimon during his years working closely with Sandy Weill expected another success story at Bank One. As Joseph Califano Jr., a longtime board member for Primerica, Travelers, and Citigroup, commented, "The day Jamie became the head of Bank One in Chicago was the day I bought stock in Bank One."

Wall Street applauded after Dimon's appointment was made known. Bank One's shares gained 13 percent on three times the normal volume. TheStreet.com hailed the decision: "Ending a short but depressing Gerald Ford–like interim regime, Bank One finally has a new leader in the form of ex-Citigroup executive Jamie Dimon. And investors, judging by their reaction to the news of his appointment, believe Dimon will be a lot more successful at cleaning up and reviving his office than Jimmy Carter was." TheStreet.com quoted a bank stock fund manager who said, "I don't think they could've picked a better leader."[10]

In his first press conference as Bank One CEO, Dimon spoke with optimism about his new job and tried to close any perception of an experience gap when it came to running a bank, noting that Citigroup's Salomon Smith Barney unit had a large retail brokerage operation, which gave him experience with retail financial services.

Dimon also came on strong as the newest player made captain, cheering for his new home team, stating that his goal was to strengthen the bank "so it is predator and not prey" as the industry continued to consolidate. He joked with reporters, quipping that in New York the press called him "Jamie," but in Chicago the press he met for the first time called him "Mr. Dimon." If he felt like a guest in his new home, Dimon tried not to show it, and was quick to dismiss speculation that he had taken the CEO position just to groom the bank for sale. "I think Bank One is a fabulous platform," he said, adding he wasn't in the job to flip the bank in a couple of years.[11]

Dimon would end up selling Bank One in a $58 billion deal four years later, a deal that would bring him back to Wall Street and eventually put him at the helm of JPMorgan Chase. On the day he took over as Bank One's CEO, however, a quick sale was definitely not in the cards. Instead, Dimon would have a tough job ahead of him.

While admitting to a few "pangs of anxiety," Dimon was ready to get back to work, having waited for what he described to *Fortune* magazine in baseball lingo as the "fat pitch"—a job that would enable him to make a valuable contribution for the long term. Now that he had what he believed to be the right opportunity, Dimon wanted to swing for the fences with a turnaround that would prove his belief that Bank One could be "one of America's great financial institutions."[12]

Taking Over as CEO

Taking over as chairman and CEO of Chicago-based Bank One in late March 2000 was Dimon's first opportunity to show his stuff since his very public firing from Citigroup in November 1998. Dimon clearly saw Bank One as a turnaround. What neither he nor the board probably knew at the time was just how extensive an overhaul that would require.

"When I got to Bank One, I only knew what I had read publicly. . . . Analyst reports don't tell you much. The annual report had poor disclosure, in my opinion. I met six directors [during the search process]; there were 22 directors. I wanted to go back to work, and it looked like a pretty good opportunity. I figured that we'll make it work," he reflected.[13]

As Dimon got down to work, he assumed a daunting task of unifying, streamlining, and strengthening. Everything from the size of the board to the size of the dividend, from boosting employee morale to shoring up the balance sheet, had to be addressed. From the start, Dimon was a tireless worker, a demanding boss, someone who saw the big picture as well as the small details. He possessed the skills to devise a plan and execute it excellently, even though that meant stepping on a few toes at times.

"He was hard on people because he was very demanding—demanding in terms of hours, demanding in terms of performance," James Crown observed. "But no one worked harder than he did. It was not a question of telling people that they should work all day Saturday; it was the fact that Jamie was going to be working all day Saturday and all day Sunday, and he expected others to be available and be prepared because there was work to do. I think we needed that work ethic. I think people were a bit complacent at Bank One relative to the urgency of the situation, although we didn't realize the urgency of the situation quite as well as we might have. Jamie was a very compelling hire."

Those who love Dimon do so with loyalty and passion. Those who dislike him do so with equal passion. As a former Bank One executive told *Time* magazine, "Jamie doesn't care who he pisses off. As soon as he walks in the room, he is by his own estimation the smartest guy there."[14]

Dimon had no time or tolerance for old rivalries or for people who wanted to do things a certain way simply because that's how they had always been done. As he reflected in a 2006 presentation after becoming CEO of JPMorgan Chase: "You can say what you want . . . and if you end up with 'because it's in the best interest of the company and the clients,' I'm fine. If you end it by saying, 'because Bank One did it that way,' I don't give a damn. That isn't a reason."[15]

While Dimon had a vision of the turnaround he would orchestrate at Bank One, he did not start out with preconceived ideas of how that would look. First he needed to engage in a fact-finding mission. "To walk into a company new, you put aside everything you think, thought, or will ever think. You evaluate everything fresh as of that day," Dimon said of his first days at Bank One. "I talked to everyone: What about this? What about that? What about this person? . . . You've got to evaluate the people making the decisions. Step out of the business and deal with the absolute truth."[16]

For Dimon, this meant asking a lot of questions and demanding answers that were more than what people thought he wanted to hear. He wanted actionable information that would help identify the scope of problems and put solutions in place. A master at posing probing questions, he pulled information out at every level, and in the process distinguished between the proverbial wheat and chaff. "If you ever go into a new situation like me, the people who are going to knock on your door first are going to be usually the biggest BSers," Dimon advised. "They're good at it."[17]

A House Divided

At the headquarters, the Bank One flag was flying. But inside the building and throughout the company were separate armies, fiefdoms, territories, and systems—lots and lots of systems. Many people in the company still identified with where they were from: First Chicago NBD or Banc One of Columbus, Ohio.

The Bank One that Dimon stepped in to lead was a house divided: bruised by internal rivalries and beaten up by the marketplace that had expected more from an acquisition spree across several states than a patchwork of loosely tied operations that were far from integrated. As the coach and new star player, Dimon was looking at a team that had not played well together. One of his greatest assets, however, was the fact that he wore the neutral jersey of an outsider.

"We ultimately decided that we wanted someone to come in who had a totally fresh look and a totally nonpartisan background with respect to First Chicago NBD/Banc One Columbus. There had been too much partisanship and too much infighting, and too little homogenization of the culture—too little culture alignment," Crown explained. "Everybody was doing things the way they were accustomed to doing them. Compensation plans were fragmented and all over the place. Business plans were fragmented. And basic things like our reporting systems and our product sets and so forth varied too greatly to be a well-run organization. We needed to bring in someone who could unify the bank."

With 22 directors—11 each from former Banc One and First Chicago—it was a board divided right down the middle. No surprise then that one of Dimon's first decisions was to cut the size of the board. Twenty-two members was simply too many and too unwieldy for making decisions.

As Dimon recalled, "One board member did say to me at one point, 'Jamie, it's almost like you're twisting their arms.' And I said, 'Guilty.' I said, 'I'm not twisting your arms for me. I'm pushing you for the company.' . . . I was trying to reduce the size of the board. You don't have a meaningful meeting with people over 20 [in number]. . . . You have to have a small crowd."[18]

The board's first reaction was to push back. Among the members were friends and associates, but Dimon persisted—and he prevailed. "He thought the board was too big, so he gave Jim Crown and me the job," Hall recalled. "Jamie said, 'Get it down to 14 for me.' We said, 'Okay, we'll do it.' It was difficult, but we did it."

Hall recalled the first year as "tough," with many changes in personnel in key places and swift actions taken as part of a sweeping restructuring. Through it all, Dimon was able to forge a team at the board level, changing what had become a divided body into one entity. "The board very quickly became a good, cohesive board," Hall commented.

The Beginning of a New Culture of Accountability

As Dimon took over, a new culture began to be infused at Bank One. The "us" and "them" attitudes had to be eliminated in order for the organization to have one team that was nimble, responsive, strategic, and competitive. Some of Dimon's moves were symbolic. For example, he claimed for himself an understated middle office along a row of other senior executives and next to the conference room, instead of the wood-paneled office that had belonged to the former CEO, McCoy. Dimon not only wanted to be accessible and visible, he also wanted to be in the midst of the action. He also halted progress on renovations on the executive floor, a project that the bank could ill afford given its financial condition.

Dimon soon had his hands into everything: every operation and line of business, expenses and contracts, compensation plans, and reporting lines. Nothing was untouchable as far as Dimon was concerned, no matter what the legacy, habit, or history was. There was no declaring something off-limits or sacred. "My attitude was different," Dimon explained. "In a turnaround, everybody's going to sacrifice. . . . I cut board compensation. I cut the board, cut charity, cut everything. Once you say, 'Well, this is different, that's different,' you're dead. And anyone could sacrifice."[19]

With his laser focus, attention to detail, and demands for excellence from himself and others, Dimon took command at Bank One. Although he had enjoyed an impressive opening act during the Weill years, his Act II at Bank One and beyond was his true proving ground. Visible and vocal, Dimon was intent on leading Bank One to become the competitive and highly profitable organization that it could be.

Chapter 6

The Turnaround
of Bank One

Aggressive accounting, a disjointed board, horrible credit problems that could have sunk the company, not enough capital, horrible customer service, disjointed systems. . . .

—JAMIE DIMON, DESCRIBING THE PROBLEMS
AT BANK ONE WHEN HE ARRIVED IN MARCH 2000

W hen Jamie Dimon arrived at Bank One, the company stock rallied about 18 percent in the first two months. Hope and expectations buoyed the share price, but an impatient and results-focused Street would soon be looking for results.

With Dimon granting no media interviews during the initial months, there was much speculation as to what he would do first. Bank One's dividend, which was high compared with its lackluster earnings, drew attention as to whether it would be cut to save capital. Restructuring charges were seen as likely; the only issue was how big they would be. All eyes were on Dimon as he rolled up his sleeves and plunged into the work to be done.

Coming to Bank One as an outsider, Dimon had no prior allegiance to one side or the other—not to the former Banc One of Columbus nor to First Chicago NBD. Thus, he could neutralize the turf battles and culture clashes that had embroiled the company, and energize and empower employees, teams, and managers to tackle the inefficiencies and capitalize on opportunities. But first, as the new CEO, Dimon had to face the reality of severe problems at Bank One that were perhaps more serious than he had imagined.

Starting with his first interview with the search committee, Dimon had laid out what he would do to improve profitability. But as he assessed the situation from the inside, the picture wasn't pretty. "Aggressive accounting, a disjointed board, horrible credit problems that could have sunk the company, not enough capital, horrible customer service, disjointed systems . . . ," Dimon recalled in a 2002 presentation, ticking off the problems he found at Bank One. "We had seven deposit systems, five wire systems, five cash management systems, two capital market systems, multiple complexity. . . . We had Windows 98, Windows 2000, Windows NT, multiple programs, backward telecom. . . . Of course our margins were half of the industry's . . . maybe less than half."

As if things weren't bad enough, Dimon saw a bigger threat on the horizon: a recession in the United States. "I thought there would be one. This was March 2000, the peak of the bull market. I was terrified by the peak of the bull market. And I was saying, 'What if this happens?' and 'You've got to be prepared for that.'"[1]

As Dimon tackled the Bank One turnaround, he pulled no punches. Even though there were those who disagreed with his approach, preferring to go after the issues one at a time, he launched a full assault regardless of the short-term hit on earnings. This is quintessential Dimon: being willing to do the right thing—the difficult thing—for the right reasons.

"The one thing about Jamie Dimon is he never talks about what the stock is today. He talks about what it's going to be tomorrow if you do the right thing. He's always focused on doing what's right," commented David Novak, chairman and CEO of restaurant chain Yum! Brands, who was one of the first new directors brought on the Bank One board after Dimon became CEO.

A hands-on executive, Dimon has a cast-iron grip at times, whether he's evaluating loan loss reserves or weighing customer satisfaction in retail branches. He asks questions of everyone, gathering information and probing for details. Exacting and thorough, he holds everyone, especially himself, accountable for results that can be measured and managed, and for risks that can be identified and controlled.

This was the leadership change he brought to Bank One, which was bound to shake up a culture that was divided along old factions between First Chicago NBD—made up of institutions that had been based in Chicago and Detroit—and Columbus-based Banc One. Within a fractured organization, Dimon faced the tough job of bringing it all together. "The word on the street was that the Banc One–First Chicago merger had been easy; the Jamie Dimon merger was the hard one because of the culture change," recalled Kathy Schroeder, who at the time was a first vice president of National Learning at Bank One.

Dimon quickly earned a reputation as a candid, straight-talking CEO, whether in presentations to board members, analysts, employees, or investors. Even when he was advised by an investor relations person at the time to couch his remarks in positive terms for fear that candor could send the share price into a tailspin, Dimon's attitude was "tell the truth and deal with it."

"If I lied to the analysts, I have also lied to the employees. I can't say, 'We've got a crisis' to the employees, and then [say] to the analysts, 'Things are going great.' I want us all to know the truth so we can then deal with it and fix it. That will make us the best company in the long run," Dimon reflected. "So that was my complete and total focus: just deal with it."[2]

From the start Dimon took swift and decisive action to tackle the problems, and he didn't care how many feathers he ruffled in the process. Sleepy managers and employees were given a rude awakening, and those who weren't on board with the plan found they were on the wrong side of the new boss. The name of the game was accountability.

New Players for the Team

As Dimon took charge at Bank One, management changes began happening swiftly and at high levels. In April 2000, the CFO resigned, becoming the first officer to leave. Verne Istock, after serving as interim

CEO and vying for that post on a permanent basis, had stepped down to the role of president after Dimon's arrival; he planned to depart as soon as the transition was completed. At the same time, the door was opening to longtime associates of Dimon who had worked with him at Travelers and Citigroup to join the ranks of Bank One. Although Dimon was prohibited from recruiting people away from Citigroup, it did not stop them from seeking him out to pursue an opportunity.

"I had a very strict noncompete that I followed to the letter. I couldn't hire you. I couldn't make you an offer. I couldn't negotiate a deal. But if you called me, I was allowed to say, 'I can't do any of this, but you're free to call Joe.' I might even go to Joe and say in a couple of cases, 'Joe, I want you to hire [this person].' . . . All these people kept coming," Dimon explained. "People came for less money, lesser jobs, and a [weaker] company."

Even though they had to move to another city, they came in order to work for Dimon, becoming an important injection of new—and neutral—talent. "A number of people were hired into senior management at Bank One because Jamie felt he was upgrading talent. At the same time, he was dismantling fiefdoms and dismantling the highly politicized atmosphere by bringing in neutral jerseys," board member James Crown observed. "If your boss is neither from Detroit nor Chicago nor Columbus, but from New York, maybe you're going to end up realizing that there isn't some political angle to what you're doing; the mission was the good of the bank as an overall enterprise."

Among the first to arrive was Charlie Scharf, who came to Bank One after spending 13 years at Citigroup and its predecessor companies, including as CFO of Salomon Smith Barney when it was part of Travelers. Scharf became the new CFO of Bank One and later led its consumer banking business. Mike Cavanagh joined Bank One in May 2000 as head of strategy and planning after seven years at Citigroup and predecessor companies, including as co-head of Salomon Smith Barney's Planning and Analysis group. In October 2000, Heidi Miller, who had been considered one of the most prominent women on Wall Street during her years at Citigroup, joined the Bank One board. Later, Miller would go from outsider to insider, becoming executive vice president and CFO in 2002, replacing Scharf when he was named head of the Bank One retail group. Then, in August 2002, Jay Mandelbaum, who had been part of the Salomon Smith Barney private client brokerage operation, joined Bank One as head of strategy and business development.

The decisions by these former Citigroup executives to join the ranks of Bank One represented a huge vote of confidence in Dimon, as well as an opportunity to be part of management headed by someone they knew and trusted. Investing their careers in Dimon's success was also powerful testimony to his leadership. "It wasn't really a choice," Scharf said of his move to Bank One in 2000. "I'm just following the best leader I've ever seen."[3]

Today, these former Citigroup executives who became members of Dimon's new team at Bank One are part of his inner circle at JPMorgan Chase. Scharf is CEO of Retail Financial Services, the consumer banking business at JPMorgan; Cavanagh is CFO and head of Global Finance; Miller is CEO of Treasury & Securities Services business; and Mandelbaum heads strategy and marketing. In these positions, all four sit on the executive and operating committees at JPMorgan.

As he took charge of Bank One, Dimon had to make decisions about managers more quickly than he would have liked or that he normally would, but time was of the essence. "I was making very quick decisions. . . . I knew this person had to go, and I thought maybe—I hadn't seen them that much—but maybe [this other person] could do the job."

John Hall, who had chaired the board's search committee that recruited Dimon, sees the willingness to make the tough people decisions as one of Dimon's key strengths as a top executive. "Evaluate the leadership and reassign people if necessary to build the strong team. If he determined that one of his direct reports wasn't making it, it didn't take him long in the nicest way he could to make a change."

In the process, Dimon needed to create cohesion among players who had been loyal to previous corporate identities and put a comprehensive turnaround plan in place. As *Fortune* noted at the time, "[The] modest infusion of talent at the top is certainly a good start, but analysts are singing in unison about the things Dimon needs to do to beget a full recovery. Among the tasks: creating a new, unified management team across the board and implementing tighter accounting policies."[4]

Welcome to Boot Camp

In order to put a restructuring plan in action, Dimon had to get up to speed—and fast. Everywhere he looked there were problems demanding his attention, from the balance sheet to information technology (IT) systems. Dimon immersed himself fully into the situation with his usual energy and zeal. Tellingly, he called the initial phase of his turnaround plan "boot camp," a term perhaps reminiscent of his early days at Commercial Credit, which they called "combat." But this was a different battle: not to build a small firm into something much, much larger, but to keep a sizable bank—in 2000 ranking fifth in size among U.S. bank holding companies, with assets of more than $265 billion—from getting deeper into trouble.

Dimon spent much of his boot camp training talking and listening to employees. "The first thing I did was meet with lots of people—breakfast, lunch, and dinner, and in between. I would say to them, 'Give me the information you're looking at,'" Dimon recalled.[5]

In a Harvard Business School case study on the turnaround of Bank One, the co-head of capital markets recalled meetings held with Dimon every day for three weeks. "He would spend one to two hours each time, going through items. What is this derivative? How do you price it? What's the risk? Literally hundreds of questions. He was testing to see if we knew the details, and if we were honest enough to admit it when we didn't. He wouldn't hold it against you if you didn't know. He just wanted to make sure you would deal with problems and move on. Finally, after three weeks he said, 'We don't have to meet every day from now on.'"[6]

Dimon scoured the data, line by line and business by business: commercial banking, investment management, retail banking, and the First USA credit card business. He compiled a list of action items on his trademark 8½ × 11 inch piece of paper, which he carried around with him. On the list went everything he (or someone else) needed to follow up with; scratched off the list were the items that had been addressed.

Dimon's charge to management was a tall order: Costs had to be reduced by $1.5 billion. The bank needed to raise capital, which was very expensive, but Dimon was not worried about the impact on the earnings per share. As he recalled, "I wanted to be around for a rainy day. I wanted a chance for survival."[7]

And then it was showtime. Dimon told analysts that in July 2000, with the release of Bank One's second-quarter earnings, he would unveil the plan to address the company's problems. As *Fortune* wrote at the time, "New Bank One CEO Jamie Dimon had better bring his A-game next month when he unveils plans for the troubled Chicago bank—or he'd better not come at all."[8] The pressure was on Dimon to perform and impress. Bank One's stock, which had enjoyed a healthy boost after Dimon's arrival, had since returned to previous lows because of lingering concerns about profitability and the health of the First USA credit card division.

Taking It to the Street

Dimon did more than make promises: He took decisive action, even though Bank One's earnings would suffer a tremendous blow. For the second quarter of 2000, the first three full months of Dimon's leadership, Bank One took a $2.9 billion pretax restructuring charge, which was larger than many analysts had expected. Write-downs and other charges amounted to $518 million in retail banking, $673 million in commercial banking, $777 million at the First USA consumer lending and credit card operation, and $963 million in corporate and unallocated charges—leaving Bank One with a loss of $1.27 billion.

Concerned with capital preservation, Dimon also cut the Bank One dividend in half to $0.21 a share. Later, in the 2000 annual report to shareholders, Dimon would call reducing the dividend "something that no corporation should ever have to do."[9]

Such news could have been greeted by the Street with pessimism, that problems were deeper and more entrenched than previously thought. Instead, Bank One shares rose 8.8 percent in one day to $32.625 in active trading. The optimism carried over into future expectations with several analysts increasing their estimates for earnings and some raising their ratings on the stock. Many analysts liked what they heard, with one in particular applauding Dimon and his team for presenting a financial and restructuring plan sooner than expected. As the analyst noted, "The speed with which Mr. Dimon and his expanding team are executing is impressive. Add to this management's focus and determination, and it looks as if the odds of Bank One not only meeting, but exceeding, have been materially enhanced."[10]

Dimon was greeted with an overall favorable reaction not only because of the scope and ambition of his turnaround plan, but also because he and his management team recognized and admitted the problems that had existed for some time at Bank One. That acknowledgment alone won him the respect of analysts who the year before had complained of a lack of credibility in the bank's management. "When I first went to the Street . . . it was pretty ugly. I mean really ugly," Dimon said. "And half of them said, 'God bless you for knowing it.' And the stock went up because [analysts said], 'At least they recognize their problems. We already knew they had them.'"[11]

While analysts were generally impressed, some skepticism remained, especially in light of daunting challenges. Another analyst was quoted as commending Dimon for "a good presentation," but added that "you have to realize that this is a battleship to turn around and Jamie Dimon is not Hercules."[12]

Indeed, later on Dimon and his team would face considerable challenges, not only inside the bank but also due to economic and geopolitical events, which bogged down but did not derail the turnaround. In the early days after the second-quarter 2000 earnings report and the analyst presentation, however, Bank One could bask in the optimism.

Dimon told the *New York Times* that he was "pretty confident" the bank would not have to take more charges to cover restructuring costs, "but it's not a promise yet." He added, "I've only been here for three or four months. But I really do feel confident that we've scrubbed pretty hard."[13]

Dimon's goal was to get everything in the first round of charge-offs, to show that no matter how big the problem or how steep the cost, management was getting control of the balance sheet. Unfortunately, that was not the case. As Dimon and his team dug deeper, there were more problem areas to address and overvalued assets to write down. "With the second round of write-downs, he was irritated," commented Harvard Business School Professor Paul Marshall, who conducted an in-depth case study of Bank One. "His feeling was when you don't get everything the first time, it says that there were more problems and we weren't smart enough to see it."

By the end of the year, Bank One would take a total of $5 billion in charge-offs, reserve additions, write-downs, and other adjustments, and post a loss of $511 million. In his first letter to shareholders as chairman, Dimon reflected on the "daunting challenges," and proclaimed 2000 to have been "an extremely difficult year."[14] But he also voiced optimism that the business was basically sound, and that having taken dramatic action, Bank One would continue on as a stronger company.

Turning Around Bank One

From the moment Jamie Dimon arrived at Bank One, he launched into a turnaround. The plan—as he outlined to analysts in July 2000 with steps already taken and those that would follow—was as comprehensive an endeavor as anyone could imagine. Every aspect of the bank's business from balance sheet to bank hours was examined, evaluated, and adjusted. Specific areas of focus in the plan, as will be discussed separately in this chapter, included credit risk, IT and operating systems, creating a meritocracy, aligning compensation with performance, improving customer service, and more.

The turnaround itself began to change corporate culture, from people operating in isolation to becoming more cohesive and accountable to each other. If there was a risk or potential risk, Dimon wanted to know about it—and who was responsible for monitoring it. "He expected people to take ownership; that was part of the culture change," recalled Kathy Schroeder. "Everybody at every level of the organization was expected to be fully accountable, and to look outside the box for new ways of doing things."

Instituting a new financial discipline, Bank One created more than 2,000 profit and loss statements—including one for every banking center—which became the basis for decision making, allocation of capital, and even employee compensation based on performance. Nothing less than a total overhaul would be adequate to reach Dimon's goal of getting Bank One back on track and growing.

Reducing Credit Risk

As Dimon focused on the financial condition of the company, his signature phrase—the fortress balance sheet—made its debut at Bank One. He first mentioned it to shareholders in the 2000 annual report as he emphasized the importance of strengthening the balance sheet, loan loss reserves, capital ratios, and credit ratings—as well as generating sufficient capital. But as Dimon began to examine the financial health of Bank One, the balance sheet was far from the fortress ideal.

"He immediately focused on the financial condition of the company. He was very concerned about the balance sheet," Hall said.

One particularly worrisome area was the credit risk faced by Bank One due to its lending practices. To reduce overall credit risk, Dimon led an in-depth assessment of exposure, particularly when the credit environment deteriorated as the economy weakened. As he told shareholders at the end of 2000, "Based on our analysis, our company has taken too much overall credit risk, has assumed too many big individual risks, and has experienced low returns relative to the capital deployed."[15] While commercial banks often use credit as a loss leader to attract other business, at Bank One that practice had led to unacceptable risks—particularly if there was no offsetting revenue stream from other business. The decision was made to reduce commercial exposure on and off the balance sheet by $10 billion to $20 billion, which would free up capital that had been earning low returns.

Dimon ratcheted up the estimates for what commercial credit costs would likely be in the near future. Costs of 40 basis points in 2000 were a "cyclical low," he said, and could very well double. Facing that potentiality and quite possibly worse, he needed to ensure that Bank One was prepared. As he warned shareholders, "In a deep recession, commercial costs can run as high as 175 basis points. While none of us would like the impact on our earnings of a recession, because of all the steps we have taken we are now prepared to weather even that kind of environment."[16]

Making Sense of Information Technology Systems

An executive with a financial industry background and who held the CFO title at several of the business units he helped to manage earlier in his career would be expected to dive deep into balance sheets and credit risks. Dimon showed the true range of his management talent as he plunged into IT systems at Bank One, spending as much as a quarter of his time with the technology team. He grasped the scope of the problem and the pros and cons of possible solutions with detail and intensity that is rare for a CEO, particularly one who did not come from an IT background. The problem was that the IT systems from the legacy banks had been preserved—yet another reminder of how poorly Bank One had integrated its previous acquisitions from an operational standpoint.

Looking back, Dimon shook his head at the memory of the lack of integration at Bank One. "You can't run a business that way. I went to a call center, and one poor lady there had four manuals—one for the Arizona system, one for this system, one for that system. . . . Our error rates were high; our costs were high. You couldn't use your cards in different branches."

Bank One was saddled with different deposit systems, loan systems, and check processing systems. "So if you said the regulators need X, we had to build it into 40 different systems, not one," he remembered.

Integrating systems not only was a huge task, but there was considerable resistance internally because no one had ever done it before (early attempts at it had failed). Nonetheless, Dimon was determined that it could—and would—be done. He began with what he decided would be the easiest place to start: Louisiana. After flying down to meet with bank operations people in that state, however, he found that his idea was met with both reluctance and fear. In fact, Louisiana had seen a 30 percent loss of business because of a previous attempt. But that was before Dimon.

He related the meetings and the conversations around the Louisiana systems conversion with energy and passion, as if it had all transpired that day and not eight years earlier. "I said to them, 'You're acting like if this fails this could be my fault.' I said, 'It's your job—100 percent. If it doesn't work, I'm blaming you. . . . Figure it out. Be responsible.'" At the same time, he also empowered the bank operations team in Louisiana with a pledge: "If you need to pull the emergency brake and stop the whole thing, I'm going to let you do it."

Needless to say, Dimon's approach to empowerment and accountability soon sent shock waves through the system, including technology and operations people who were charged with the overall conversion process. "I fly back to Chicago. I'm in my office late at night and two people responsible for the conversion walk in and quit. I said, 'What are you quitting for?' They said, 'Jamie, we heard that you told the people there that they could stop the conversion whenever they wanted.' I said I did. They said, 'It will never work.'"

Then came the fear and complaints from the two people who wanted to quit: The Louisiana staff would stop the project; they didn't know what they were doing. Dimon listened at first and then he explained things his way: "I said, 'You got it backwards. They now have skin in the game. They're not going to pull that brake unless it's an emergency; maybe there's a good reason.' I said, 'You don't fully understand that I made them your partner.' . . . I told them the story about the '100 percent,' and then I said, 'I'm going to blame you 100 percent, too.'"

In the end, the conversion project worked beautifully and was celebrated with a party, awards, and gifts. "And that team—the same team—it was like having the 101st Airborne Division after that."

As Dimon rallied his troops to undertake the system conversion, the process would be neither easy nor cheap, but it had to be done. As Dimon outlined for shareholders in the 2000 annual report, "Converting to uniform operating systems—and doing it quickly— will help us run our business more efficiently, provide better customer service, and put us in a strong position to aggressively grow internally or by acquisition. Ultimately, it should save Bank One hundreds of millions of dollars a year."[17]

Creating a Meritocracy

"If there is one thing that grinds my gut," Dimon commented in a 2002 presentation, "it's bureaucracy." The man who had been one of the "refugees from bureaucracy" at Commercial Credit had no patience for organizations that rewarded people for time spent in a chair. His ideal was to create a meritocracy. As Dimon explained it, "All I wanted to do is pay and promote those who . . . are good. If they are bad, they have to go, and they have to be demoted if they have to be moved. And that is the hardest management decision, demoting someone—'good old Joe.' . . . And the other hard one, which is more insidious, is when a job opens up [and] people say, 'Who should have that job?' Does someone deserve a job because he's a good guy? Of course not. . . . If we had a really good person in that job, would it wake up the whole area—like treasury, or finance, or analysis? Absolutely it would."[18]

The antidote to the malaise of bureaucracy, Dimon believed, was establishing a meritocracy: rewarding people for their efforts and contributions, whether they made a measurable impact on the bottom line or did something less tangible such as recruiting or mentoring. In the Dimon meritocracy, people were responsible and accountable for controllable performance. That meant delving deeply into numbers, measures, and metrics, from how Bank One was performing compared to peers such as Wells Fargo or Fifth Third Bancorp to how it accounted for loan loss reserves and derivatives. Dimon's approach resulted in quite a bit of boat-rocking as he shaped the team from the top down, setting an example of hard work and accountability for the entire organization.

"These were powerful messages, powerful cultural changes," board member James Crown observed. "In my experience with these kinds of cultural shifts, people fall into one of three groups: There are those who have desperately been hoping for change; they intuitively understood some of the institution's problems. They accept the new program instantly, and really start to perform. And there are those who are stuck in their orthodox way of doing things and can't imagine another approach. They need to change jobs. Whether they leave or are asked to leave, they are never going to fit into the new system. Then there are those who have to adapt, who need to have a little time to come around. But if you can work with them and help them adjust, you can preserve certain relationships, institutional memory, and some of the legacy benefits of having seniority. People started to sort themselves into those groups: those who left or were asked to leave, those who figured it out instantly, and those who adapted and stayed."

Dimon believed in asking anyone questions and expected thorough answers. If someone couldn't answer the question right away, that was okay; but the answer had better be forthcoming soon. If there was a problem, Dimon wanted to know about it. Many employees were impressed not only that Dimon wanted their input, but that he listened intently. The impression he gave was of gathering information with an open mind in order to see things the way that employees who were deeply involved in daily operations experienced them.

There were times, however, when Dimon's hands-on style felt intrusive. According to one story told about Dimon, because his office at Bank One was near a conference room, he felt free to sit in on virtually any meeting and had a habit of dropping in on any gathering. This led some people to inquire when Dimon was going to be out of town before scheduling a meeting in the conference room. If he was in the office, they would find another place to meet.

Aligning Compensation

Also as part of his meritocracy plan, Dimon set about bringing compensation into alignment with performance, having the right people in place, and setting high standards that were linked to how much a person earned. Prior to Dimon taking over, compensation at Bank One was not well linked to performance and there was a lack of cohesiveness throughout the organization—another vestige of the patchwork of acquisitions and mergers.

"Different executives had different deals for different reasons," Crown explained. "Those reasons could have been a carryover obligation from the acquisition when their firm was bought, or could have come from a special relationship with the CEO who folded a compensation plan into the deal. For certain executives their compensation was the product of special, customized negotiations. Whatever it was, compensation wasn't linked to performance, certainly not the performance of the bank as a whole. It was totally segmented and not really appropriately sized or aligned to drive shareholder value."

Dimon's compensation philosophy was to tie pay closely to the performance of the bank, essentially making people partners in the success of the organization. He also led by example, cutting his own compensation. For example, supplemental pension plans, which were customary in commercial banking, had been a way for making up for more moderate levels of base salary. Supplemental pension plans had become quite lavish and, in Dimon's view, completely inappropriate, especially given the performance of Bank One.

"He cut everything back. He cut out all these extras and amenities that he felt were outsized and out of line," Crown continued. "He worked to make sure that everybody had basically the same deal for the same reason, based on their value to the company and their success at their job, rather than where they had come from [in a merger] or what they had negotiated separately."

With Dimon in the CEO seat, senior management would put their money where their mouths were. If they said pay for perform-ance, their own compensation was on the line. If they said everyone is a stakeholder in the success of the organization, they led the way. At the end of 2000, Bank One senior management did not receive any bonuses—even those members of the bank's planning committee who had guarantees. "This company cannot and will not pay the senior peo-ple more when the company does worse," Dimon told shareholders. "Now we will be the first to sacrifice, as is appropriate. The higher the manager, the more his or her compensation will be tied to the compa-ny's performance—no excuses. Leadership is an honor, a privilege, and a responsibility to do the right thing and set the right example."[19]

Waste Disposal

With $1.5 billion in expenses to be reduced at Bank One, Dimon was on a search-and-destroy mission when it came to wasteful spending. Gone were the pagers, cell phones, multiple subscriptions to the *Wall Street Journal*, and other perks. In aggregate, they added up, but more important was the symbolic impact of the cutbacks. If anyone doubted that there was a new boss in control and he meant business, then the cancellation of a gym membership or a magazine that had previously been paid for by the company was a noticeable sign.

"Jamie didn't like the term cost cutting. He referred to it as waste cutting, and that's what it was," Crown recalled. "He found all sorts of places where the bank was not using money well. We had hun-dreds of cell phone bills we were paying for employees who were no longer there and so obviously no longer using those cell phones. Magazine subscriptions, expense accounts, and club memberships and that sort of thing not only were expensive in the aggregate, but really sent a bad message; they were symbols of complacency and privilege."

With vendor contracts, in an effort to stop the waste that came from overpaying, Dimon took things into his own hands—literally.

Imagine the surprise of a top executive at a telecommunications, software, or other company who suddenly got a call from the new chairman of Bank One. This was no courtesy call or overture to have your person call my person. This was Dimon himself who had probably spent hours poring over the details of the contract with the same intensity and focus that he brought to everything, wanting to know about service, terms, contract provisions, and so forth.

"Jamie would do things like look at the service contracts . . . and quickly conclude that we were supposed to get 'most favored nation' pricing and we weren't. We were supposed to get a certain quality of service and we weren't. And we were supposed to get some sort of help from them to solve problems and those problems were not yet solved," Crown remembered.

Dimon called the CEOs of those companies and insisted that whatever services or goods Bank One had at some point in its past contracted for actually be delivered. Otherwise, Bank One would take its business elsewhere.

"He would do that up and down the line with every vendor of size and importance. I think it shook people up that, not only was the CEO calling to state the bank's case, but he knew precisely what the contract said, what the promise was, and what was going on in the system that might be falling short. It was a very detailed level of knowledge— not common for most CEOs," Crown continued.

The Case of the Flickering ATM

Dimon's pursuit of wise spending and getting what the bank paid for was not a one-time salvo as the turnaround was launched. It was an ongoing campaign. A case in point was an ATM machine in a bank branch that was not functioning properly; the screen was flickering. Dimon's wife, Judy, noticed it first and, after it remained that way for months, let him know about it. She also informed him that she had called the phone number at the ATM to report a problem; however, the machine had not been repaired.

When Dimon inquired about the ATM, he was first told that there wasn't a problem with it because the machines were monitored. Dimon countered that, yes, there was a problem; his wife had noticed it months before. When he asked who monitored the ATMs he was told "an outside vendor." Finally a crew was dispatched to check on the ATM.

This was not an acceptable response for Dimon, who believed that the outside vendor that had been hired to monitor the ATM shouldn't have let a problem persist for several months without addressing it. "What did I say?" Dimon recalled. "'Fire the vendor.'"[20]

Bolstering Customer Service

Nothing got under Dimon's skin like poor-quality customer service on the retail level. The field, as he called it, was where Bank One encountered its customers. Without better, prompter, more efficient, and more welcoming service, Bank One would lag its competitors. Moreover, Bank One's branch hours were not competitive with other banks'—a problem that Dimon discovered after he was on the job nearly a year.

"I thought I was a good CEO, but I missed it! How did I miss this basic thing?" Dimon recalled.

Dimon painted a vivid picture of the resistance encountered when the team tried to change branch hours. "People said, 'Well, studies were done—consultant studies.' . . . 'You've got to change everyone's hours, the delivery times of cash.' . . . I said, 'Folks, we're here for the customer. It doesn't matter.'"

Still the pushback continued, with a reminder to Dimon of his drive to reduce expenses whereas changing the bank hours would be costly. "I said, 'Excuse me, we are going to win in the marketplace. I'm not looking at the study, and I'm not doing a study. You are going to be open in every single market equal to your competitors, whatever that is.'"

Then came the final argument: Extending the branch hours would hurt employee morale. "I said, 'I don't give a sh— about employee morale.' I didn't mean that. What I meant was . . . you've got to compete. Never stop doing the right thing for the business to save a few bucks. Working hard and winning in the marketplace boosts employee morale."

Dimon took that same approach when it came to the Bank One call centers, refusing to sacrifice quality of customer service even in the midst of a firmwide cost-reduction campaign. "One call center was answering 80 percent of their calls in 40 seconds. That was their standard. I said, 'You're kidding me. Change it right away—today.' They said,

'We're going to have to hire a hundred people.' I said, 'I don't [care]. Hire a hundred people.' . . . Can you imagine waiting on a phone for 40 seconds before someone answers it? Who waits that long? When they call back the second time, they're angry. And what's the turnover in the call center? Huge! They hate working for the company."

When the initial response was "to do another study," Dimon replied, "Forget the study. That's how we're going to run our business."

Straight Talk from the New CEO

The actions that Dimon took in his first nine months as CEO—from April through year-end 2000—were summarized in a clear and detailed letter to shareholders, which earned the praise of none other than Warren Buffett, whose own epistles to Berkshire Hathaway investors are classics in investor communication. If anyone was expecting a "rah-rah, let's hear it for the home team" speech from Dimon in his first official communiqué with shareholders, they were in for a surprise. If they thought that the native New Yorker, who had quickly become a fixture in the Chicago business community, was going to tell it like it is, they were in for a treat.

In a detailed five-page letter to shareholders, Dimon laid out the actions that had been taken thus far and the priorities for future actions. He also pledged five promises to shareholders, not of guaranteed results, but of transparency and accountability:

1. We will share with you the truth, and offer honest assessments of our businesses and our prospects.
2. We will relentlessly follow our business principles.
3. We will act with integrity and honor.
4. We will always try to do the right thing, not the easy or expedient thing.
5. We will work hard and with fierce resolve to make this a company of which our shareholders, employees, customers, and communities can be proud.[21]

Dimon's letter to shareholders set a standard for clear communication with investors, respecting their right to know not only the accomplishments that every company likes to trumpet, but also the problems and the risks that the organization faced. Explaining his style of communicating with shareholders in a 2002 presentation, Dimon paid tribute to the Oracle of Omaha. "Warren Buffett talks about when you disclose financial information that you should disclose it as if you are speaking with your intelligent sister. Explain it to her. You'll find nothing that complicated in business. And so full disclosure is also: Did you explain it to them? What is the risk? What could go right? What could go wrong?"[22]

The Fortress Balance Sheet Debut

In order to survive as an independent regional bank—and not one seen as ripe for a takeover—and thrive as something bigger one day, Bank One needed strength at its core: its balance sheet. In the 2000 letter to shareholders, Dimon unveiled his "fortress balance sheet," a phrase that has become one of his signatures in management style, philosophy, and action. The fortress balance sheet not only guards against threats, such as adverse market conditions or a downturn in the economy, but it also puts the bank in a stronger position to take advantage of opportunity.

In his first year at Bank One, Dimon's drive was on the defensive side, especially increasing loan loss reserves for more protection against bad loans and defaults. As he told shareholders, Bank One's loan loss reserves at the beginning of 2000 had been 1.4 percent of loans, among the weakest in the industry. By adding nearly $2 billion to reserves, Bank One ended the year with loan loss reserves of 2.4 percent, among the strongest in the industry. Other measures of its balance sheet strength included raising its Tier 1 capital ratio—a core measure of the financial strength of a bank—to 7.3 percent.

"Jamie fully lived by the notion of 'what gets measured gets done'; what is measured can be improved. So there was an awful lot of emphasis put on clarity in financial reporting," Crown recalled.

On the offensive side, Bank One was able to avoid a credit downgrade, and by cutting the dividend improved its capital retention. With excess capital, the bank's ability to use it in any number of ways—investing in its businesses, buying back stock, or making an acquisition—was now possible.

In the last paragraph of the letter, just above a picture of Dimon smiling assuredly (in his shirtsleeves, no jacket), he saluted the 80,000 employees. And perhaps in response to the analyst's comment about the superhuman effort needed to address the problems at Bank One, Dimon noted: "They've made Herculean efforts to turn this company around and to build the platform for enduring success."[23]

While Dimon credited his team, there was no doubt who had a strong grip on the wheel.

Restoring Profitability

Dimon had proven himself capable of making the tough choices of slashing overhead costs, reducing payroll, halving the dividend, and shoring up the balance sheet. And over the course of 2001, Bank One was back in the black after a series of cuts and write-downs, but now investors were impatient for what would follow.

"To thrive in the eat-or-be-eaten financial services arena, [Dimon] knows the bank has to expand. And shareholders are becoming increasingly impatient that it hasn't done so," *BusinessWeek* reported in October 2001. "Investors have pushed the company's stock down from $39 in June [2001] to about $33 now, and about $5 more than the price before Dimon joined on March 27, 2000." Dimon, meanwhile, had promised to be "on the acquisition trail," but cautioned that it would be "in a prudent way."[24]

While Bank One did post a profit in 2001, earning $2.6 billion with return on equity of 13 percent, it was still a difficult year. As Dimon told shareholders candidly, "Despite the recession, we should have done better. Our credit costs were worse than you should expect, and worse than most of our competitors. On most other measures, however, we made good progress in positioning ourselves for 2002 and beyond."[25]

Dimon detailed for shareholders in his 2001 letter the steps taken to improve financial discipline, and pledged that actions would continue to be governed by conservative accounting and properly managed risk. He gave three specific examples: On- and off-balance-sheet credit exposures in the large corporate business had been reduced by $38.5

billion or 26 percent. The bank stopped buying brokered home equity loans that it did not underwrite and that had certain high-risk characteristics, even though this segment had been the most profitable and rapidly growing part of the bank's home equity business. Auto lease production was substantially reduced from $500 million per month to $50 million per month, with the entire auto lease portfolio reduced to $6.1 billion from a peak of $11 billion, and with plans to cut it further to $2.5 billion.

The examples show a level of detail that is typical of Dimon's view that shareholders have the right to know—and the ability to understand—how a bank manages its businesses. Dimon also explained the rationale for such actions, taking a short-term hit for a long-term benefit. "We know these actions can slow short-term growth, but we value a clean balance sheet over growth at any costs," he told shareholders. "We want our growth to be solid and healthy."[26]

As of the end of 2001, Dimon declared that the "boot camp" phase was over. The bank's fortress balance sheet was evidenced in many measures, including Tier 1 capital ratios that rose to 8.6 percent in 2001 from 7.3 percent in 2000. Now Bank One could aggressively engage in building the company, he promised, but the fulfillment of that pledge would still have to wait.

The following year, Dimon called 2002 the end of the "fix-it chapter" for Bank One. In a letter that highlighted more accomplishments than prescriptive actions taken, Dimon noted the $3.3 billion profit posted in 2002, compared to the $2.6 billion earned in 2001. Tier 1 capital rose even further to 9.9 percent and loan loss reserves amounted to 3.2 percent, which were among the highest of all major banks. The defensive posture of the bank had served it well during the economic decline of the early 2000s, and when recovery occurred, credit costs were expected to decline.

In a tumultuous time economically and with the financial world rocked by accounting scandals from Enron to WorldCom, Bank One appeared poised for better things thanks to Dimon's leadership, which earned him some well-deserved accolades, including the 2002 CEO of the Year title from Morningstar, Inc., the independent investment analysis firm. As Patrick Dorsey, director of stock analysis for Morningstar, commented then, Dimon proved "you don't need a grand strategy to run a great business—you just need to get the basics right. Jamie Dimon has transformed what once was considered one of the most poorly run banks in the country into a solidly profitable firm with a bright future."

Morningstar noted that, since Dimon took office in March 2000, Bank One stock had increased in value more than 30 percent. Further, in 2002, the company's stock fared far better than competitors', dropping 4 percent compared to an average loss of 13 percent in share value for banks in general. "Dimon's handiwork is obvious," Dorsey said. "He has made Bank One a much better financial institution by focusing on basic business principles—keep costs low, serve customers, and focus on profitability rather than growth at any cost."[27]

By the end of 2003, Bank One had reached a milestone. From a loss of $511 million in 2000, it earned a record $3.5 billion in 2003. In response, the stock price was up 85 percent from March 2000. As analysts and investors alike had waited for the answer to "what's next?" for Bank One, Dimon delivered up a surprising reply. Rather than making an acquisition, Bank One itself was being acquired in a $58 billion deal with JPMorgan Chase. In his 2003 letter to shareholders, Dimon explained that, for the first time in years, Bank One was strong enough to contemplate several options. "We could continue on our current path, purchase a franchise, or merge with another company. . . . After looking at and weighing the risks and rewards of each option, we concluded—and are very confident—that the proposed merger with JPMorgan Chase provides us with a truly unique opportunity to build one of the world's great financial institutions."[28]

While Chicago would lose one flagship bank to a New York institution, the result was a financial powerhouse—and Jamie Dimon was headed back to Wall Street.

Chapter 7

Back on Wall Street

Two or three times I felt deep anxiety about this deal. It's terrifying. Do you push the button or not? But if you don't and this opportunity is gone when you want it later, you've made a horrible mistake. So I pushed the button.
—JAMIE DIMON, DESCRIBING THE DECISION
TO SELL BANK ONE TO JPMORGAN CHASE

J amie Dimon may look, act, and speak like a New Yorker, but he had found a home in Chicago. "My wife and I love Chicago. . . . I didn't want to go back to New York. I was fine," Dimon remarked in 2006, two years after the $58 billion merger deal that brought together Chicago-based Bank One with JPMorgan Chase.[1] In fact at the time he made that comment, Dimon was still commuting from Wall Street back to Chicago, where his youngest daughter was finishing high school at The Latin School, a private preparatory academy. (The Dimons have since relocated to New York. Their 15,500-square-foot brownstone mansion in Chicago's Gold Coast neighborhood was listed for sale in May 2007 with an asking price of $13.5 million, which was later reduced to $12 million.[2])

Certainly no one could question Dimon's commitment to Bank One, not after investing nearly $60 million of his own money (supposedly half his net worth at the time) into its stock when he took over as chairman and CEO, and not after his tireless drive to turn the bank from a $500 million loss to a record $3.5 billion profit. But no matter how much he seemed at home in the Windy City, the Queens-born and Manhattan-raised Dimon was still one step away from the big game of New York–based financial services. And Wall Street wanted him back.

The transaction that brought together JPMorgan Chase and Bank One in 2004 was widely applauded as providing exactly what each party needed. The combination of the two firms created the second largest banking conglomerate in the United States, with $1.1 trillion in assets, 2,300 bank branches in 17 states, and top-tier positions in retail banking and lending, credit cards, investment banking, asset management, private banking, treasury and securities services, middle-market, and private equity. The Bank One–JPMorgan Chase matchup created a financial superstore capable of rivaling Dimon's alma mater, Citigroup. The businesses weren't the only prizes in the package. Dimon himself was a jewel in the crown: a strong and accomplished successor to JPMorgan Chase chairman and CEO William Harrison Jr.

As *Fortune* magazine noted at the time, "The main reason the deal is getting kudos is that it brings Jamie Dimon back to where he belongs, to the big stage. He's returning from the wilderness of regional banking to face the biggest challenge of his career: running an immense, complicated new creation, the hybrid of a giant investment and commercial bank. It's a role Dimon was born to play—and one in which he has no doubts that he'll succeed."[3]

Reflecting on the transaction that brought Bank One and JPMorgan Chase together, Harrison said Dimon becoming his successor was an excellent fit. "The stars were very aligned on a very natural transition that could take place," he commented, adding, "Jamie, in my opinion, was the best guy out there." His endorsement of Dimon was further strengthened by the fact that had the Bank One merger not occurred, Harrison said he would have "recommended that the board go get Jamie as my successor."

Dimon's ascension to the top job at JPMorgan Chase was guaranteed, but not immediate. According to the merger terms, Dimon would become CEO when JPMorgan Chase leader Harrison retired in mid-2006. As the two banks combined, Dimon, who would turn

48 in March 2004, was stepping into the No. 2 role as president and chief operating officer. But this was not a return to the old days with Sandy Weill, when Citigroup was built without an official succession plan other than the widespread assumption that Dimon would take over—that is, until he was fired suddenly. Dimon had an agreement that he would become CEO of JPMorgan (unless the vast majority of the board was to oppose that move for some reason) and also had carte blanche to dive into operations.

In Act II of Dimon's career, which began with his recruitment to Bank One, the merger with JPMorgan was a notable high.

"When Jamie left [Citigroup] and was without a job, and then he went to Bank One, people didn't always understand what a talent he was," commented Steve Burke, president of Comcast Cable and a member of the JPMorgan Chase board of directors. "Once people saw what he did at Bank One and then what he accomplished at JPMorgan, they realized what the rest of us had been seeing in Jamie all along."

Whether Dimon felt redeemed or vindicated that he was moving into the house that J. Pierpont Morgan built, he wasn't feasting on any of it—at least publicly. All he'd acknowledge for the press at the time of the merger was, "We'll give Citi a run for its money!"[4]

While Dimon was certainly a plus, he was not the only rationale for the deal. Acquiring the retail strength of Bank One was a major consideration. As Harrison explained, "We were convinced that scale, if managed properly, was a huge competitive advantage in our business."

The previous combination of JPMorgan and Chase in 2000 had increased the company's foundation in businesses such as investment banking, private banking, and treasury services, Harrison added, "but it had not given us the scale in retail. We believed that was also very important."

Examining the field, the potential strategic players for a merger, in addition to Bank One, included names such as Wells Fargo, Wachovia, or U.S. Bancorp. Since timing is everything in making a deal, the synchronicity of developments at Bank One and JPMorgan Chase enhanced the pairing of the two. At Bank One, 2003 marked a high point after its turnaround. On the other side, the JPMorgan-Chase combination announced in late 2000 had taken "a while to digest," Harrison explained. "Our board was comfortable in 2003 that we could look at other possibilities, which led to a big retail play if you could find the right partner."

Bank One had the retail scale that made it attractive to round out the JPMorgan Chase businesses, along with a strong and capable management team. "In the form of Jamie Dimon and his key partners you had people who had come out of mostly Citi and who understood our business, compared with Wachovia or Wells Fargo or U.S. Bancorp that mainly had retail experience," Harrison added.

In order for the deal to succeed, however, Dimon and Harrison would have to work together: two executives with distinctly different personalities and management styles. But Harrison welcomed Dimon from the beginning, knowing that his company would be in good hands in the future. And in the interim, the combined firm was in for a shake-up that the new president was bound to create.

The House of Morgan

As mergers and acquisitions shaped the financial services industry, Jamie Dimon's career path has intersected some of the biggest and best-known names in the business. At various times, he's been part of the top leadership of Smith Barney, Shearson, Salomon Brothers, and Travelers, all of which were gathered under the Citigroup umbrella. Today, as head of JPMorgan Chase, Dimon oversees operations that have a long history and a pedigree going back to 1799 with the Bank of the Manhattan Company that was founded by Aaron Burr and in its time became one of the leading banking institutions in the country.

Several prominent names have merged into what is now JPMorgan Chase through the Chase operations: Manufacturers Hanover, Chemical Bank, and The Equitable Trust, of which the Rockefeller family was the largest single shareholder. The prominent name on the institution today—JPMorgan—pays homage to J. Pierpont Morgan, who in 1871 founded Drexel, Morgan & Company, along with Philadelphia banker Anthony Drexel. The firm, later known as J.P. Morgan & Company, became one of the most powerful investment banks in the world, headed by J. Pierpont Morgan, who was arguably the premier financial statesman of his era.[5]

The House of Morgan catered to the elite of finance and business, which added to its prestige and mystery. As Ron Chernow noted in his epic *House of Morgan: An American Banking Dynasty and the Rise of Modern Finance*, "The old House of Morgan spawned a thousand conspiracy theories and busied generations of muckrakers. As the most mandarin of banks, it catered to many prominent families, including the Astors, Guggenheims, du Ponts, and Vanderbilts. . . . Since it financed many industrial giants, including U.S. Steel, General Electric, General Motors, Du Pont, and American Telephone and Telegraph, it entered into their councils and aroused fear of undue banker power. The early House of Morgan was something of a cross between a central bank and a private bank. It stopped panics, saved the gold standard, rescued New York City three times, and arbitrated financial disputes."

The Glass–Steagall Act of 1933 broke apart commercial banking and investment banking. While J.P. Morgan stayed in the commercial banking arena and Morgan Stanley was spun off as an investment house, the "truest heir" to the House of Morgan, Chernow wrote, is "J.P. Morgan and Company."[6]

By the 1980s, J.P. Morgan had shifted its focus from commercial banking for the bluest of blue bloods into investment banking. But the firm remained staunchly independent and seemed to buck the trend of mergers going on around it. In fact, before being acquired by Chase, J.P. Morgan had not done a major deal since it merged with Guaranty Trust Company of New York in 1959.[7]

Chase, meanwhile, had gone on a shopping spree, merging or attempting to merge with other players in an effort to become larger and full-service. Under the leadership of Harrison, who became CEO in 1999, Chase bought San Francisco–based Hambrecht & Quist in late 1999 for $1.35 billion, netting for itself an independent investment bank that catered to Silicon Valley. The 22 percent premium offered for Hambrecht & Quist led to criticism that Chase might have overpaid. The same red flag was raised when Chase bought British investment bank Robert Fleming Holdings for $7.7 billion in April 2000, in a deal aimed at strengthening Chase's presence in Europe and Asia.

Even with these two deals, Chase let it be known that it was far from reaching its goal of gaining breadth and depth in the business. Wall Street and Chase executives alike were looking for a "transformative" deal, as the bank's reported attempts to merge with the likes of Merrill Lynch, Morgan Stanley Dean Witter, or Goldman Sachs had not been successful.

All around Wall Street, firms were being snapped up: UBS bought PaineWebber for more than $12 billion, and Credit Suisse acquired Donaldson, Lufkin & Jenrette for $12.8 billion. Chase needed to partner with someone significant—even if it meant paying up to do so. In September 2000, Chase reached an agreement to acquire J.P. Morgan & Company in a nearly $31 billion deal. With total assets of $650 billion at the time, the Morgan-Chase combination ranked second to Citigroup at $800 billion. Harrison was named CEO of the combined firm, which was called JPMorgan Chase.

For Harrison, the creation of JPMorgan Chase was a crowning achievement of his career to date. As he told the *New York Times*, "This is the first merger I've been part of where I feel our core business is complete." But the high price that Harrison paid for J.P. Morgan looked inflated when the Wall Street climate turned dismal in 2001. At the time, deal makers and analysts were already speculating that Harrison would have to do another large deal to diversify. In the third quarter of 2001, Wall Street's malaise dragged JPMorgan Chase's profits down by two-thirds, to $449 million from $1.4 billion a year before. Nonetheless, Harrison remained resolute in his optimism: "While there are pluses and minuses to operating in a weak economic environment, we have a much stronger platform to manage with during this difficult time."[8]

Other troubles would soon dog JPMorgan Chase, including accusations that it—along with other Wall Street firms—had allegedly aided Enron in misrepresenting its financial condition. Enron, the high-flying energy trading firm, came to symbolize the scandals and malfeasance that tainted corporate America in the early 2000s. In 2003, JPMorgan and Citigroup agreed to pay nearly $300 million in fines and penalties related to their roles as advisers to Enron, which allegedly portrayed borrowed cash as revenues generated from businesses. In a settlement with the Securities and Exchange Commission, JPMorgan agreed to pay $135 million, while Citigroup paid $101 million. The banks also agreed to pay $50 million to the state and city of New York.[9]

By 2003, JPMorgan Chase had considerably strengthened its businesses across the board. In his letter to shareholders in the 2003 annual report, Harrison highlighted several corrective steps to improve risk management and address factors that had caused the bank's performance to suffer in 2001 and 2002. The problems—none of which were principally related to the merger of JPMorgan and Chase—were excessive capital committed to private equity; overconcentration of loans to telecommunications companies; and large exposure to Enron. "We dealt decisively with each issue in 2003," Harrison told shareholders, including to "put Enron behind us through the settlement that our firm and others reached in 2003 with the Securities and Exchange Commission and other regulatory and government entities."[10]

With the House of Morgan put back in order—and Bank One proclaiming a turnaround—the time was ripe for a merger.

The Deal That Almost Didn't Happen

While the deal to combine Bank One and JPMorgan Chase had synergies that made it look predestined, it almost didn't happen. Dimon reportedly faced a difficult decision selling to JPMorgan Chase. The problem: the price.

Having been criticized for overpaying for acquisitions, including when Chase bought J.P. Morgan & Company, Harrison wanted a "market deal," meaning to pay the going rate for Bank One shares. Dimon, however, was looking for a premium of at least 20 percent, especially given the fact that Bank of America had just paid an astounding 43 percent premium in October 2003 to acquire FleetBoston. This put Dimon in a quandary: whether he should hold out for more money from another buyer. As he said at the time, "When Harrison wouldn't pay a big premium, the board and I talked extensively about selling the company to the highest bidder, especially in light of the Fleet deal."

What changed Dimon's mind was his own history. Back in his early days with Sandy Weill, acquisitions were made for little or no premium. "It's true that when you have a low-premium deal, you have a better platform to build value, because you can build the business instead of slashing and burning simply to save enough to pay for the premium," Dimon explained at the time. His conclusion was that potential long-term returns from the combination of Bank One and JPMorgan

Chase would more than compensate for a low premium paid at the acquisition.[11]

Then Harrison gave in a little, agreeing to a 10 percent premium. When JPMorgan Chase's stock price increased, so did the value of the deal, which called for an exchange of shares. That put the premium for Bank One at 14 percent. Even though the asking price was less than what Dimon had originally wanted, he decided to proceed. "Two or three times I felt deep anxiety about this deal," he described then. "It's terrifying. Do you push the button or not? But if you don't and this opportunity is gone when you want it later, you've made a horrible mistake. So I pushed the button."[12]

The combination of Bank One and JPMorgan not only created the second largest banking franchise in the United States, as measured by core deposits, but also established a platform with top positions—first, second, or third—in several key banking business categories. As board member David Novak recalled, "When you looked at Bank One and JPMorgan, one plus one equaled three. The opportunity was there to create the best in the industry."

For Harrison, the rollout of the deal in January 2004 was particularly satisfying. He recalled a long day of meetings with analysts and employees, after which he returned around 11 o'clock at night to his home in Connecticut. "I walked in and told my wife that this was the most satisfying day of my 39 years in the business . . . because CEOs of public companies have three important priorities: one is quarterly earnings, two is strategic planning, and three is your successor."

With the acquisition of Bank One and bringing Jamie Dimon on board as the CEO successor, Harrison had advanced all three. As he put it, "Quarterly earnings would take care of themselves. Strategic planning had been advanced forward, and I had the best successor I could have found in the business world."

Two Leaders, Two Vastly Different Styles

While much was made of the transaction's built-in succession plan, in the interim a smooth transition and working relationship between Dimon and Harrison were essential. Two people more different in style and temperament could not be imagined: Harrison, described as a Southern gentleman, did not fit the stereotype of the New York banker. As a basketball player for the University of North Carolina who entered a training program for Chemical Bank, he had never expected a Wall Street career. Dimon, a fast-talking New Yorker, thrives in the competitive, intense environment of financial services and had been "reading annual reports in high school."[13]

One of the reasons the arrangement worked is that Harrison gave Dimon the free rein he needed to complete the integration of the merger. Put another way, given Dimon's intensity, energy, and drive, he was likely to run right over anyone in his path to accomplish what needed to be done. Knowing that, Harrison graciously stepped out of the way.

The working relationship between Harrison and Dimon was eased by the fact they had known each other previously and had spent a significant amount of time together during four or five months of negotiations. "People ask me quite often, how did we get along so well? The practical side of this is you put two companies and two CEOs together and most of the time they don't get along," Harrison observed. "I was 61 years old. I was very happy to have a great guy like Jamie taking over the firm. I wasn't driven to have to continue to be CEO. That was all behind me. I wanted to make sure we had a partnership. And Jamie wasn't concerned, because he was doing his job. It was a very nice structure that eliminated any possibility of ego problems and 'two cooks in the kitchen.'"

A Smooth Transition

For Bank One, which had been built by mergers of regional banks in the Midwest, the prospect of another marriage could have made for some prenuptial jitters—given its history of culture clashes and a lack of integration among operations. By comparison, the matchup with JPMorgan Chase was smooth sailing. "I have lived through three significant bank transactions—the three being when First National Bank of Chicago joined with NBD, when First Chicago NBD joined with Banc One Columbus, and then the Bank One merger with JPMorgan Chase. From the perspective of a director, the integration of Bank One with JPMorgan Chase was by far the most compelling, the most comfortable,

and the most professional," remarked James Crown, a Bank One director who now sits on the JPMorgan Chase board.

"The management and directors at JPMorgan Chase were more
open, easier to work with, and more quickly ready to get down to
business than either of the other two; and it just had to do with the
culture and the tenor of the organization. It was a good fit right from
the beginning at the board level. It was respectful, professional, and
nobody was made to feel like they didn't belong or their views were
unwelcome in an integrated organization," he added.

As Bank One joined the fold, if there were questions as to how
Dimon would regard the existing JPMorgan staff, those particular concerns would be quickly put to rest. Dimon treated all parties equally—
which meant he demanded the most out of everyone. For some, that
had to be an eye-opener and potentially a shock. But for Dimon, it was
just business as usual.

"With Jamie, it's all about your ideas and it's about your business
results," commented board member Steve Burke. "It sounds simple, but
the bigger the company and the higher up you go, the more sophis-
ticated they are at playing the game of 'what does the big boss want?'
Jamie has been able to cut through all that stuff and create an environment based on doing what's right for the business."

Delving into JPMorgan Chase

As Dimon dug into the operations as the new president, the top of his
to-do list was the execution of a plan to cut $2.2 billion in unnecessary
costs. If successful, JPMorgan Chase stock would likely rise—giving the
company currency for future transactions. As board member Novak
observed, "With Jamie at the helm of an organization like JPMorgan
Chase combined with Bank One, we would have a chance to create a
masterpiece in the industry."

The job facing Dimon as president and chief operating officer was
monumental, not only bringing Bank One into JPMorgan Chase, but
also focusing on the bank's culture and operations. In particular, the
combination of J.P. Morgan & Company and Chase four years earlier
resulted in a clash that had yet to be fully resolved. As a former Chase

private banker who had been with the firm for more than 20 years in New York and overseas remarked, the previous merger between Chase and Chemical Bank was "very smooth in many ways because there was a similarity of culture. But the J.P. Morgan and Chase merger was horrific. The J.P. Morgan bankers came in as if they had taken over Chase, when it was Chase that had taken over them."

The bane of most large companies is bureaucracy, which dilutes management's attention away from identifying problems, managing risks, and capitalizing on opportunities. "Senior management doesn't know what's going on several layers below them," commented Tom Brown of Second Curve Capital, LLC. Not so with Dimon, who has his hands on every part of the business and his nose in each profit-and-loss statement. "I'm a proponent of not being big," Brown added, "but if there's anybody who knows how to run a big company like JPMorgan Chase, it's Jamie Dimon."

JPMorgan Chase board member Robert Lipp, who had previously served on the Bank One board, recalled the early days of the merger when he was serving on the risk committee of the combined board of directors. Dimon, who was then president of JPMorgan, sat in on one particular risk committee meeting. "Let's just say that the risk people who presented that day are not here anymore. There was this little lackadaisical attitude," Lipp explained. "Jamie would ask questions about what's the real data. He would dig into a particular trading position, for example. He wanted to know what the numbers were. The risk people didn't have the numbers. He'd ask for the correlation between this and that, and they said, 'We'll get back to you.' He told them, 'I want it tomorrow.' It was a wake-up call and it was the right thing to do."

Leading by example and demanding that managers own the results of their teams, departments, units, and business lines, Dimon improved the organization's ability to measure and manage right down to smaller units and even individual bank branches. Individual budgets and year-over-year performance were tracked at every business unit. Execution of Dimon's plan required that the people he had in place embrace his vision and strategy. "Whether you are running a big or small organization, you have to see that the right people are responsible; that you are able to encourage people, and pay them well to do well," Lipp added.

Some Difficult Conversations

The JPMorgan Chase 2004 annual report, which featured a photo of Dimon and Harrison side by side, highlighted key achievements for the year and evidence of the bank's financial strength, from merger-related cost savings of $400 million to a Tier 1 capital ratio at a strong 8.7 percent. Dimon's "fortress balance sheet" also made the annual report headlines, telling shareholders, "We want a balance sheet of unquestioned strength." Hand in hand with financial strength is accountability, a principle that Dimon stressed at Bank One and emphasized in his new corporate home.

As explained in the 2004 annual report, the management team from each business line met with top executives to discuss financial performance, revenue growth, risk management, competition, productivity, innovation, and other initiatives. "In the beginning these meetings were somewhat painful for most of us," stated the letter to shareholders signed jointly by Harrison and Dimon. "Too often, they ended with more questions than answers. Many managers were asked to dive more deeply into the numbers and be more tough-minded about the reasons why certain initiatives were not on target. Although they aren't yet where they should be, our meetings are becoming more open, candid, and focused."[14]

Steve Black, co-head of the JPMorgan Investment Bank (who had worked with Dimon back at Smith Barney) observed at the time that Dimon had brought a new style of leadership to JPMorgan Chase: "For every single thing we do at the entire company, there will be a level of discipline brought to bear that no one has ever seen before. And it will be different." Commenting on Dimon's work ethic, he added, "It's a combination of inquisitiveness, of wanting to know every single part of how something works and being willing to go look in every nook and cranny for every bit of efficiency you can get."

Although Dimon can be intrusive, his close associates know he doesn't mind when others disagree with him, and that he's willing to back down when proven wrong. As Black added, "I'm not going to say he's perfect, or that he doesn't step on toes, but you can tell him something, and he's perfectly willing to say, 'You're right. I didn't pay attention.'"[15]

While capable of injecting himself into any business meeting, discussion, problem, or strategy, Dimon's style is not to run everything himself. Rather he creates a high level of accountability in those who are closer to the business operations. "The boss's job isn't to make the decision," Dimon commented in a presentation made in 2006. "The boss's job is to make sure the best decision is made. I can't make the best decision half the time because, honestly, [they] know more than I do. So I make sure the right people are there."[16]

Information flow is critical to the success of any organization, especially one as complex as JPMorgan Chase. Profitability, risk management, changes in the business environment, and more must be quantified and understood—and readily shared with the rest of the team. As Lipp observed, Dimon will cut off any presentation that's full of too much "baloney" and demand specifics. "He'll say, 'I want to know this and I want to understand that, so get back to me. I want to know tomorrow what these specific issues are.' That was Jamie 20-some-odd years ago, and it's him today."

Getting Bigger, Stronger, and Leaner

By 2005, JPMorgan's workforce had been cut by 12,000 people, or some 7 percent. Gone was a $5 billion outsourcing contract to IBM, as well as executive perks such as country club memberships and first-class travel. At JPMorgan Chase, Dimon continued the drive to eliminate unnecessary spending that he launched at Bank One.

What especially riled Dimon when he arrived at JPMorgan Chase was, as he saw it, how executives there had let pay "get totally out of hand." Dimon announced he was drastically reducing compensation by 20 percent to 50 percent over two years. "I'd tell people they were way overpaid, and guess what? They knew it already."[17]

Even after the compensation cuts, many managers stayed on with the firm. Dimon also sought feedback on people's performance in order not only to discover what they should be paid, but also to see if there were some hidden stars in quiet corners, as well as chest beaters who didn't deserve the hype.

Dimon's search-and-destroy mission on excesses focused on anything that didn't grow the business, improve shareholder value, or just plain make sense. Nothing incensed Dimon more than when money was spent on outside consultants and vendors when the company could have done just as well with internal resources. For example, when Dimon arrived at JPMorgan Chase, the company had contracted with 500 executive coaches to help people become better managers, to provide feedback, to give guidance on career development, and so forth. "They didn't make us a better company," Dimon commented in a 2006 presentation.

His solution? To end the contracts "cold turkey." "I'm not against executive coaching. I have used them on occasion. But 500? . . . Who should have been doing that? The boss. Management—what the hell was management doing?"[18]

Dimon's intolerance of waste even finds its way into stories about him that are legendary. Such is the limousine story, which people seem to enjoy telling although it is not true. (The genesis of the story is a much-scaled-down incident that occurred when Jamie was CEO of Smith Barney back in his Citigroup days.) As the story goes, Dimon came upon a long line of limousines idling at the curb outside JPMorgan Chase's Park Avenue headquarters. He tapped on the window and asked the driver who he was waiting for.

When the driver replied, "Who are you?" Dimon pulled out his business card and introduced himself. He then explained to the driver that this would be the last time he would be waiting for Mr. So-and-So. He then did the same at every driver's window down the line.

Now, that never really happened at JPMorgan. But the fact that this story is told so often and considered quite believable reflects Dimon's persona. It's completely plausible that he would personally interrogate a row of drivers in hired limousines. While it makes for a funny anecdote, it carries a big truth: that unnecessary waste and extravagance would not be tolerated, particularly by the new executive in charge.

Dimon Takes Over

When the JPMorgan Chase–Bank One deal was announced, the expectation was William Harrison would stay in the CEO position for two years as the merger was completed and the businesses combined. By October 2005, however, the transition was ready to be made official—six months ahead of schedule by mutual agreement. The official handover was set for the end of 2005 when Dimon, aged 49, would become

CEO and Harrison, 61, would retire. By all appearances, the announcement was a mere formality. As the *New York Times* noted, "The decision to speed up the handover . . . came about after Mr. Harrison and the board recognized that giving Mr. Dimon the top job would formally acknowledge what had been Wall Street's worst-kept secret for many months: that Mr. Dimon is already running the show."[19]

In his first letter to shareholders as CEO in JPMorgan Chase's 2005 annual report, Dimon set a tone reminiscent of his first letter as a CEO back in 2000 at Bank One. He laid out principles, many of them identical (in spirit, if not in exact wording) to what he had proclaimed at Bank One, such as promising to "share with you the truth and offer honest assessments of our businesses and our prospects" and to "do the right thing, not necessarily the easy or expedient thing." While such wording may look like corporate spin or shareholder-speak, for Dimon these are foundational principles that underscore his leadership and his management style.

Exhibiting the same candor with JPMorgan Chase shareholders that he had shown at Bank One, Dimon explained that while various businesses were well positioned, they were not yet meeting expectations. "Any way one analyzes our businesses, for the most part our costs are too high, our returns on capital are too low, and our growth is not what it could be. We are underperforming financially in many areas. We need to understand the reasons and focus our energy on making improvements, not excuses. We cannot afford to waste time justifying mediocrity. Each line of business now assesses its performance in a rigorous and very detailed way. Each compares results to targets in a variety of areas, including sales force productivity, customer service, and systems development."[20]

By 2006, Dimon had better news to share with investors: earnings from continuing operations of $13.6 billion, up from $8.3 billion in 2005. Return on equity excluding goodwill, a key measure of how well a business is operating, rose to 20 percent from 13 percent. Such strength was crucial—especially given the storm that was just beginning to brew.

Integrating the Mortgage Business

In hindsight, the full impact of the move becomes apparent: integrating home lending and investment banking, two businesses that in the past had nothing to do with each other. At JPMorgan Chase the home lending unit had become one of the largest originators and servers of mortgages in the United States. The investment bank, meanwhile, had become increasingly involved in the mortgage business as well—namely, selling mortgages that were packaged and sold to institutional investors. In the past, virtually none of the mortgages that originated in-house were sold by the investment bank. By 2006, that trend had completely reversed, with some $25 billion in mortgages from the home lending business sold by the investment bank.[21]

Better integration of the two businesses in 2006 made sense from a business opportunity perspective. Home lending could offer a wider variety of mortgages and be more competitive on rates as well. Plus, the investment bank gained the competitive advantage of a homegrown crop of mortgages to package and sell. By 2006, JPMorgan's mortgage securitization activities had grown significantly, including some subprime collateralized debt obligations (CDOs).

There was another reason for mortgage lending and investment banking to be more closely tied: Better sharing of information allowed an early warning on the subprime debacle—which was first noticed in home mortgage servicing—to be signaled to the investment bank. While JPMorgan has had its share of losses from the mortgage meltdown and the credit crisis, such integration and sharing of information on a detailed basis enabled Dimon and his team to greatly reduce the risks on the balance sheets.

In October 2006, according to a 2008 *Fortune* magazine profile, JPMorgan Chase had detected the first whiffs of smoke from what would be the conflagration that would engulf Wall Street. The JPMorgan mortgage servicing business that handles some $800 billion in home loans for itself and others noticed that late payments on subprime loans were rising. Moreover, loans originated by other institutions were performing much worse than JPMorgan's subprime mortgages, which indicated to Dimon that underwriting standards across the industry were deteriorating.

Meanwhile, Bill Winters and Steve Black, the co-CEOs of JPMorgan's investment bank, noted that the cost of credit default swaps, which act like insurance against bond failures, had risen significantly. "We saw no profit, and lots of risk, in holding subprime paper on our balance sheet," Winters told the magazine.

As *Fortune* chronicled, that prompted a phone call in October 2006 from Dimon to William King, who then headed J.P. Morgan's securities products, while he was vacationing in Rwanda. His message: "Billy, I really want you to watch out for subprime! We need to sell a lot of our positions. I've seen it before. This stuff could go up in smoke!" In late 2006, JPMorgan sold more than $12 billion in subprime mortgages that it had originated, and the trading desks got rid of subprime paper on their books and mostly stopped making markets in subprime paper.[22]

"That was just pure sharing of information. We saw it [subprime assets] deteriorating dramatically in what we own. We also knew that would mean that the other tranches [based on loans underwritten by others] would be even worse," Dimon observed.

Summarizing 2006 for shareholders, Dimon categorized "the good, the bad, and potentially the ugly" in subprime mortgages. Included in the "good" category was the sale of subprime loans, which the bank would otherwise have held and serviced. By selling them, JPMorgan reaped the proceeds and made the default potential someone else's problem. The "bad" included loan default rates that were still higher than expected and underwriting standards in subprime that should have been more conservative—even at the cost of being less responsive to market competition.

Dimon's words on the "ugly" contained a warning that foresaw problems from "recent industry excesses and mismanagement in the subprime market," adding that "bad underwriting practices probably extended into many mortgage categories."[23] But even in these frank words there was no hint of the devastation that would soon spread across Wall Street as default rates soared, home prices fell, mortgage-backed portfolios declined in value, and several financial giants faced credit losses and liquidity problems that brought firms to their knees.

The financial crisis has claimed several big-name victims: Bear Stearns, which was bought by JPMorgan Chase for fire-sale terms; Lehman Brothers, which filed for bankruptcy; and Merrill Lynch, which ended its long history of independence by selling itself to Bank of America.

Among the badly bruised was Citigroup, which has had to write down tens of billions of assets and seek capital infusions. Compared to the watchful JPMorgan Chase crew, Citigroup apparently didn't see the problem in subprime mortgages erupting into anything bigger because liquidity was so abundant. As then-CEO Charles O. "Chuck" Prince told the *Financial Times* in July 2007, Citigroup, a major provider of finance for private equity deals, was not pulling back. That comment led to a now infamous quote: "When the music stops, in terms of liquidity, things will be complicated. But as long as the music is playing, you've got to get up and dance. We're still dancing."[24]

In November 2007 the music stopped for Prince, who had been handpicked by Sandy Weill to be his successor as CEO of Citigroup. Prince stepped down after Citigroup reported a $5.9 billion write-down and a sharp drop in its profits.

The Storm of 2007

In a 15-page letter to shareholders in the 2007 annual report, Jamie Dimon reviewed financial performance and offered insights and lessons from what he called "the storm of 2007." He reiterated that JPMorgan had steered clear of SIVs, which had grown to a $500 billion industry segment. Within the investment bank, exposure to subprime loans was controlled by reducing positions or actively hedging them. Even so, in 2007, JPMorgan's losses on subprime mortgages and subprime-related CDOs amounted to $1.4 billion. While significant, the number pales by comparison with other CDO exposure on Wall Street. (For example, in mid-2008, Merrill Lynch sold $31 billion of CDOs for an average of $0.22 on the dollar.[25])

JPMorgan's relatively safe position as the storm of 2007 raged into 2008 and beyond reflects Dimon's ongoing strategy: identify risks, know the worst-case scenario, and always be prepared for the unthinkable to happen. While the payoff for such financial conservatism is obvious now, it was an unpopular stance a few years ago when competitors were minting money by following riskier strategies.

"Those are the toughest management decisions to make—deciding not to go into an area that other competitors are growing in aggressively. Sometimes you're right, as in the SIV case when Jamie was right. But you have to have the courage of your convictions to state, 'Our analysis says this doesn't make sense,' and be willing to look foolish to the investment community by not doing something," observed fund manager Tom Brown.

"The board of every public company will always gravitate toward measures like market share and growth, and so it's very difficult for a public-company CEO to say, 'We're losing market share,' or 'We're not growing as fast in market share because we think they're making a mistake.' That's a lot tougher decision than to buy Bear Stearns," Brown added.

When Dimon and his top executives informed the board of their investment strategies, they received strong support. "Jamie had enough confidence in himself and his team to succeed so that they didn't need to cut corners to maximize quarterly income in 2006 when the seeds of [the credit crisis] were planted," observed board member Steve Burke. He was "prepared to leave some money on the table" rather than risk pursuing an opportunity today that could pose a risk problem tomorrow.

Such thinking was revealed in Dimon and his management team even before the credit crisis hit the headlines—and the marketplace. In the spring of 2007, investment bank co-CEOs Steve Black and Bill Winters presented an overview of the business to the board, including the risks that they saw associated with SIVs and certain CDOs. Black and Winters explained that not pursuing these opportunities would be frustrating, and top competitors were likely to make more money. But when the cycle turned and credit problems worsened, a conservative approach would pay off.

The Wall Street Statesman

Jamie Dimon returned to Wall Street to take the helm of JPMorgan Chase. In the process, he has thus far successfully steered the company through one of the most disastrous times in the financial industry since the Great Depression.

For William Harrison, the recent management of JPMorgan Chase has proved the wisdom of his own decisions late in his career: buying Bank One and bringing Dimon in as his successor. As he watches the fortunes of the company he created by bringing together two of the most respected names in banking—JP Morgan and Chase—Harrison can do so with confidence and pride. "I can't imagine how a

CEO in today's world with all these problems would feel turning over a company and it not doing well. You would just feel awful about that." Harrison mused. "I was very excited when we did the deal to have a guy like Jamie running [the company], and he's done nothing but impress me with his talent and leadership since that time. And then in these difficult times as an industry and a country over the past months, to have a guy with Jamie's leadership skills and technical understanding is just a huge plus for JPMorgan."

While colleagues and peers point to Dimon's intelligence, experience in financial services, and detail-oriented management style, perhaps more than anything it is his emphasis on risk management—both analytically and at the gut level—that differentiates him from the pack. "Jamie is operational, detailed, and has the capacity to understand risk, which is especially important in this day and age and makes a huge difference in an organization like this at this time," commented board member Lipp.

Risk management does not hamper Dimon and his team, but rather guides them forward to grow and seek opportunity while never losing sight of the downside. Such thinking is contained in the business principles of JPMorgan Chase. As explained in a 10-page document, the principles listed are "aspire to be the best," "execute superbly," and "build a great team and a winning culture." Unless there is action behind such principles, however, they will remain only words on a page.

Sitting in a conference room on the executive floor of the JPMorgan Chase headquarters, in the midst of one of the worst crises ever to hit not only Wall Street but the global markets as well, Dimon cut through to the heart of the matter. "You can say it all you want, but unless you do it, no one gives a damn."

Part Three

WEATHERING
THE STORM

You've got to have disciplined reporting and a disciplined review of [what's] reported. And then it's got to be widely shared with smart people who also have experience and judgment. You will minimize problems. You'll still have them, by the way, but they should hopefully be smaller and fewer.

—JAMIE DIMON

Chapter 8

The Dimon Fortress

We believe we have to be prepared for tough times. And a fortress balance sheet . . . means strong loan loss reserves, conservative accounting, and paying a lot of attention to all the assets and liabilities on your balance sheet.

—JAMIE DIMON

As a CEO, Jamie Dimon has an impressive list of accomplishments: the turnaround of Bank One, the strengthening of JPMorgan Chase, and the completion of two strategic acquisitions in the midst of the worst financial crisis since the Great Depression. The question then is: How has he managed such feats?

If there were one secret to Dimon's prolonged success, it could arguably be his strict adherence to maintaining what he calls a fortress balance sheet. "It's not a philosophic bent. It's a strategic imperative," Dimon reflected in early October 2008, as the ongoing financial crisis and rising fears about the depth and duration of an economic recession took a toll on the stock market.

Indeed, when times are tough, the wisdom of embracing disciplines such as strong loan loss reserves, using conservative accounting, and focusing intently on the assets and liabilities on the balance sheet seems obvious. Not to take such a stance would seem as foolish as, say, failing to renew the insurance after a tornado has ripped through the property. Of course, if you didn't have insurance in the first place—because the sky seemed so blue and the sunshine so bright you thought there would never be a storm—then that's a different matter entirely.

What has distinguished Dimon and his management team is their unwavering adherence to the conservative financial approach of the fortress balance sheet regardless of the economic climate. They are alert and prepared, while still being nimble and aggressive to take advantage of market opportunities. The fortress balance sheet may keep them out of areas that they deem to be too risky or without a business purpose, which may trim profits in the short term. Dimon and his team are willing to leave a little behind for the sake of a stronger balance sheet longer term and the ability to withstand the torrents when things suddenly turn stormy and unpredictable.

That attitude in action has won praise for Dimon and his team at JPMorgan Chase, which in December 2008 was named one of "The World's Most Influential Companies" by *BusinessWeek*—joining nine other firms that also earned this distinction. Said *BusinessWeek*, "It is a testament to the times that CEO Jamie Dimon has become a towering figure in finance. As rivals were leading the charge into esoteric mortgage-backed products, he shied away. . . . But the conservative banker has had greatness thrust upon him. By shunning the deals that sent others crashing, he helped JPMorgan emerge as the king of banking. Even as its own fortunes suffer amid the turmoil, regulators trust it. Politicians cite the bank as a model of the kind of management needed to save Wall Street from future bouts of greed. And some rivals have looked to it for survival."[1]

The fortress balance sheet mentality demands constant preparedness, knowing that no matter how good things are now, they can and will eventually turn for the worse. As a modus operandi, it means rigorous analysis of the numbers, identifying the risks and potential risks, maintaining a detailed view of every business and product line at all times, and sharing information across the firm. The fortress balance sheet demands nothing less than full attention to the reality of the situation and a constant focus on the risks that lie hidden, just below the surface.

Strong Defense, Strategic Offense

The phrase *fortress balance sheet* evokes powerful images, like the walled Edinburgh Castle that towers over the Scottish city; Windsor Castle, chosen by William the Conqueror for its strategic site on the river Thames; or the Alhambra of Spain, a citadel protected by mountainous terrain. Each was built as a fortress, combining strength and strategy—a formidable defense against attack and providing a favorable, offensive position.

The same can be said for the fortress balance sheet, which has become a signature phrase for Dimon. In his first letter to Bank One shareholders, he painted a vision of "a fortress balance sheet with unquestionable strength" at a time when the Chicago-based institution was still in need of a financial overhaul. After JPMorgan Chase acquired Bank One in 2004, then-CEO William Harrison and Dimon told shareholders in a letter they co-authored that, "With a fortress balance sheet, we can withstand—perhaps even benefit from—difficult times and be deliberate in our capital allocation decisions."

In the midst of the financial crisis, that is exactly what JPMorgan Chase has done. Dimon and his team were able to undertake the Bear Stearns acquisition after a whirlwind of weekend negotiations, amid great uncertainty over the value of the assets being purchased, because the company was well prepared.

"They had the balance sheet strength to pull it off, the management ability to analyze Bear Stearns, and Jamie had the CEO guts to pull the trigger on the deal," observed Tom Brown, founder of Second Curve Capital. "Somebody may have had one of two of those attributes, but nobody except JPMorgan had all three."

Similarly, when Washington Mutual failed and the Federal Deposit Insurance Corporation (FDIC) was looking for a buyer (as will be recounted in Chapter 9), JPMorgan Chase had been the steady, patient player that was prepared to make a move, even though it was still in the midst of integrating Bear Stearns.

Dimon's strict focus on capital has been a hallmark of his career that spans more than two decades. Having managed companies through downturns and recessions, and now emerging as a Wall Street statesman at a time when the entire financial services industry has been threatened, Dimon combines the fortress mentality with superb execution. As board member David Novak observes, "Jamie is so focused on being rock solid, and focused on making money today and being able to make money tomorrow."

The Signature Phrase

Dimon did not coin the phrase, although he mentions it so often one might think so. Rather, the fortress balance sheet is attributed to J. Richard Fredericks, a former Montgomery Securities analyst who became a managing director of Bank of America and was later appointed as U.S. ambassador to Switzerland and Liechtenstein. In a *Fortune* article printed in 1985 on the consolidation among regional banks, Fredericks observed that Banc One Corporation, based in Columbus, Ohio, had what he called "a fortress balance sheet," which would likely make it an acquirer instead of an acquiree.[2] Curiously, Banc One would, in fact, engage in an acquisition spree, eventually merging with First Chicago NBD in 1998 to form Bank One. (And that acquisition, as stated in Chapter 5, eventually led to a management change and the recruitment of Jamie Dimon as the CEO.)

Nor is Dimon the only one to use it. For example, Wachovia Corporation cited the phrase as one of its goals for 2002 to create shareholder value, and in its 2003 annual report to shareholders said "maintaining a fortress balance sheet and strengthening our external debt rating" would be among the measures used to determine whether it had met its "overriding goal to be the best, most trusted and admired."[3] Then in late September 2008, Wachovia found itself dealing with the heavy burden of a portfolio of risky home loans and pressure from the federal government to find a merger partner. First to the plate was Citigroup, with a $12 billion plan to buy the banking assets, backed by the FDIC pledging billions in loss protection. Then Citi was bested by Wells Fargo, which reemerged as an interested party, and bought all of Wachovia for $15 billion in an all-stock transaction.[4]

When American International Group (AIG) was under siege due to mounting losses on its mortgage-related positions, it, too, turned to the fortress balance sheet. As *Fortune* magazine noted: "Martin Sullivan, the chief executive of American International Group, picked the right time to build what he calls a 'fortress balance sheet,' because bad bets in the mortgage markets have him and his board under siege."[5] A few months later, facing mounting losses and a liquidity squeeze, AIG was bailed out by the federal government with a loan of up to $85 billion—the first step in what would later become a $150 billion rescue and investment in the company.

Although JPMorgan Chase has not been without its losses from the credit crisis, Jamie Dimon's leadership has demonstrated his commitment to the fortress balance sheet as an operating principle in good times and in bad. A balance sheet that is fortified with capital can withstand the losses that mount when borrowers default and assets decline in value. Having ample capital provides the wherewithal to act when opportunities appear, particularly when others cannot. And when the cycle turns again, the next time to the upside, the strength of the fortress will add momentum that allows the strongest players to outpace those that are still in recovery.

It Always Pays to Be Prepared

"Always have a column called 'worst ever' and make sure you can survive under that," Dimon advised University of Chicago Graduate School of Business students in 2006, a time when JPMorgan Chase was enjoying strong growth in revenues and profitability.[6]

Dimon's perspective came from the events he had already witnessed in his career, starting in the very beginning. "The day I went to work out of business school, do you know what the prime rate was? Twenty-one and a half percent. Before that, the highest it had ever been was 9 or something like that. No one ever thought it was going to 20. Inflation was at 12, . . . 30-year bond at 14¾," he reflected in another college campus presentation in 2006, this time at Northwestern University's Kellogg School of Management.[7]

Dimon's career has also spanned several major market upheavals, including the stock market crash of 1987, the implosion of hedge fund Long-Term Capital Management (LTCM) in September 1998, and bursting of the bubble in technology stocks in 2000. Dimon was a top executive at Salomon Smith Barney when LTCM, which was thought to be perfectly hedged, faced massive losses after Russia defaulted on its domestic debt. Suddenly, LTCM's supposedly hedged positions went haywire. To prevent a meltdown of the system, the Federal Reserve brought together the nation's big bankers—including Dimon—to work out a solution. The result was that 11 banks contributed $300 million apiece to the bailout of Long-Term Capital, which was forced into liquidation.

Then came September 11, 2001, with deadly terrorist attacks striking at a time when the United States was in a recession and a financial bubble had burst. As Dimon remarked in 2006, many CEOs thought at the time they were facing a "perfect storm." Dimon, however, took a different view. "It wasn't even close to being one."[8]

The financial crisis of 2007–2008, however, certainly qualifies: the first decline in the overall U.S. housing market since the Great Depression; rising defaults among borrowers, particularly those in the subprime category; evaporating values for risky mortgage-based assets; a contagion of financial losses and fears as once-solid firms teeter on the brink of bankruptcy or fall over the edge; and on top of it all, a recession in the United States and several other countries that could be prolonged and deep.

Through much of 2008, even while credit conditions deteriorated they did not look dire—not until September when firms began to crumble and a former stalwart, Lehman Brothers, went bankrupt. Just a couple of months before, in a July 2008 interview on the *Charlie Rose* show, Dimon had sounded optimistic about the credit crisis, saying he hoped "we have hit bottom, but I don't know that for a fact." Even so, Dimon had remained cautious: "At JPMorgan, we try to prepare for all kinds of weather. We aren't guessing what the weather is going to be like. I have never seen anybody really try to pick the true inflection points of the economy—when it is going to start growing, what makes it stop growing or stop shrinking, et cetera. I just want to be prepared."[9]

"Being prepared" is a continual refrain for Dimon. Although today he sits in the top spot at one of the largest financial institutions, with more than $2 trillion in assets, Dimon's training in managing capital and risk goes back to much leaner days when he was part of the management team at consumer lender Commercial Credit in the mid-1980s. "Back then, we used to think that $500,000 was a huge issue. We would spend hours going over a few hundred thousand dollars," recalled Bob Lipp, who worked with Dimon at Commercial Credit, and today is a board member at JPMorgan Chase.

As the CFO at Commercial Credit, Dimon was always concerned about the potential impact of loan delinquencies and how well the firm was protected in case that challenge materialized. "He was always very conscious that reserves were appropriate," Lipp remarked.

Longtime Wall Street executive Hardwick "Wick" Simmons, who is a former CEO of Prudential Securities and of the NASDAQ stock market, commented that the need for the fortress balance sheet approach grows out of one's experience of having to operate without one. "And the fact that you like to sleep at night," Simmons quipped, adding on a more serious note: "For someone now running a major bank, the fortress balance sheet is an important concept with which to put your own house in order."

Ironically, while risks need to be mitigated in order to maintain financial strength, a fortress balance sheet also allows management to take on risks when circumstances call for it. "Jamie just showed that with the Bear Stearns acquisition. He could take risks when no one else was in line to step up because he had what he understood to be a fortress balance sheet," Simmons added.

Dimon's penchant for preparedness has earned him the admiration of associates and board members alike. Although he strives for growth both organically from existing operations and from acquisitions, he will never compromise on protecting the balance sheet from trouble, whether forecasted or unforeseen.

"He is wise beyond his years," board member Novak commented. "Jamie realizes that times are not always great. The best banks are prepared and the best companies are prepared to win in the good and the bad times. . . . He's very focused on Tier 1 capital being around 8.5 percent so there is capital available. That's why he's very focused on liquidity: how much is on the balance sheet in core deposits. He's always mindful of that because he's very prepared for the day when things get worse."

As important as having a strong defensive balance sheet is to prepare for the downturns, the discipline to maintain that strength cannot

thwart growth by refusing to take any risk. "You don't just want a balance sheet that's all Treasury bills. You won't earn enough for shareholders," observed Elinda Fishman Kiss, PhD, a professor of finance
and the Ralph J. Tyser Teaching Fellow in Finance at the University of
Maryland, who has also worked for several banks, the Resolution Trust
Corporation, and the Federal Reserve. "You need to take some risk,
but not just shoot from the hip."

As JPMorgan Chase has demonstrated, it does take risks in the
marketplace, whether participating in the subprime market as a lender
or in its investment bank. But it tries to protect its downside as much as
possible by keeping manageable positions and hedging to guard against
unfavorable market moves. Furthermore, as Dimon told shareholders in
his letter in the 2007 annual report, the company views its risky positions on a gross basis, rather than on a net basis with offsetting positions.
"Relying solely upon a net basis implies that it is not possible to lose
money on both sides of a complex trade," Dimon explained. "We know,
however, that this is quite possible."[10]

Analyst David Trainer, CEO of New Constructs, an independent
research firm, lauded Dimon for maintaining a prudent course in
the face of competitors who were following a different and—in the
short term, at least—a more lucrative path that later proved to be pitted with unforeseen risks. "He stays true to what is best for shareholders and best for the business, without falling prey to the temptation of
the times. And that is often an underappreciated characteristic on Wall
Street where the predominant mentality is 'What have you done for
me lately?' and 'How are you making money for me now?'"

No Resting on the Laurels

While Dimon certainly credits his team at every opportunity—
particularly for the hard work of integrating two major acquisitions in
a very short period of time—he focuses on the downside, preferring to
be self-critical and emphasize what could have been done differently in
order to learn from the past and be better prepared for the future.

As Dimon noted in a July 2008 television interview, "So here is a
good chance to make it really clear when you are reading about this

stuff [JPMorgan's performance compared to competitors]. I don't think we are doing that great . . . . You are never going to do stuff perfect in life. It is irrational for anyone to think every time you get up to bat, you will hit a home run. You are going to make errors."

Errors can be minimized, as Dimon acknowledged, with risk management measures such as thorough reporting, complete transparency, separate accounting for trading and operations, and people in place who can be trusted to do the right thing. Another imperative is to look at just how bad things can get, with real numbers attached. "Foreign exchange can move 10 percent in one day; credit spreads can gap out 300 basis points in one day; the stock market could fall 25 percent in one day—because they did," he added.[11]

Underscoring risk management is an operating environment that affirms—by word and deed—taking the high road. Tom Terry, managing director of JPMorgan and CEO of the company's Compensation and Benefit Strategies unit, recalled the culture he encountered after JPMorgan acquired Terry's national actuarial consulting firm in 2006. "I was really struck by the bank's strong belief that 'doing the right thing is always the right thing to do.' It's that simple."

The management style at JPMorgan encourages full disclosure when problems arise or results are not what is expected. "There is an amazing orientation toward full disclosure here," Terry added. "That ethic really encourages team problem solving rather than team problem hiding. So as a manager, I get to tap everyone's expertise and knock out problems a lot faster."

Another example is the JPMorgan Chase operating committee meetings, which are "not warm and fuzzy gatherings," as one executive remarked, but rather an opportunity to review each business unit and discuss problems. As each unit lays out its challenges, others chime in with their advice and perspective to help devise a solution or strategy. "Jamie really believes in getting the bad stuff out on the table. He's not going to point any fingers," the executive added. "It's really about accountability and having an open, frank, and respectful discussion. If Jamie senses there's any politics involved or if there's any backstabbing, you're dead."

Dimon's management style, from his self-described fanatical stance on reporting to his continual focus on the downside, is part of the fortress balance sheet mentality. Although he believes in learning from mistakes, there is nothing quite as inspiring as success. Here JPMorgan serves up an important lesson for other banks on what can be done to fortify their own balance sheets.

Advice and a History Lesson

In the midst of one of the worst months in the history of the financial markets, September 2008, JPMorgan Chase published on its web site a paper on "Building a Fortress Balance Sheet: Protect Your Bank's Financial Health While Positioning It for Growth." A how-to plan on fortifying balance sheets, the paper outlines the struggles confronting smaller and midsize banks that face increased regulatory pressure to raise capital above what would be considered a well-capitalized level and scarce funding available from sovereign wealth funds and private equity investors.

The paper also sent an urgent warning to banking executives that while many hoped the worst was behind them, their troubles were far from over. "In addition, investors are causing waves in the market as they try to get their arms around potential credit losses at banks and predict just where the bottom is. Blend this with high oil prices, inflationary concerns, falling consumer confidence, and home price depreciation and you suddenly have the formula for the market volatility we're experiencing. And don't be alarmed if we continue to see more of this as the market tries to find a floor on valuations," it stated.[12]

Indeed, just a month later, the stock market would experience several severe declines, including a few days with 700-point drops. JPMorgan's timing to assure and empower others with lessons from its own practices couldn't have been better. The white paper revealed the basic tenets of the JPMorgan fortress balance sheet creed, emphasizing:

- Offensive skills to raise capital and seize growth opportunities.
- Defensive skills to protect asset quality and fortify balance sheets.

To illustrate the concept, the JPMorgan Chase paper offered the example of Le Marechal de Vauban, a distinguished soldier and military engineer in seventeenth-century France who displayed unique genius for the offensive as well as the defensive. The paper went so far as to put forth "The Vauban Model," with its emphasis on a strong, protective defense, which then enables a strategic offense.

A quick study of history reveals the parallels between the military leader who from the late 1600s to the early 1700s helped protect French territory with impenetrable defenses and staged strategically brilliant offensive moves. Vauban started his career as a military cadet during civil war in France. After being captured, Vauban was recruited into the royal army because of his abilities. Appointed a "king's ordinary engineer," Vauban proved his talent during several military campaigns. He then rose to prominence after his engineering skills caught the attention of Louis XIV, who personally witnessed many of the sieges he directed.

As an engineer, Vauban's most notable accomplishments included several fortresses to protect France's northern border. The fortresses contained supplies for French armies on campaign, and also presented enemies with obstacles that required costly and time-consuming attacks to overcome. Vauban's genius on the offense enabled troops to move forward with successive advances until the ramparts gave way—or the enemy surrendered. When he wasn't engaged in battle, Vauban could be found surveying, inspecting, and checking the fortresses, making sure all was ready should a battle ensue.[13]

Stress Testing Assets

As Vauban knew, a strong defense is possible only if one is well prepared ahead of time, with fortifications that have been strengthened long before a siege is on the horizon. Similarly, one of the pillars of the fortress balance sheet approach is to stress test assets, which is the equivalent of determining what force of attack the walls can withstand.

The JPMorgan white paper advised that banks should evaluate their defensive strength by determining potential losses by asset type (e.g., home mortgages, commercial real estate, commercial and residential construction, and so on) in progressively worse scenarios. The first is the "base case," reflecting the actual charge-offs on a loan portfolio in the current environment. The second is a "stress case," showing the potential charge-offs among heavily leveraged assets, such as construction loans. The third is the "worst case," with high levels of charge-offs across all asset classes—such as home mortgages, commercial and residential construction, commercial real estate lending, and credit card and other consumer loans.[14]

A bank that has ample capital is like an army on the march with more than enough provisions and ammunition. Obstacles are more easily overcome, and even a long siege can be withstood. And when opportunities arise, an offensive can be launched.

Having Real Capital

A balance sheet becomes fortified when it has ample capital and, more important, quality capital. As Dimon explained, it's not enough to boast a strong Tier 1 capital ratio if loan loss reserves are inadequate. "But it goes much deeper than that. The loan loss reserves have to be strong—at that level, for that product, for that security, in that state. So you have to know real product profitability, real P&L [profit and loss], real costs, real margins, so that you can really survive." Dimon also made a direct link between the fortress balance sheet and his drive for "fanatical reporting—real, detailed, fair, accurate reporting."

Hand in hand with maintaining quality capital is knowing how and when to deploy it. Dimon proposed a hypothetical scenario of a business earning 21 percent, but if it were less leveraged—and therefore would be exposed to less potential risk—it could earn 18 percent. "So what?" he commented, clearly implying that the 3 percentage point difference in return is not worth the risk of being more highly leveraged.

Using the 18 percent return scenario, Dimon demonstrated the real value of the fortress balance sheet mentality: protecting against undue risk while still earning a solid return. "If you were investing in your business, growing customers, growing accounts, but you're slightly less leveraged on the balance sheet, you're building a great company," he asserted. "Everything you build is actually worth more, as opposed to, very often, people build stuff and try to sell it and it's worth nothing."

A critical part of building value for the future is maintaining investment in the operation, even if the cost reduces profits in the near term. To do otherwise would be akin to skimping on airplane maintenance in order to save money: It might work in the short term, but after a while would become dangerous. "To me you don't actually have a good business if you're earning your profit by not investing in systems for the future. You're kidding yourself," Dimon observed.

Value is created strategically over time, with a hawk's eye on the risks and conservative expectations for the rewards. Dimon sees examples of this in other industries where value is created through precision. "Look at the mature companies: Johnson & Johnson, Wal-Mart, GE. . . . They are learning institutions; they are always getting better. They are always adapting."

Colleagues say the same could be said for Dimon and his team as they manage risks, evaluate opportunities, and fortify a balance sheet to protect the downside and to wage a strategic offensive move or two.

"One of the pleasures of serving on the JPMorgan board is to see Jamie and his team in action," said Steve Burke, a longtime friend of Dimon's and president of Comcast Cable. "You can't go to a board meeting without learning something. You can't watch Jamie's interaction with his people and not see how wonderful that is and not come away having learned something and become inspired to do your own job better."

"My Grandmother Could Do That"

While JPMorgan's profits in 2008 were down significantly from the prior year, it has not had the huge losses or the need for resuscitative capital injections that some other firms required. "The fact that they have been able to increase reserves when most people are depleting theirs, and they had a very small amount of write-offs versus their peers—that says it all from a financial perspective. JPMorgan is not destroying value like others," Trainer commented.

As the JPMorgan team has also demonstrated, there is much more art to controlling risk than tightening one's belt during the downturn. The far more critical component is how risks are managed when things are going well and opportunities arise, especially those in the form of a new market or an innovative product. As Wall Street has experienced time and again, financial innovation creates risks that are not adequately recognized until it is too late.

"People at JPMorgan make fun of me because I say, 'My grand-mother could do that,' bless her soul. My grandmother could own risky assets and hold them and see what happens and earn a nice spread. That's not a business. Sometimes it's a completely reasonable thing to do, but it's not a . . . strategy," Dimon commented in a television inter-view. "We do some of that—don't get me wrong—but carefully."[15]

The real issue is knowing what kind of growth to pursue, and distin-guishing between growth that adds value for the long term and growth that ends up destroying value. In the 2007 letter to shareholders, Dimon cautioned against pressure on people to "grow, grow, grow . . . when market conditions are good." When market conditions turn, the result can be "dangerous outcomes for all businesses—and especially for vola-tile businesses like investment banking that takes risks."

He added, "It is easy to grow a business when taking on additional risk—but that is often the worst thing to do. Growth expectations need to be rational. We know there are times when we should not strive to grow certain areas of the business. This is an operating philosophy that protects us from the costly consequences of bad growth."[16]

Lessons from Warren Buffett

In 2007, when the credit crisis was only an unpleasant ripple compared to the massive earthquakes and devastating aftershocks to follow, Dimon described the triggering events as the bursting of the housing bubble, bad mortgage underwriting standards, and speculation in mortgage-backed investment products that spread risk throughout the system. Quoting Warren Buffett, Dimon wrote, "'When the tide goes out, you can see who's swimming naked.' In this crisis, as the tide went out, we saw sub-prime concerns first, then mortgage-related collateralized debt obliga-tions (CDOs), structured investment vehicles (SIVs), Alt-A mortgages, mortgage real estate investment trusts (REITs), the impact on monolines [which insure bonds and other finance products], and, finally, very unfor-tunately for us, home equity loans. And the tide is still going out."[17]

Dimon often cites Buffett, who is the model for his straight talk to shareholders. (Dimon is also among the many leaders in business who have consulted with Buffett.) These days, it's good company. Just as Dimon has been heralded in the media as a strong and steady player on

Wall Street, Buffett is the grand master of fortitude and calm. Buffett's $5 billion investment in Goldman Sachs in late September 2008 was seen as a singular vote of confidence in the market.

Yet it wasn't so very long ago when people questioned Buffett's wisdom, suggesting that perhaps his time had passed. The reason? Buffett, the quintessential value investor, avoided Internet stocks. When the latest dot-coms were going public and soaring to new heights at supersonic speed, some people thought Buffett had lost his touch. When the technology bubble burst and numerous Internet names faded into oblivion, suddenly Buffett looked to the masses to be a sage once again (although his fans never doubted his wisdom for a moment).

"During the tech bubble, they all said Buffett's time was past. He couldn't handle tech. He was an artifact. It was time to put him in the mothballs," analyst David Trainer said. However, Buffett "turned out to be right. Think about that. For a long time, a year plus, people said, 'He doesn't get it. Warren Buffett can't keep up.'"

Dimon had a taste of the same treatment a few years ago when competitors were dazzling Wall Street with profits gained from SIVs and heavy exposure to CDOs. By comparison, JPMorgan's results looked a little lackluster. By 2007, however, the game had changed dramatically. When the banks that had boasted big profits were suddenly reporting stunning losses, JPMorgan's prudence earned kudos from Wall Street analysts and pundits while Dimon's corporate alma mater, Citigroup, was facing serious problems.

"Contrasts between Dimon's JPMorgan Chase and [CEO Charles "Chuck"] Prince's Citigroup couldn't be sharper right now, even though the banks, among the biggest in the world, are squarely in the same mortgage-securities and leveraged-lending businesses that got hammered by the summer's market turmoil," *Forbes* reported in October 2007, citing quarterly earnings at the time that were above expectations for JPMorgan and down 57 percent for Citi. "In the last few days, Citi has rearranged the management of its investment bank, yet cries in some investor corners for the ouster of Prince as Citi's chief executive and/or the break-up of the firm have gone unheeded. There have been no such calls for the removal of Dimon or the break-up of JPMorgan."[18]

Commenting on the bank's quarterly results at the time, Dimon observed: "We always believed in a fortress balance sheet."[19]

A year later Dimon was still counting on the discipline of the fortress balance sheet to carry the day in the midst of deteriorating credit conditions. After JPMorgan announced third-quarter 2008 earnings that were 61 percent lower than a year ago (although above what analysts had expected), Dimon assured investors that the company would withstand the uncertainty in the capital markets, the housing sector, and the economy, and the likelihood of lower earnings in the future. Its loan loss reserves and Tier 1 capital ratio—two pillars of the fortress balance sheet—made it "well-positioned to handle the turbulent environment and, most importantly, to continue to invest in our businesses and serve our clients well."[20]

The Long-Term View

The crisis of 2008 yields rich lessons for those willing to pay attention to what has mitigated risk and what has failed miserably. These are lessons that will be evaluated for years to come, Dimon believes. One of the obvious ones to him was the mistake of ignoring bubbles that were created when asset values inflated beyond reasonable levels. As he noted, "I made a joke that we should have a bubble-watch section in our risk management team, so you're always asking, 'What has gone up a lot lately and what are the risks?'"

Knowing where the risks are and, even better, where they are likely to develop in the future keeps the fortress strong. Preparedness is everything, to be on guard against attack—in this case adverse conditions and unforeseen events. Even in the midst of a long siege, the fortification holds. And then when the battle turns in one's favor, the shift can be the offensive to gain ground.

Chapter 9

Taking Over WaMu:
A Sign of the Times

We [view] this franchise for the long term—not for next year or the next five years but for the next hundred years.

—JAMIE DIMON

I t was late September 2008, and the credit crisis had deteriorated to the point that pundits were predicting economic fallout that could rival the Great Depression. Bitter battles raged on Capitol Hill over the Treasury Department's proposed $700 billion Wall Street bailout, which had been defeated in its first round and would need considerable political wrangling to pass on the second. Financial institutions were merging, acquiring weaker players, getting government bailouts, and, in the case of Lehman Brothers, going bankrupt.

In the midst of the financial and economic trauma, Washington Mutual officially became the largest bank failure in U.S. history. The collapse of the $307 billion thrift institution eclipsed the implosion of $40 billion Continental Illinois in 1984. Even adjusted for 2008 dollars, Continental's assets of $67.7 billion on an equivalent basis placed it far behind Washington Mutual as the biggest bank bust.[1]

Washington Mutual came to an end as an independent institution on September 25, 2008, when the Federal Deposit Insurance
Corporation (FDIC) stepped in to take control of the 110-year-
old thrift and promptly sold off most of it to JPMorgan Chase for
$1.9 billion—thereby assuring continuity for insured and uninsured
deposits alike. It was a straightforward deal without any taxpayer
money and with all of the proceeds going to the FDIC. Washington
Mutual, which called itself "the bank of everyday people" and went by
the nickname of WaMu, was now part of a global financial powerhouse
that boasted more than $2 trillion in assets.

Six months earlier, the Bear Stearns rescue deal had sent shock
waves through the financial markets. By comparison, the acquisition of
Washington Mutual assets barely caused a stir. It's not that the acquisition wasn't important; the market was just too stunned to register much
of a reaction. While keenly strategic for JPMorgan and its Chase retail
network, the WaMu deal is important for another reason: it demonstrates
the fortress balance sheet in action. The operating philosophy of building strength in the good times and staying strong during the bad times, as
outlined in Chapter 8, was illustrated in September 2008 when the financial markets were crumbling, yet JPMorgan Chase was on the offensive.

In an interview two weeks after the Washington Mutual deal was
announced and closed, Jamie Dimon explained that the Seattle-based
thrift had always been at the top of the JPMorgan wish list. "We look
at everything. I give a little chart—the board has it and the management
team [has it]—of all potential acquisitions around the world in different
businesses. WaMu has always been number one at the right price."

While it looked like JPMorgan was once again in the right place
at the right time and at the right price when a financial company was
about to fold, Dimon refuted the notion that it was an opportunistic
deal. "It was opportunistic in that we were ready—there, poised. But it
was completely strategic in that this is the one that completely made
sense for the company . . . just exactly what we needed and wanted,
and the price was right."

JPMorgan Chase director James Crown added that for the past several years, senior management and the board had been on the alert for
strategic opportunities that would leverage the company's strengths.
"That would include paying attention to a franchise like Washington

Mutual. It would be on a long list of things that the company would be interested in."

Welcome WaMu

As Washington Mutual changed hands, a welcome sign from JPMorgan Chase went up on its web site, with an assurance that all WaMu customer deposits—including checking accounts, savings accounts, and certificates of deposit—were backed by JPMorgan. For WaMu depositors who had staged a run on the bank, withdrawing more than $16 billion in about a 10-day stretch in September, the JPMorgan Chase statement should have helped them breathe more easily. Still, news stories published the day after the deal closed contained anecdotal quotes from WaMu customers who were closing accounts, spreading their money around in several banks, and voicing concern about the banking system in general. Yet having the lights on and the branches running the day after the FDIC seized Washington Mutual demonstrated that the system still worked. And this time, it worked the old-fashioned way, without bailouts or taxpayer money. A bank faltered, the FDIC stepped in, and someone else took it over in a seamless fashion.

The JPMorgan team had been looking at Washington Mutual for some time. In March 2008, JPMorgan had offered to buy Washington Mutual for $4 to $8 a share, or $7 billion to $9 billion, the *Wall Street Journal* reported. Those talks did not progress when Washington Mutual opted to remain independent and accepted $7 billion in fresh capital from a group of investors led by Texas Pacific Group (TPG), a private equity firm.[2] Like the rest of Washington Mutual investors, TPG did not recoup any of its money when the bank failed.

Not everyone has cheered the JPMorgan acquisitions, seeing a large bank getting even bigger at the apparent expense of the weaker. In the press, Dimon and the bank he runs have been compared to vultures picking over the carrion, which even in its harshness does point out the necessity of stronger players being able to absorb the weaker ones to the benefit of the system. "Vultures serve a very valuable purpose, both in the natural world and in business," Bert Ely, president of bank consulting firm Ely & Co., was quoted by *MarketWatch* as saying.

"It's crucial for the banking industry and the economy for the Jamie Dimons of the world to be there in times like this."[3]

Even as *MarketWatch* described the tough stance taken by Dimon and his team to manage the bank through the crisis, including as it made acquisitions, there was more praise than criticism. In fact, *MarketWatch* named Dimon as a finalist for its 2008 CEO of the Year award—the only financial industry executive to be honored. (Winner of the *MarketWatch* 2008 CEO of the Year award was Brian Goldner of Hasbro, the toymaker.)[4]

While JPMorgan was first looking at Washington Mutual in March 2008, it did have its hands full with the Bear Stearns transaction, which Crown called a "speed merger." In time, the Washington Mutual deal would be "more of an effort at courtship," he added; "two very different rhythms, two very different companies."

A number of other banks were said to have looked at Washington Mutual: Citigroup, Wells Fargo, Banco Santander, and others. But it was JPMorgan at the front of the line to complete the deal that it had long wanted. In an investor conference call, JPMorgan executives mentioned bidding for Washington Mutual, although it was not clear just how that process had transpired. In the end, JPMorgan Chase emerged as the deal maker when the federal government had a troubled financial institution on its hands to sell. This earned praise from FDIC Chair Sheila Bair, particularly for JPMorgan's willingness to take on questionable loans on the WaMu books. "Some are coming to Washington for help, others are coming to Washington to help," Bair commented.[5]

The acquisition received a nod from Wall Street as another good move for JPMorgan to build its business for the future when some others were unable to hang on for another day. UBS analyst Sandra Goldschneider wrote in a report that "JPMorgan's skilled management team waited patiently for the most attractive opportunity to expand the company's retail banking presence in a shareholder-friendly way."

She applauded the upside potential for the Washington Mutual deal, which she saw as being beyond JPMorgan's conservative estimates. "We continue to view JPMorgan as one of the best-run and most uniquely positioned franchises within US Financials. While each integration carries its own risks, we think the JPMorgan team is among the most capable."[6]

Under the leadership of Dimon, JPMorgan demonstrated that not only was it weathering the credit crisis storm, but it was also able to take over weaker firms—and bolster the company's future growth prospects. JPMorgan's strength stemmed from the philosophy and operating principles of Dimon's fortress balance sheet mentality, which enabled the company to remain on the offensive while others either were trying to plug holes in their capitalization or were looking to be acquired.

Washington Mutual Runs into Trouble

The trouble for Washington Mutual had stemmed from its specialization in home mortgages, credit cards, and other retail lending products and services—all of which were impacted by lower home values and rising defaults on mortgages and other loans.

In Washington Mutual's 2007 annual report to shareholders, Kerry Killington, who was then chairman and CEO, stated that the bank had expected a downturn, "but it hit with much more severe consequences than anyone anticipated."

"Over the course of my 30-plus years in banking and finance, including 18 years as CEO of WaMu, I have managed through many cycles. But this is the most difficult period I have seen for the [housing] market, and WaMu in particular," Killington stated in his letter to shareholders dated March 2008.[7]

Killington's comments would prove to be an understatement for the country's largest savings and loan institution and for the executive himself. After posting its largest loss ever in the second quarter of 2008, Washington Mutual shares plummeted to $3. As recently as June 2007 the bank's stock had been over $30 a share. In early September 2008, Killington, who was credited with building Washington Mutual into one of the biggest financial institutions in the country through a series of acquisitions, was asked to leave.

Just days later, Washington Mutual announced more dire news on its financial condition, predicting additional charge-offs for bad loans in the third quarter. Further, Washington Mutual had to mark down the value of its preferred stock holdings in faltering mortgage giants Fannie Mae and Freddie Mac by 90 percent to $282 million. Washington

Mutual was put on probation by the Office of Thrift Supervision, and Standard & Poor's, the credit rating agency, lowered the firm's credit outlook as the housing market worsened. Things at Washington Mutual were going quickly from bad to unbearable.[8]

The downturn in the housing market crushed the performance of Washington Mutual's mortgage portfolio, leading to three consecutive quarters of losses totaling $6.1 billion. As market conditions worsened, Washington Mutual experienced a run as depositors withdrew billions of dollars. The Office of Thrift Supervision stepped in to seize the bank, stating that it had insufficient liquidity to meet its obligations and was found to be in "unsafe and unsound condition to transact business."[9]

The troubles at Washington Mutual then opened the door to JPMorgan Chase, which was waiting in the wings to do a deal with the FDIC.

A Strategic Fit for JPMorgan

With patience and precision, JPMorgan Chase got exactly what it wanted, especially geographic expansion, gaining an important presence in California and Florida and increasing its market share in existing fast-growing markets, including New York, Texas, Illinois, Arizona, Colorado, and Utah. As Dimon told analysts and investors on a conference call the night the Washington Mutual deal was announced, "It obviously will add a whole bunch of states—California, Florida—and enhance states we're already in."

By acquiring Washington Mutual, JPMorgan Chase expanded the geographic footprint of its retail banking business. Combined with WaMu it had the No. 2 retail branch network with 5,400 branches in 23 states and established a bigger base for its business banking, commercial banking, credit card, consumer lending, and wealth management businesses. After the transaction, JPMorgan could boast 14,300 ATMs, 24.5 million checking accounts, and $1.433 trillion in mortgages served. It had also extended its reach to 42 percent of U.S. households, up significantly from 25 percent previously. It could now offer its products and services, from debit cards to online bill paying, to a new group of customers, as well as services for business banking and small businesses.

But it wasn't growth just for the sake of growth; it was a strategic move for the future.

"Often when you're running a company as big as JPMorgan, the business model is always under scrutiny," Crown added. "Does it make sense to be this big, to have this diverse a product line? We have always been able to analyze that, and the answer is yes."

Taking a Look at WaMu

Unlike the flurry of weekend negotiations and a $29 billion federal guarantee to back troubled assets in the Bear Stearns deal, JPMorgan was able to take its time—relatively speaking—with the Washington Mutual transaction. How much time, executives wouldn't say exactly, except to indicate that it was enough to do thorough due diligence. As JPMorgan Chase retail banking chief Charlie Scharf told analysts and investors on a conference call explaining the deal, "We spent an awful lot of time going through an awful lot of detail coming up with what our estimates are. These were not estimates that came together in a 12- or 24-hour time period. They are estimates that came together over a substantial period."

JPMorgan had some 75 people involved in the process of evaluating Washington Mutual and also committed the resources of its investment bank to evaluate WaMu's mortgage loan portfolio. "It was one of the most thorough things we've ever done," Scharf commented.

After deciding that, indeed, WaMu was what it wanted, the JPMorgan team played to win not for a short-term uptick, but for the long haul. "We bid to win because we wanted to win for a lot of obvious reasons," Dimon told analysts and investors.

Just as Dimon was cautionary about the Bear Stearns deal when it was first announced, he underscored the risks in the Washington Mutual deal, particularly in the asset values. The key questions were not only what the WaMu banking business was worth under current conditions, but also its value if the economy went into a deep or even severe recession. That same risk, however, created a potential reward—in this case, an opportunity for JPMorgan to make a move when others either wouldn't or couldn't. This decisive preparedness has been a hallmark of Dimon's career and a particular strength of his management team.

"Some people obviously couldn't do the work or bring themselves to be comfortable. Some people maybe couldn't raise the capital," Dimon told analysts and investors. "When you bid on something like this, there is always a risk. That's what created this opportunity, but that still remains a risk. . . . We don't know exactly what the future is going to hold. We're pretty sure we did the right thing for the shareholders."

Right from the start, by buying the deposits, assets, and certain liabilities of the Washington Mutual banking operations, JPMorgan expected to add significantly to earnings. "We think this deal is extremely financially compelling," Dimon said. "It's accretive immediately and it's substantial—it's 50 cents [per share in added earnings]. Some people say 'accretive immediately' and they're talking about two years out and 2 or 3 cents. This is more than that, and it will grow over time as cost savings and other things come in."

In addition, JPMorgan projected cost savings of $1.5 billion, with the majority of its anticipated synergies achieved by the end of 2010—the same target date for completion of branch conversions.

Taking on Washington Mutual, JPMorgan Chase also acquired a large loan portfolio, of which some $31 billion had to be marked down—an amount that represented the company's estimates for credit losses in the future from the WaMu portfolio. Concurrent with the Washington Mutual deal, JPMorgan Chase raised $11.5 billion through a common stock offering to allow the company to maintain a strong balance sheet and capital ratios going forward. It was an "offensive capital raise," Dimon said. "We're not raising capital to fill a hole. We're raising capital to go on the offensive."

After the Washington Mutual acquisition and the capital raised through the stock sale, JPMorgan's Tier 1 ratio, stood at a strong 8.9 percent. Having high Tier 1 capital is part of the JPMorgan financial discipline, which includes not only having ample capital, but having quality capital along with strong loan loss reserves, and using conservative accounting. This is the essence of the rainy-day scenario, of preparing for the inevitable downturns, especially those that turn out to be prolonged or severe.

"You have a buffer to deal with problems. You know you're always going to have them," Dimon observed at an FDIC forum in July 2008. "It's almost impossible to be in a cyclical business and think you're going to avoid them."[10]

"First-Class" Banking Meets "Whoo Hoo!"

In many ways, buying Washington Mutual is a continuation of JPMorgan Chase's strategy in retail banking that began when it acquired Chicago-based Bank One in 2004 in a deal that also brought Dimon to JPMorgan Chase as the successor CEO. "Once JPMorgan bought Bank One, it had to adopt the Starbucks model, with a branch on every corner," commented money manager and economist Rob Stein of Astor Asset Management LLC in Chicago and author of *The Bull Inside the Bear* (John Wiley & Sons, 2009).

Although Washington Mutual does have some less-than-desirable retail locations and branches that will need to be upgraded and converted to the Chase model, the initial plan called for JPMorgan to close less than 10 percent of combined units. Scharf saw the WaMu acquisition as an opportunity to take the best locations among the two networks. "We're looking forward to treating this like a real merger, taking the best of both and winding up with a combined business which is hopefully run better . . . than each of us had going into this."

What will be interesting to see is how JPMorgan manages the combination of culture and marketing messages. The old J.P. Morgan & Company catered to an aristocratic clientele, and woven into its history were scions of business and industry. Describing its culture on the corporate web site, JPMorgan Chase quotes J. P. Morgan Jr., who in 1933 advocated "at all times the idea of doing only first-class business, and that in a first-class way."

By contrast, WaMu used the marketing catchphrase "Whoo hoo!" (spelled with "Wh" to avoid confusion with Homer Simpson's exclamatory "Woo Hoo!" which is trademarked). "We're informal, friendly, and fun," Washington Mutual stated on its web site. "We take our customers' money seriously, but not ourselves. We even call ourselves by a fun name that started out as a nickname years ago: WaMu."

A month after the merger, a combination of messages began to emerge. The Washington Mutual web site in late October declared, "WaMu & Chase, Safe and Secure," with the slogan "Same friendly attitude. Way more muscle."

The messages appeared to be working: In its third-quarter 2008 earnings conference call, JPMorgan Chase executives reported that the

Washington Mutual deposit base had stabilized and was increasing, with positive net inflows of cash on seven of the first nine days of October.

In terms of the customer base, while WaMu may have more to do with Wal-Mart, and the JPMorgan Chase image may be colored by its blue-blood past, on the retail level the banks' customers have a lot of similarities. "The mass banking business is the mass banking business," Scharf told analysts and investors. "People are often surprised when we talk about the new accounts opened at Chase. The average checking balance will be $500 or $700 initially. . . . Our branches serve a very wide rage of individuals, as do Washington Mutual's."

A significant contrast, however, was apparent in Washington Mutual's loan policies, compared to the far more stringent procedures at JPMorgan. As the *New York Times* reported, Washington Mutual and its "Power of Yes" slogan had allegedly led to the writing of questionable loans to borrowers, a practice that contributed to the downfall of the thrift. "At WaMu, getting the job done meant lending money to nearly anyone who asked for it—the force behind the bank's meteoric rise and its precipitous collapse this year in the biggest bank failure in American history," the *Times* reported.[11]

One thing is certain: after being acquired by JPMorgan, WaMu was in for an overhaul of its procedures for making loans. (JPMorgan did not comment in the *Times* article on Washington Mutual loan operations before the acquisition. "It is a different era for our customers and for the company," the *Times* quoted a JPMorgan spokesman as saying.[12])

The Chase retail operation, meanwhile, has unveiled an expanded mortgage modification program to help troubled borrowers avoid foreclosure. In addition to Chase customers, the program was also offered to those who had mortgages written by WaMu and EMC Mortgage Corporation, a lending unit of Bear Stearns.

A Somber Picture

Despite the optimism over the opportunity to buy Washington Mutual, the JPMorgan presentation to analysts and investors included some sobering projections: the possibility of a deep recession in the United States and housing prices falling substantially from the already-low levels of September 2008.

Discussing the Washington Mutual deal with analysts and investors, the JPMorgan team put forth some what-if scenarios and how each would affect the expected profit boost from Washington Mutual. Or as Scharf explained, the purpose was to look at "how wrong could we be, and if we're wrong what does it mean?"

This echoes Dimon's view—repeated many times over the years—that he does not worry about small fluctuations, but about cataclysmic shifts. In 2006, before the credit crisis erupted, Dimon remarked, "I think as a company you have to be prepared to deal with all eventualities."[13]

Buying a troubled bank in the midst of a devastating credit crisis requires a stoic view of just how bad things can get. The markdowns on Washington Mutual loans totaling $31 billion were based on "some pretty severe estimates," Scharf explained: unemployment at 7 percent; an additional 8 percent decline in home prices in the United States from September 2008 levels, with Florida falling another 16 percent and California by 10 percent.

Seeing the potential for economic conditions to worsen, the JPMorgan team put forth more dire scenarios and projected the impact on the Washington Mutual loan portfolio. In a deeper recession with unemployment rising to 7.5 percent, the additional projected drop in U.S. home prices would be 11 percent, with Florida declining by another 21 percent and California by 14 percent. If a severe recession developed with unemployment at 8 percent, U.S. housing prices would decline by 20 percent from current values, with Florida falling by an additional 36 percent and California by 24 percent. To put these numbers in perspective, JPMorgan's estimates call for a peak-to-trough decline in home prices of 25 percent across the United States given current conditions, worsening to a 28 percent decline with a deeper recession and to 37 percent in a severe recession.

As economic projections become pessimistic, estimated losses from the Washington Mutual portfolio would rise from $31 billion at the time of the deal to $42 billion in a deeper recession and $54 billion in a severe recession. To offset these potential scenarios, JPMorgan had a cushion—in this case the expected earnings accretion from buying Washington Mutual. In the worst-case scenario, the additional losses from the loan portfolio would wipe out projected earnings gains from the Washington Mutual acquisition for three years. That means that in a severe recession the

Washington Mutual acquisition would be a breakeven proposition for a few years. Thus, the projected earnings boost from Washington Mutual—of $0.50 a share in 2008, $0.60 in 2010, and $0.70 in 2011—created a buffer for the company should the economy go into a severe recession.

As 2008 came to a close there was no end in sight for the recession that was declared by the National Bureau of Economic Research to have begun in December 2007. In a CNBC interview in December 2008, Dimon shared his outlook for a potentially tough 2009, given "a dramatic downturn in almost every single economic indicator there is." If one bright spot in his dismal outlook could be found, it was that a depression seemed unlikely. "You now have the governments and the central banks of the world putting every ounce and every fiber to stop the snowballing [downturn in the] economy, and they've already pulled out the financial system. . . . I think they're going to do what they have to do. We know a lot more than we knew the last time we had a depression."[14]

Failure and Takeover: A Sign of the Times

The Washington Mutual deal was a sign of the times for several reasons. For one, it was yet another failure at a time when the once-mighty were falling. In September 2008, panic gripped the banking sector and a flurry of transactions and bailouts occurred, making it hard to keep track of the players without a scorecard. While the initial events were sobering, the aftermath indicated that the financial crisis was far from over.

- The U.S. government took over Fannie Mae and Freddie Mac, the mortgage financing giants that together held $5.4 trillion in guaranteed mortgage-backed securities and debt outstanding.
- Merrill Lynch & Company agreed to be acquired by Bank of America Corporation in a $50 billion all-stock transaction. Bank of America CEO Ken Lewis had considered buying Lehman Brothers as it headed toward bankruptcy, but a lack of government backing squashed that deal. Instead, Lewis and Merrill CEO John Thain negotiated a deal whereby Merrill Lynch—and Thain, himself—would become part of Bank of America. Then, in January 2009, after

the Merrill operations contributed to an unexpectedly large loss at Bank of America, the institution received a $20 billion capital injection from the U.S. government and Thain agreed to resign. The $20 billion in federal funds—along with the $25 billion handed out by Treasury to each of the top banks in October 2008—brought the government's investment in Bank of America to $45 billion.

- Lehman Brothers filed for Chapter 11 bankruptcy protection in what became the largest failure of an investment bank since the collapse of Drexel Burnham Lambert 18 years earlier. Barclays, the British Bank, had been in talks to buy all of Lehman, but instead purchased its American investment banking business and its New York City headquarters. Nomura Holdings Inc. of Japan acquired Lehman operations in Asia, Europe, and the Middle East.

- Insurance company American International Group (AIG) was granted an initial $85 billion from the U.S. government to avert bankruptcy, which turned out to be only the first wave of federal assistance. The total package for AIG climbed by year end to $152 billion, which amounted to one of the largest bailouts of a single private firm.

- Citigroup agreed to buy the banking operations of Wachovia Corporation in a $2.16 billion deal with the FDIC providing tens of billions in loss protection. Citi was then upstaged by Wells Fargo in a bidding war for Wachovia, which was won handily by Wells Fargo in a $14.5 billion deal without any FDIC backing. By early 2009, Citigroup was on the defensive, announcing it will spin off its Smith Barney brokerage unit to Morgan Stanley and sell its Japanese retail brokerage operation. Citi also replaced its chairman.

- And also in September 2008, the Federal Reserve agreed to convert the last two large independent investment banks on Wall Street, Morgan Stanley and Goldman Sachs, into traditional bank holding companies, which would give them access to consumer deposits as a key source of funding. In addition to being overseen by the Securities and Exchange Commission (SEC), the Federal Reserve would regulate the parent companies of the two banks; the U.S. comptroller of the currency would oversee the national bank charters; and the FDIC would become involved as the companies seek higher volumes of federally backed deposits.[15]

Bailouts and Bank Investments

And if that wasn't enough for one month, the banking landscape was about to change further with the passage of the $700 billion Wall Street bailout proposed by Treasury Secretary Henry Paulson. The original stated purpose was to purge the system of illiquid assets and allow liquidity to flow to businesses and consumers (although in deployment, the bailout has morphed to include a host of rescue measures).

The next move was for Paulson to call the nation's top bankers together to present a plan whereby the government would invest a total of $250 billion in several financial institutions through the purchase of preferred securities. While the move to partially nationalize the U.S. banking system may seem shocking, it is not without precedent. In the 1930s, the Reconstruction Financial Corporation (RFC), which was established by the Hoover administration, lent money to banks. Its role as a financier was expanded later by Franklin Delano Roosevelt, who approved direct government investment in banks.

"In 1933, the RFC was authorized to make preferred stock investments in financial institutions. No fewer than 6,000 American banks sold preferred stock to the government via the RFC program," explained Richard Sylla, economics professor at New York University.

Sylla estimated that the $3 billion invested by the RFC in the banks was equivalent to 3 percent of the U.S. gross domestic product (GDP) in 1928. Today, 3 percent of the U.S. GDP would be $400 billion to $500 billion.

The expectation was that the banks would use the money to increase lending to consumers and businesses in order to ease a liquidity squeeze in the marketplace. But early indications were that the liquidity tap had not been turned on, and that some banks might be using the funds to make acquisitions. While some consolidation could be good for the system if weaker players were absorbed by the stronger ones in order to prevent failures, it did appear to run contrary to the bailout plan expectations—and to the Treasury secretary's own pronouncements.

Appearing on the *Charlie Rose* show, Paulson said the objective of the investment program was to encourage healthy banks to use the money received from the government to increase lending and thereby improve liquidity in the marketplace. "We need the banks to deploy the money, not to hoard it. The way to have that happen is to have, first of all, the banks have plenty of capital. It's all too easy when you're going through a period like this for banks to say, 'I've got plenty of capital.' They don't need to raise it. [They] shrink their balance sheets, pull in their horns. They need to be well capitalized. They need to feel confident."[16]

After the first injection of U.S. government investment money arrived, the banks were given a stern warning from Washington: start lending, because the regulators were watching very closely. Still, there were indications that some of the federal money might go for acquisitions, not loans. For example, after PNC Financial Services Group received $7.7 billion in return for company stock, it announced the acquisition of National City Corporation for $5.58 billion.

Before the PNC deal was announced, Paulson said in the *Charlie Rose* interview that acquisitions would be possible—although he repeatedly stressed that the purpose of the program was for the government to invest in healthy banks as a way of bolstering confidence in the financial system. "There will be some situations where it's best for the economy and the banking system for there to be a consolidation. But again, this is something that regulators are looking at very closely."[17]

Asked in a JPMorgan Chase third-quarter earnings conference call about the government's expectations for using the money, Dimon said, "It's clear that the government would like us to use the capital to facilitate clients and make loans and stuff like that. We want to do that, too. So we have a common interest in this."

Although Dimon has declined to account for exactly how the $25 billion that JPMorgan received from the government has been and will be spent, he told CNBC that commercial loan balances for JPMorgan Chase had risen 18 percent in 2008. In addition, credit card loans, student loans, and large corporate loans were also up.[18]

In remarks at the Yale CEO summit in December 2008, Dimon noted that JPMorgan had $60 billion in the interbank market, in which banks lend to each other. "That's a lot of risk," he added.[19]

From Wall Street to Main Street, perhaps the biggest frustration has been that despite dramatic actions taken to shore up the financial sector, great uncertainty remains. Just days after the inauguration, Congress gave President Barack Obama permission to spend the second $350 billion of the Wall Street bailout amid indications that additional funds to rescue banks and financial institutions might be necessary. In a statement before the Senate Finance Committee during hearings on his appointment to become Treasury Secretary, Timothy Geithner urged aggressive action and voiced support for the Obama team's stimulus plan. Yet even as an $800 billion economic recovery package was debated in Congress, the outlook was for a long and potentially painful recovery. Meanwhile, in an apparent show of confidence, Jamie Dimon reportedly bought 500,000 shares of JPMorgan Chase stock for $22.93 each—a total investment of about $11.46 million, according to the *Wall Street Journal*.[20]

More Acquisitions in the Future?

With ample capital, JPMorgan Chase has made hints about deploying some for strategic deals if the right opportunities came along. Thus, Washington Mutual also became a sign of the times not only because of its failure, but because of what followed: namely, consolidation with weaker players gobbled up by stronger ones.

Banks profiting from the tumultuous times is not without historic precedent. J. Pierpont Morgan himself, after quelling the Panic of 1907 by corralling bankers to save troubled thrift institutions, wanted a quid pro quo for his good deeds. In order to save Moore and Schley, a speculative brokerage that was $25 million in debt, Morgan arranged for U.S. Steel—described as his "favorite creation"—to buy the firm's stake in Tennessee Coal and Iron Company. In a scenario that sounds eerily current and familiar, the fear was that if Moore and Schley had to liquidate that stake, it could cause a stock market collapse; and if Moore and Schley went down, that could hurt other investment houses as well. Morgan arranged for U.S. Steel to buy the Tennessee Coal stake from Moore and Schley—as long as a $25 million pool of financing was secured from trust company presidents to protect the weaker firms. As soon as President Theodore Roosevelt approved U.S. Steel's takeover of Tennessee Coal and Iron before the stock market opened up, the criticism started—including that Roosevelt had been duped into overriding his antitrust policies and that the $45 million price tag for Tennessee Coal was too low compared to a potential property value of $1 billion.[21]

As history has shown, panics and opportunities seem to go together as the stronger consume the weak in Darwinian fashion. This time around, the criticism rests on whether the big will keep getting bigger thanks in part to government money, while smaller institutions—including those that are healthy—fall prey to consolidation.

Waiting for What Comes Next

As 2008 drew to a close—ending a year that was both cataclysmic and transformative for the financial services industry—one can only wonder what might be next for JPMorgan Chase and its CEO. In the third quarter earnings conference call, Dimon had commented that some of the government's capital could be deployed "to benefit our shareholders," which appeared to indicate that future acquisitions were possible. (In late December, JPMorgan announced that it would acquire UBS Commodities Canada Ltd., the Canadian energy operations of UBS AG, as well as UBS's global agricultural business for undisclosed terms. That deal was expected to close in the first quarter of 2009.)

Given the experience of the integration team that has taken on Bear Stearns and Washington Mutual deals just six months apart, there is no doubt that the House of Dimon has the ability to make another move—as long as it makes strategic sense. Don't look for JPMorgan to do a deal just because it can or something is available. Given the fact that Washington Mutual had topped the JPMorgan acquisition wish list and the bank had pursued the deal not once but twice before being successful, expect the same criteria for any future acquisitions if and when they materialize.

Dimon has earned a reputation as a deal maker, starting with his Sandy Weill days and continuing through his sale of Bank One to JPMorgan Chase, and then the more recent acquisitions of Bear Stearns and Washington Mutual. But at heart, he is all about managing businesses for growth while maintaining financial strength to guard against the downturns that are inevitable in the cyclical banking business.

Showcasing Dimon's reputation among some leaders in the financial services industry, Thomas A. James, chairman of Raymond James Financial Inc., commended the JPMorgan CEO for the close attention paid to operations.

"The distinguishing thing about Jamie Dimon is that he is very sensitive to the operating issues. He believes in homogenizing systems. He believes in assuring that his management team has very high-quality people who work hard and are dedicated to the company for which they work," said James, who is a past chairman of the Financial Services Roundtable and worked closely with Dimon on industry issues. He further credited Dimon with making sure that processes are in place to analyze current and projected conditions and make informed decisions.

Dimon's stewardship of the JPMorgan Chase operations, particularly in the midst of risky credit and economic conditions, bodes well for the company not only to survive the current crisis, but to emerge in a stronger condition that could catapult its growth in the future. As analyst David Trainer, president of independent research firm New Constructs, commented, "Jamie Dimon is in a position to scoop up assets on the cheap. That's how you create value for the long term. That's Jamie Dimon managing a bank the way Warren Buffett manages money."

As history has shown, what happens after the deal determines the ultimate success. It's one thing to make an acquisition, and another to integrate it well. Here Dimon shines the spotlight on his team. "It was an unbelievable thing to watch the people accomplish the WaMu acquisition, managing the portfolios. A lot of these same people were dealing with clients and mortgages and issues, trying to do the right thing for clients every day," Dimon said in the third-quarter earnings conference call. "It makes you really proud to watch what the people here are able to accomplish. That portends very well for what can be accomplished in the future."

Chapter 10

Navigating
Financial Storms

I think there will be lessons learned for a long time.
—Jamie Dimon

F irst there is a bubble, the rapid inflating of prices that goes beyond normal, rational supply and demand. After the bubble and the burst, a sobered investment community faces the lessons it ignored during the good times when investors tried to convince themselves that the expansion could go on forever. They quote the wise words of the late John Weinberg, former senior partner and chairman of Goldman Sachs: "Trees don't grow to the sky." They ruminate on the observation of former Federal Reserve Chairman Alan Greenspan when he spoke about "irrational exuberance."

They've learned their lesson. It will be different the next time.

And then it happens all over again.

This time it was a bubble mania in housing, a market drunk on liquidity, and financial innovation in pursuit of reward without adequately modeling for risk. And this time, the burst was so violent that it devastated the credit market, sent the world financial markets into chaos, and nearly brought Wall Street to its knees. Considering Wall Street's tumultuous past—from the Crash of 1929 to the 1987 crash, the 1998 meltdown of Long-Term Capital Management, and the bursting of the technology stock bubble in 2000 (just to name a few)—there is no reason to think the future will be any different. And given Wall Street's insatiable appetite for financial innovation, the likelihood is high that new products and derivatives created in the future will be just as risky and potentially unmanageable as what we've seen in the past.

Richard Bookstaber, Wall Street risk management executive and author of *A Demon of Our Own Design: Markets, Hedge Funds, and the Perils of Financial Innovation*, observed that financial innovation certainly produces positive effects. Among them are improved efficiency in the market; increased liquidity; freer flow and wider distribution of information, and faster reaction to it; near-instantaneous trade execution; and lower transaction costs. "And, whether developed with the intent of better meeting the demands of investors or, more cynically, to stave off commoditization and maintain profitability, we are awash in new and innovative instruments," he noted.[1]

Innovation, however, also carries a price, including increased complexity in the marketplace. Interconnected markets coupled with the complexity of derivative instruments add to the unpredictability of market behavior. The marketplace is not rational and therefore cannot be easily modeled. Market crises can and will occur, and no matter how devastating the most recent one, there is the potential that those in the future will be even worse.

Reflecting on the causes and effects of the latest financial crisis, lessons emerge. Some are obvious: the need for better oversight and risk management. This is easy to say, but not so easy to carry out in the midst of complex transactions or in an environment where the laurels go to those who are currently reaping the biggest rewards. Other lessons raise the need for more regulation, particularly in the $55 trillion credit default swap market. As we have also learned, the interconnectedness of the marketplace shows just how dependent the system is on the health of all the players. When Fannie Mae and Freddie Mac went into conservatorship or Lehman Brothers failed, the results were staggering losses for other firms.

And there is a call for greater leadership: the kind that will stand up to the herd mentality and hold to convictions of what is and is not a good business opportunity, regardless of what others are doing. Again, this is easy to say, but more difficult to practice in a Wall Street environment where for many firms *this* quarter is all that matters. The often-repeated quote by former Citigroup CEO Charles "Chuck" Prince was a sad anthem of the times: ". . . as long as the music is playing, you've got to get up and dance."[2]

Wall Street needs more leaders who are willing to sit this one out when the music isn't to their liking. A fundamental shift of this magnitude will require a culture change not only within firms, but throughout the industry, to value managing risks as much as generating immediate rewards.

A Brief Postmortem of a Complicated Crisis

Examining the events and developments before and during the financial crisis reveals a host of causes and contributing factors. The more obvious ones are housing prices that inflated into a bubble and a marketplace awash with liquidity that led to massive levels of lending and serious deterioration in underwriting standards, particularly in the subprime category. Securitization that was supposed to reduce risk actually increased it as debt was packaged, sliced, diced, and then resold in what was made to look like safer investments. A wide variety of investors were caught up in the securitized debt frenzy, from investment firms to pension funds, all seeking increased returns.

The housing bubble spurred financial innovation with the creation and proliferation of new investment products and derivatives. Structured investment vehicles (SIVs) were set up to profit from the spread between short-term and long-term debt. Collateralized debt obligations (CDOs) were created from pools of debt such as mortgages that were then divided into segments or tranches based on credit quality. There were even derivatives of derivatives such as CDO-squareds, using pools of CDOs to create more CDOs.

As debt instruments expanded, so did the use of credit default swaps, which are supposed to act like insurance against the risk of default.

The buyer of a swap seeks protection against the potential default on a particular bond by paying a periodic fixed fee to a seller. The seller then promises to pay the buyer should a default or other credit event occur. In essence, credit default swaps were supposed to protect against counterparty risk, which, given the crumbling of Wall Street firms from Bear Stearns to Lehman Brothers, was no longer an outlying event on a bell curve of probabilities.

In the 1990s, credit default swaps focused on municipal bonds and corporate debt, and then later expanded into securitized instruments such as CDOs, and even became outright speculative bets on whether a particular player might default. The fear then developed that the swap market was a time bomb ticking under Wall Street as it cleaned up the financial crisis mess.

What has become painfully clear is the widespread cost of the financial crisis to virtually everyone, from Wall Street firms to pension funds to individual 401(k) retirement plans to investors' accounts. As Markus K. Brunnermeier, the Edwards S. Sanford Professor of Economics at Princeton University, wrote in his in-depth study entitled "Deciphering the Liquidity and Credit Crunch 2007–08": "The bursting of the housing bubble forced banks to write down several hundred billion dollars in bad loans caused by mortgage delinquencies. At the same time, the stock market capitalization of the major banks declined by more than twice as much. While the overall mortgage losses are large on an absolute scale, they are still relatively modest compared to the destruction of about 8 trillion dollars in stock market wealth that has occurred since the market's all-time high in October 2007."[3]

Contemplating what will likely come next, some major lessons emerge. In interviews with several executives, questions were raised: What have we learned? What leadership qualities are necessary in the future? The responses are worth pondering as the industry, perhaps working in concert with regulators, contemplates the way forward.

Bubbles Are Trouble

Jamie Dimon summed up the lessons this way: "I think it was a mistake that assets bubbles [were] ignored. I think that was a terrible mistake."

The housing bubble not only was ignored for years, but even when it looked like it might pop, the likely outcome was grossly underestimated. When housing prices reached such high levels that a pullback seemed inevitable, virtually no one expected a sharp nationwide decline. The last time a decline in the national housing market occurred was during the Great Depression, but that was seen as an anomaly. More recent history appeared to prove the point that the U.S. real estate market was regional; if and when there were downturns in one area, there would be stability or even gains in another.

Alan Greenspan, as Federal Reserve chairman, several years ago had drawn the same conclusion. In testimony before Congress in 2002, he noted: "The ongoing strength in the housing market has raised concerns about the possible emergence of a bubble in home prices. However, the analogy often made to the building and bursting of a stock price bubble is imperfect. First, unlike in the stock market, sales in the real estate market incur substantial transactions costs and, when most homes are sold, the seller must physically move out. Doing so often entails significant financial and emotional costs and is an obvious impediment to stimulating a bubble through speculative trading in homes. Thus, while stock market turnover is more than 100 percent annually, the turnover of home ownership is less than 10 percent annually—scarcely tinder for speculative conflagration. Second, arbitrage opportunities are much more limited in housing markets than in securities markets. A home in Portland, Oregon, is not a close substitute for a home in Portland, Maine, and the 'national' housing market is better understood as a collection of small, local housing markets. Even if a bubble were to develop in a local market, it would not necessarily have implications for the nation as a whole."[4]

If the housing market were, indeed, regional—made up of pockets of local housing markets—then the experiences of the more recent past would be a reliable predictor of the future. Except, of course, the housing market was not.

Housing and Banking—Regional No More

A fundamental change in banking and housing hit Wall Street where it really hurt: in its investment and risk models. As Brunnermeier explained in an interview, models used data that reflected what existed in the past: namely, a regional housing market and a regional banking industry. Over the past decade, however, the regional housing markets in the United States had become more correlated.

Assuming that the housing market was still regional, Wall Street gained a false sense of confidence that creating portfolios of loans from coast to coast would mitigate risk. In simplest terms, rather than hold only subprime loans from, say, the Northeast, mortgages were gathered across the United States and put into one pool. The thinking was that the regional mix was a safeguard, that a downturn in one area would be offset by gains in another. The fundamental shifts to national housing and banking markets in essence undermined the risk models that were based on faulty assumptions. As Brunnermeier put it, "The past data wasn't so reliable anymore. It was from a different world."

Add to that another factor: the originate-and-distribute model in mortgage lending that was a sharp departure from decades past when a local bank granted loans to local borrowers, and therefore could monitor risk and detect potential problems much sooner. But recently, when loans were packaged and sold off to third parties, the originator's job was done; what happened to the loan was no longer that party's concern. The originate-and-distribute model met with strong demand for securitized products. While the original rationale was to transfer risk from banks to other parties, there was "unprecedented credit expansion," which "helped feed the boom in housing prices," Brunnermeier explained in his study.[5]

Part of the attractiveness of securitized and structured products was the ability to meet the needs of different investor groups. Risk could be shifted to those who could bear it and spread among many market participants, thus allowing for lower mortgage rates and lower interest rates. Slicing and dicing the debt enabled them to be further tailored; for example, a pension fund that was only enabled to invest in triple-A rated securities could buy triple-A rated tranches of portfolios based on single-A rated securities. As long as the rating agencies gave the debt tranche their blessing, investors felt secure.

The securitization process was also based on a skewed perception that risk was posed only by the likelihood of default, which was seen as statistically low based on past events. But models did not take into account the possibility of a widespread, correlated decline in housing values that would affect even the more senior tranches of the structured products. Consequently, the prevailing thinking was that the top tranches were very secure because of the credit quality of the borrowers. Believing the top tranche to be completely secure—once again, based on the premise that the U.S. housing market as a whole could not decline—investment firms borrowed against these supposedly high-quality holdings to buy even more securitized debt.

In his study, Brunnermeier established the many links between increased securitization, the decline in lending standards, and the demands for more loans because of the appetite for securitized products. "By early 2007, many informed observers were concerned about the risk of a 'liquidity bubble' or 'credit bubble.' However, they were reluctant to invest based on an expectation that matters would soon change. . . . [I]t was perceived to be more profitable to ride the wave than to lean against it, and so no individual player had an incentive to stop playing the game."[6]

When the housing market declined on a nationwide basis, debt across the board was affected. For one thing, default rates went up. But in addition, borrowers could no longer refinance their mortgages, because the prices of the collateral—houses—had stopped rising. In many cases, what was owed on the mortgage exceeded the value of the property.

The obvious question then becomes: Why didn't people see it? Surely someone must have observed these changes in housing and banking and theorized that the models should be adjusted. "Some people saw it. Others didn't," Brunnermeier said. The problem is that Wall Street relies on data regressions that constitute so-called hard information based on past experience. Therefore, the conclusions drawn using real, historical data are difficult to refute.

Even the Best Model Can't Predict Everything

Imagine this scenario on Wall Street: Someone approaches the investment committee or the risk management department with observations that challenge the model, but there is a lack of hard data. The person's only ammunition is so-called soft information based on that individual's perceptions of reality, not backed by historical experience. How can that type of evidence stand up to the irrefutable data of the past? Wall Street, which employs legions of PhDs to devise investment and risk models, doesn't pay much attention to anecdotal soft information warnings when the hard data makes the case.

"There was no incentive to deviate," Brunnermeier explained. And why would anyone want to change course when market conditions were so favorable: a booming housing market and a steady stream of mortgages of every type and flavor, from prime to exotic subprime? Further, firms that might be tempted to take a step back and question the models could suffer a talent drain as the investment gurus and risk managers sought new pastures that were greener with more cash.

When there is a disconnect between models and the real world, the result can be disaster. Consider what happened at American International Group (AIG), where models used to gauge the risk of more than $400 billion in credit default swaps appeared to have been inadequate. As the *Wall Street Journal* reported, "AIG relied on those models to help figure out which swap deals were safe. But AIG didn't anticipate how market forces and contract terms not weighed by the models would turn the swaps, over the short term, into huge financial liabilities."[7]

No one expects Wall Street to throw out the models used to identify opportunities and gauge risks, but rather to recognize their imperfections. As Dimon noted in his 2007 letter to shareholders, "Risk models are valuable tools, but they have limitations. Because they are backward-looking by design, they tend to miss certain factors. The value of stress testing [to determine how assets are likely to perform under worsening conditions] is also a function of time frame."

As valuable as risk management tools and models are, Dimon said they are only a part of good risk management. "Good, sound, old-fashioned human judgment is critical. Strong risk management entails constant reporting and review, exposure by exposure, and the ability to size up exposures instantly with the right systems."[8]

Blame the Underwriting

Innovation linked to the housing bubble wasn't limited to financial instruments. With easy credit and a marketplace hungry for more debt to securitize, there were also mortgage innovations. The traditional

30-year, fixed-rate mortgage gave way to nontraditional loans. Mortgage innovations included adjustable-rate hybrid mortgages (which have interest rates that reset periodically and could be hiked sharply after an initial starter period); interest-only loans that never build homeowner equity; and negative amortizing mortgages (in which the amount owed increases because initial payments do not cover all the interest on the amount borrowed).

The purpose of these mortgages may seem dubious now. But they appealed to the borrower in need of nontraditional financing, who was convinced that housing prices would keep rising so refinancing down the road would take care of any debt problems. As Federal Deposit Insurance Corporation (FDIC) Chair Sheila Bair observed, "We know that those innovations were very popular for a short while as home prices were rising. But now it's abundantly clear that they would fail under virtually any other market conditions. The way those mortgages were structured is just one of many aspects of our mortgage finance system that ran amuck."

The way forward, Bair stated, was to return to basic principles of mortgage lending, starting with protection of the consumer. "Protecting the consumers from such perils is not simply a do-good public service," she added. "In fact, consumer protection and safe and sound lending practices are two sides of the same coin. Lenders who put their retail customers at risk also put themselves, their investors, and our entire financial system in danger."[9]

What's needed is the examination of lending practices—not to restrict credit, but to keep the system safer and more secure for all. It profited no one, neither borrower nor lender, for high levels of credit to be extended to those who became overly burdened with a debt they could not afford. Such practices by banks and other lending institutions were spurred by competitive pressure to lend aggressively and the wave of securitization that put a gap between originator and the one who bore the risk. Now the marketplace as a whole is paying the price, from steep losses on mortgage-backed assets to tighter availability of liquidity.

"None of us benefit from having a failure in the mortgage market as a result of unfettered securitization of any kind of collateral, which no one could evaluate. That's not good for individuals or anyone, and not for us. It's a shame," commented Thomas A. James, chairman and CEO of Raymond James Financial, a Florida-based diversified financial services company. "Some of the individual companies did a better job of it than others. JPMorgan and Bank of America are examples [of better management], and Wells Fargo is another. There are numerous other smaller banks that did a much better job of managing risks than others."

As Tom Brown of Second Curve Capital observed, the problem came down to bad judgment on the part of banks and other lending institutions, with lax standards and practices such as underwriting no-documentation loans. "When you make 1 out of 100 like that, okay, that's fine. When it's 25 in 100, that was a breakdown in the system."

Beyond the individual companies adhering to high operating and risk management standards, James believes the financial industry itself must do a better job of self-policing and working with regulators. In turn, regulators must be willing to take on an educational/advisory role, as well as enforcement. More open dialogue is needed between regulators and private industry participants—not just in times of crisis, but on an ongoing basis. He offered the example of the rise of subprime mortgage lending. While some banks became heavily involved in making loans to higher-risk borrowers, industry regulators did not sound an early warning alarm when subprime rose from 5 percent to 10 percent and then to 30 percent (and some cases higher) of new loan originations. "The regulators did not say . . . that trend is unhealthy," James added. "While everybody would like to support housing for everybody in the U.S., it's not going to benefit people who cannot afford to pay back the loans. We don't want to get people into situations that aren't good for them, and you don't want to make the financial system fragile because we don't have the right risk management, controls, and processes."

At an FDIC forum in July 2008, Jamie Dimon laid the blame for the mortgage mess at the feet of banks themselves. He didn't fault regulations; accounting rules such as FASB 157, which requires fair value measurements for assets based on market valuations; mark-to-market requirements, which have triggered steep write-downs; or any other factor that may have played a contributing role. "It was underwriting," he said simply.

Ten years ago when housing prices were rising, loan-to-value ratios went to 90 percent and above. Looser standards were applied to appraisals and income verification. As long as property values continued rising, the deterioration in underwriting fundamentals wasn't an issue. "It was completely masked by the fact that prices had gone up. Then they started going down, and what happened? Now we've learned," Dimon added.

The question now becomes: Has the industry learned enough to keep from repeating the problem in the future? "We should really write a letter to the next generation and tell them, if you have a time when housing prices go up, don't ever go to 100 percent [loan-to-value ratios]," Dimon said.[10]

Launch New Products Cautiously

With so much innovation in financial products, securitizations, and mortgage lending, there were bound to be problems. In fact, a certain amount of failure is expected with every product rollout.

"New products have problems," Dimon also observed at the FDIC forum. "That was true in almost every financial product we've ever seen that has its own series of problems. [It] goes back to equities and options and . . . this time obviously subprimes and CDOs and a whole bunch of others."

Because problems are a given, the likelihood of failure must be adequately taken into account. Rollouts must be structured as staging grounds to test, learn, and refine. Dimon recommended that new products be introduced more slowly and with a deeper financial cushion behind them. "In the next round—and there will be another round of them one day—let's remember that, and maybe make sure more capital is held against [the new products]."[11]

Tom James also urged the financial industry to undertake a more in-depth analysis of operational issues as new products are launched. He gave the example of his own firm, where multiple committees look at the impact of a new product not only on clients and the particular business limit, but also more broadly throughout the company. "Internally in companies, you must have a series of committees that work on the introduction of even slightly changed products or services that the firm offers, because often the implications of the changes are not fully appreciated by the departments that instigated them, and other departments that are indirectly impacted need to be prepared for them."

The problem is not a new one; financial innovation is as old as trade routes and the first currencies. Therefore, innovation will always be with us, as will the potential for discombobulating results, whether a brief shudder that goes through the markets or a massive upheaval. As author Charles R. Morris explained in his book, *Money, Greed, and Risk: Why Financial Crises and Crashes Happen*, published in 1999: "The story of finance is therefore one of innovation, crisis, and consolidation. Industrial, commercial, or technological change calls forth an innovation—paper trade credits, private-company stocks and bonds, retail stock markets, junk bonds, collateralized mortgage obligations, derivative instruments. In every case, the innovation solves an immediate problem—expanding trading, financing railroads, restructuring companies, stabilizing pension portfolios—and also triggers a period of greatly increased risk and instability, until institutions catch up."[12]

Therefore, as future innovations are rolled out, the industry needs to acknowledge that risks are difficult to model or predict; that the unexpected can and will happen; and that even the strongest of players can suddenly become weakened.

Risk at One Firm Affects Others

Testifying before the U.S. Senate just weeks after the Federal Reserve and the Treasury Department brokered JPMorgan Chase's 11th-hour purchase of Bear Stearns, Fed Chairman Ben Bernanke stressed the complexity and interconnectedness of the financial markets. Therefore, as he saw it, "the sudden failure of Bear Stearns likely would have led to a chaotic unwinding of positions in those markets and could have severely shaken confidence. The company's failure could also have cast doubt on the financial position of some of Bear Stearns' thousands of counterparties and perhaps of companies with similar businesses."[13]

While his point may very well have been to justify the federal government's intervention in the fate of an investment bank, his comments home in on a fundamental concept: Risk at one firm has an impact—and a potentially devastating one—on others. Unfortunately, the size of that impact is often unknown, which can increase fear in the market-place until it reaches panic levels. Fearing that a firm has too much risk, other parties may refuse to trade with that firm. Investors and customers alike may pull out their cash, staging a run on the bank—which happened at Bear Stearns. What's needed, therefore, is a way to judge the spillover risk from one firm to others and to the marketplace in general.

Internally, financial institutions use value at risk (VaR) to evaluate what is likely to happen to their portfolios. As a statistical measure, VaR estimates the potential loss from adverse market moves and provides a consistent measure of risk across multiple businesses. While financial institutions rely on VaR to monitor their own risk, it cannot be used to effectively estimate the risk that firms face because of their counterparties and industry peers.

"Before, we only focused on the risks of individual banks. Now, externalities have become very much the focal point," Markus Brunnermeier said. Toward that end, he and Tobias Adrian—a research officer at the Federal Reserve Bank of New York—developed a measure they call CoVaR to gauge the amount of spillover risk that institutions face because of other firms.[14] CoVaR would help the industry determine the potential fallout from actions such as when a bank maximizes profits by taking on risky businesses. "I expect banks to adapt new risk measures such as CoVaR very soon," Brunnermeier said. As recent events such as the failure of Lehman Brothers and the bailout of AIG have shown, risk at one firm is never confined to one place.

More Regulation Is Coming

In the midst of the worst financial crisis in 70 years, it's no surprise that talk soon turned to the likelihood of more regulation. Add to that a Democratic president and a Democratic Congress in 2009, and the financial sector is most certainly in for a regulatory overhaul. Given the fact that Wall Street firms have appealed to government for help in the form of loans, guarantees, and bailouts—and Goldman Sachs and Morgan Stanley have traded their status as independent investment banks to become bank holding companies that are subject to more regulation—the time may be ripe for such a move by lawmakers.

"People seem to think they want no regulation until problems happen. We like being able to walk through airports and come at the last minute, but after 9/11 we take off our shoes and get our packages inspected. We keep going back and forth on regulation and deregulation. Luckily we live in a country where we can go back and forth," said Elinda Fishman Kiss, professor of finance and the Ralph J. Tyser Teaching Fellow in Finance at the University of Maryland.

One area that may very well see further regulation is the vast credit default swap market, in which transactions are done in secret and often anonymously. Without any regulation, it is impossible to track the transactions that swap these instruments from buyer to seller, and often repeatedly. Although Congress declined to regulate the swaps in 2000, there have been calls to reverse that decision and increase market transparency and surveillance.

Christopher Cox, writing a *New York Times* op-ed piece at the time he was Securities and Exchange Commission (SEC) Chairman, stated: "Congress needs to fill this regulatory hole by passing legislation that would not only make credit default swaps more transparent but also give regulators the power to rein in fraudulent or manipulative trading practices and help everyone better assess the risks involved."

Cox also called for Congress to support federal regulators to mandate the use of clearing and settlement organizations and/or exchange-like trading platforms for credit default swaps. "As it is now, it is often impossible even to know who stands on the other side of a swap contract, and this increases the risk involved. We at the SEC are already working with the Federal Reserve, the Commodity Futures Trading Commission, and industry participants to accomplish these goals on a voluntary basis, using the authority we currently have."[15]

Only time will tell what new regulation of the financial services industry will look like. That it is coming, however, no one disputes. For its part, the financial industry stresses the need to maintain the competitiveness of the U.S. financial services industry and sees a danger in too much regulation that could force business to other corners of the global marketplace with less regulation. As The Financial Services Roundtable noted in a report, written by a blue-ribbon panel co-chaired by Jamie Dimon and Wells Fargo Chairman Richard Kovacevich, "Regulatory reforms to enhance the competitiveness of U.S. financial markets and firms do not have to conflict with the broader public policy goals of financial system stability and security. To the contrary, ensuring the competitiveness of U.S. financial markets and firms complements the systemic objectives of financial regulators."[16]

Dimon echoed this sentiment in his comments at the FDIC forum: "The regulatory response . . . has been thoughtful, and I think it's important to continue that way. We have a new Congress coming up [in 2009]. And we have to worry about unintended consequences of regulation. . . . We can't hurt the United States companies and, on the other hand, [regulators] want to do the right thing. And they have to balance this other major risk, by the way, which is the more you regulate here, the more things go over there. So you have to be careful how you create that [regulatory structure], because I'm not sure that it's good public policy to be forcing a lot of things onto unregulated markets."[17]

Regulators must also keep pace with the speed at which the financial services industry innovates, as well as how business is carried out among multiple parties in complex transactions. To this point Sandy Weill, former chairman of Citigroup, observed, "One thing we have learned from this crisis is the regulators are going to have to have more knowledge about the businesses that they regulate. What is coming out of this crisis is the Treasury or the Fed, in no special order, having supervisory, regulatory oversight of what's happening in the marketplace and what's happening in derivatives. This is not just supervision of the banks, but also the investment banks that are a major counterparty to all the other transactions."

Bolder, Braver Leaders

The few lessons outlined here, while hardly an exhaustive or comprehensive list, point to another need, which encompasses all others—that is, bold and brave leadership on Wall Street: people who are willing to stand up and question the prevailing attitudes of the day and forge their own way against the herd mentality. Although it starts with the top, watchfulness and questioning must be valued and promoted throughout the ranks. Such behavior should be recognized and rewarded. Otherwise, Wall Street appears doomed to repeat its past mistakes.

Longtime Wall Street executive Frank Zarb did not hesitate to answer when asked what leadership qualities are needed today and in the future. "We need senior managers who not only measure the risk in each bucket, but who have the seniority to go to the boss and say, 'Bucket 6 was good two years ago, but we need to get out,'" said Zarb, whose resume includes being a partner at Lazard Freres, past CEO of Smith Barney, and a former chairman of the NASDAQ stock market. "The industry is moving toward that: bringing in more senior-level people who worry about risk."

Dimon, who during his years at Primerica was Zarb's chosen second-in-command at Smith Barney, elaborated on Zarb's comments. Stressing the need for in-depth, detailed reporting, he said, "You've got to do it in a way that's always getting better so that you can actually see Bucket 6. And Bucket 6 isn't just [your responsibility], because you might not know the significance of Bucket 6, but [someone else] might know."

Disciplined reporting and review of every facet of the business and across all product lines allow risks that are detected one place to be applied more broadly. As JPMorgan illustrated, the early warning on subprime defaults from its retail mortgage servicing department triggered the investment bank to scale back its holdings. By sharing information, JPMorgan avoided some of the risks that hurt other firms, particularly those with larger CDO exposure. But it wasn't just the information alone: JPMorgan had the foresight and courage to act on it.

Making such a move counter to the trend and ahead of the crowd takes conviction and also strength of character. "You have to stand up and do your own analysis, even though in the short term it may be very costly. Essentially you have to stand up against the herd mentality," Brunnermeier observed.

Standing up against the crowd is also important inside the company—to be brave enough to speak out about unacceptable risk and to be empowered to suggest the need to change strategy. "You hire people you trust because your mind isn't big enough," said Hardwick "Wick" Simmons, who over the course of his career has been CEO of Prudential Securities and of the NASDAQ stock market. "At vulnerable points, whether overseas or in fast-moving businesses, you always put your best and most trusted players in place . . . people who also must be willing to take on the CEO. You've got to have people who aren't afraid to stand up and take you on."

Rewarding Risk Management and Return

Wall Street leadership needs to encourage a culture change around risk management as well as return, providing incentives and rewards for both behaviors. Otherwise, the message to employees will be that returns are all that matter, regardless of the risks that are undertaken. Compensation is a powerful means to define and reinforce corporate culture. If pursuing the upside, and not protecting the downside, is all that is rewarded, then that's what the culture will reflect.

David Trainer, founder of New Constructs, said the "hedge fund mentality" has overly influenced Wall Street, creating an asymmetrical relationship between risk and reward. "People get rewarded for taking too much risk."

The time has come to reward behaviors that identify and mitigate risk. As events of the past year have painfully exhibited, no matter how lucrative the short-term upside is, it is not worth the long-term devastation that results from taking dangerously high risks. "I'd like to see Wall Street and the market in general be more efficient in terms of allocation of compensation and allocation of value to those who create the most cash profits *over time*," Trainer added. "At the end of the day, our society gets better when we do more with less. . . . Far too often the focus in a predatory environment is only on the short term."

Compensation needs to reflect a corporate culture that not only rewards the creation of return, but also provides incentives to those who identify and mitigate risks. In the past, corporate compensation—in the name of alignment with corporate goals and shareholder interests—emphasized generating returns to the extent that executives were encouraged to take on high levels of risk, thanks to the incentive plans that rewarded them handsomely. "The best and worst thing about incentive plans is that they work. By rewarding people for taking high levels of risk—surprise!—they took them," commented Donald P. Delves, founder of The Delves Group, a Chicago-based executive compensation consulting firm that works closely with boards and corporate management to design pay-for-performance compensation and incentive plans.

The challenge now, Delves added, is to create compensation systems with offsetting or even competing incentives, whereby some people are rewarded for creating appropriate return and others are rewarded for mitigating risk and applying appropriate judgment to evaluate risk and allocate capital. "Unfortunately, it's very easy to reward high levels of performance. It's harder to reward people for mitigating risk, but that doesn't mean it can't be done," he said.

Second, compensation systems should do more than just reward the upside, but also impose meaningful downside consequences for certain actions such as taking on inappropriate levels of risk that create future losses, Delves added. "The reality is for the investment banker or the loan officer there is only an upside. If the investor wins, they win. If the investor loses, the banker just doesn't win. There has to be an upside and a downside, so that the gain and pain of the banker is felt equally with the gain and pain of the investor."

Eyes on the Road, Hands on the Wheel

Corporate culture is set at the top. Regardless of what mission statements and corporate principles state, it starts with the attitude and actions of the CEO and other top executives. What they value is emulated by those the next level down and then by those the next level down from that. To be effective leaders, Wall Street executives must be fully engaged in the business and be accountable to their boards, shareholders, employees, and clients for the day-to-day operation of the company—not just the year-end results.

When the boss is distant or removed from the business, employees notice. The message becomes it doesn't matter what they do or it's every person for him/herself. Criticisms leveled at Bear Stearns upper management after the firm failed focused on their supposed detachment from everyday operations and not acknowledging the severity of problems faced by the firm.

Steve Burke, president of Comcast Cable and a JPMorgan Chase board member, offered Dimon as an example of Wall Street leadership that is engaged and accountable. "When you see Jamie in operation, he really knows what's going on in the business. A lot of time the people who are running businesses act like they are like the King of

England: They go to state functions, but they don't know what's going on in different parts of their organizations."

Wall Street leadership may be at 50,000 feet at times when taking the broad view, but it must also be in the trenches. "I think people want to see you're willing to work as hard as they are," commented Dimon, who is known for putting in very long days.

Above all, Wall Street leadership needs to be accountable for the mess it has created as well as for the solutions and safeguards that stem from the lessons learned. To that point, Lazard Ltd. Chairman and CEO Bruce Wasserstein, speaking to reporters in June 2008, blamed the turbulence in the financial markets on too much risk taking and not enough common sense among executives.[18]

Perhaps the best advice comes from a retired bank executive who died in the midst of the credit crisis: a former chairman and chief executive of J.P. Morgan, Dennis Weatherstone. In his obituary, the *New York Times* credited him with laying the groundwork for transforming J.P. Morgan into a diversified global bank and called him a "a prototype for today's Wall Street chiefs." His advice, repeated by former associates who knew him, reflected a man who had a rare mix of savvy and common sense. As they told the *Times*, "'Investment has to be rational,' he used to say. 'If you can't understand it, don't do it.'"[19]

Chapter 11

A Wall Street Statesman

*[Leadership] isn't all about making the biggest paycheck. When I hand
JPMorgan off to the next generation, I've made it better than it was. It
wasn't all about me.*

—Jamie Dimon

J amie Dimon's leadership is rooted in his innate gifts: among them,
high intelligence, an analytical mind, and the ability to grasp details
on a granular level while never losing sight of the big picture. He
has also been shaped by the professional choices made throughout his
career. The first was to deviate from the predictable path that would
have led from Harvard Business School to a major Wall Street firm, and
instead to choose the corporate world where he could learn more. Then
he became part of a small executive team at a backwater company
in Baltimore. It takes a tremendous sense of self to turn down Goldman
Sachs and later become the chief financial officer of a company probably
few people had ever heard of. But, working closely with Sandy Weill,
Dimon helped build that company into Citigroup.

Even after being fired as president of Citigroup, Dimon probably
could have gone just about anywhere. Yet he chose to leave New York
to become CEO of Bank One, a regional institution in desperate need

of a turnaround, where he could truly make a difference. It was another career-defining moment.

Everywhere he has been, Dimon has pursued the same goals: identifying and controlling risks, reducing unnecessary expenses, and pursuing excellence. He demands a lot from others in the process, but no more than he asks of himself. This is the essence of his management style—frank, transparent, detailed, disciplined—that allows him to run a company of the size and scope of JPMorgan Chase. And in the course of that day-to-day leadership he has put himself in the position he's in today: a Wall Street statesman.

"I really think he'll be the outstanding business leader of his generation," said Joseph A. Califano Jr., a former board member of Travelers, who spent 31 years in Washington, including as secretary of the Department of Health, Education, and Welfare in the Carter administration. "If I were elected president, I would do everything in my power to get Jamie to be the secretary of the Treasury. The economic problem is so stunning, and he's the best guy in the country."

Dimon was reported to be on President Barack Obama's list of possible candidates to head Treasury, but in the end the post went to Timothy Geithner, president of the Federal Reserve Bank of New York. (Given Dimon's distaste for bureaucracy, one wonders how he would rise to that challenge.)

While Dimon garners the respect and admiration of many in the industry and the business community at large, another type of praise is heaped upon him. "He's a regular guy," Califano added, a sentiment voiced by several others.

Although he has a healthy ego, Dimon doesn't focus on what he's done well or what he has accomplished. In an interview, he never once mentioned having been one of the youngest executives on Wall Street when he was named CEO of Smith Barney back in his Primerica/Travelers days; nor does he mention that, at 52, he is young for being a seasoned CEO at the helm of one of the strongest firms on Wall Street.

Rather, Dimon talked about his teams: the people who have been engaged in the day-to-day tasks of integrating two major acquisitions. One has been especially exhausting: merging Bear Stearns, a troubled investment bank, in the midst of the worst financial crisis in 70 years. If anything was heroic in Dimon's eyes, it was the work of the integration teams.

Leadership, as Dimon defines it, is not about the individual, nor is it accomplished for one's self. Rather, leadership must benefit the whole, whether an organization or society at large. As he told an audience at his undergraduate alma mater, Tufts University, where he was presented the Light on the Hill award in 2006—the highest award students can bestow on a distinguished alumnus—leadership "isn't all about making the biggest paycheck. When I hand JPMorgan off to the next generation, I've made it better than it was. It wasn't all about me."[1]

As an individual and a Wall Street executive, Dimon sets an inspiring example. He stands for a kind of leadership that has been lacking on Wall Street. Instead of emphasizing profits at all costs for today, Dimon targets the longer term and stresses accountability at all levels. He emphatically believes in doing the right thing for the right reasons, even when the result is painful in the short term. Perhaps most important, Dimon doesn't rest on what has been done well, but instead concentrates on what could have been done better. He won't focus on the victories, but on the problems and defeats. He is aware of his own failings, and equally cognizant of the weaknesses of his organization. Being self-critical is a quality he values.

"You have to set the standards. First, you've got to get it out there, and then you have to do it all the time," Dimon reflected. He compared the consistency of setting and keeping standards to a person training for a marathon. "You don't just get into shape and stop. You've got to set the standard you want. We set a pretty high agenda for ourselves and eventually I expect you to do it."

The Hard Work of Being a Leader

Jamie Dimon works at being a leader. He is purposeful and driven but for all the right reasons: to build an organization that is strong, of which employees, board members, shareholders, and customers can be proud, and that will survive the downturns and crises that are part of the cyclical business of banking and emerge well-positioned when the cycle turns to the upside.

"He works very hard. I'd like to see him not work so hard, but he thrives on it," said Bob Lipp, a JPMorgan Chase board member who has known Dimon for more than 20 years, including when they were part of the management team at Commercial Credit. "It's not easy being in his job. I think he's comfortable in it, but it's not a lot of laughs being the CEO of a big public corporation."

The performance of JPMorgan Chase throughout the financial crisis has distinguished Dimon from the crowd. As previously stated, the company has had its share of losses created by subprime mortgage defaults, the decline in asset values, and some misjudgments in its own loan portfolio and elsewhere. But compared to many of its peers, JPMorgan has been the far better performer. This has been no accident, but the result of a strategy that was consistently executed year after year, with detailed reporting, risks that were uncovered and managed, and the willingness to walk away from businesses that didn't make sense.

"I think when you see how well he has done in his career and where he has gone, to me it's a lesson to people: If you are honest and you have great integrity and great confidence, and you consistently do the right thing, you will succeed in business," commented JPMorgan Chase board member Steve Burke.

Consistency is one of Dimon's corporate values, and it is also a personality trait. Associates who have known him for years and consider him a friend say he hasn't changed all that much (although age and experience have mellowed him a bit). He's still the same man who in his late twenties was a brilliant student at Harvard Business School and in his thirties was the diligent and dependable right-hand man to Sandy Weill. The drive and the passion he had then are still present, even though he sits behind the CEO desk at JPMorgan Chase. He's still a worker with a job: to make JPMorgan Chase the best company it can be.

Family, Humanity, and Then JPMorgan

Asked about his priorities, Jamie Dimon quickly responds "my children, my family—but especially the children I'm responsible for, even though they're kind of on their own." Dimon and his wife, Judy, have three daughters ranging in age from their late teens to mid-twenties.

"They're way up here," Dimon replies, holding his hand high above a conference room table. "Right next to that is humanity. Honestly, we're not all here just for ourselves."

Dimon gestures about two feet lower. "And then way down here is JPMorgan. I don't mean that in a bad way, and it may seem contradictory as in 'Okay, Jamie, you spend 80 hours a week at JPMorgan.' But no, it's not."

As Dimon sees it, doing a good job as CEO of JPMorgan Chase is the best way he can further his top two priorities. "If I do a good job here—and I really believe this—if this is a vibrant, healthy company and people can get jobs and make careers better; if we can give more money away, and give opportunities to people. We treat [others] with respect. We treat our customers well. What else can I do? And maybe one day there is something else I can do . . . maybe sit on the board of a hospital."

Dimon also gives of his time whenever possible in another pursuit he loves: speaking to students at business schools. "Maybe one day I'll go teach," he mused. "I'd really get a kick doing that, but it would not be enough right now."

Right now, Dimon has his hands full running a company with $2.3 trillion in assets and has leadership positions across its array of businesses. While not everyone would want to work for someone like Dimon— he can be blunt and demanding—those who are in his inner circle are very loyal. That loyalty goes both ways, as board member David Novak related. "You know Jamie is going to be there. He's not a guy who is going to chase something else next. He's loyal to this company."

Public Service in Thought and Action

While he does spend countless hours a week at JPMorgan, Dimon's leadership also extends into other areas about which he is passionate. For example, he serves on the board of the National Center on Addiction and Substance Abuse (CASA) at Columbia University, a national organization dedicated to studying and combating abuse of all substances in all sectors of society. Califano, who is the founder of CASA, spoke of Dimon's dedication to the board despite his job pressures, and his willingness to do whatever he can to help. For example, several years ago when CASA was considering moving from space it rented in the Carnegie Hall Tower in Manhattan, the suggestion was made to buy space—which, over time, would make more sense for the organization. Dimon immediately pitched in to help, working with the CASA staff to arrange a private placement of tax-free bonds.

"He just did it. He worked with the staff here and made it happen," Califano said.

Dimon has a strong sense of public service, in thought as well as action. Steve Burke recalled when he and Dimon, a lifelong Democrat, were in Harvard Business School right after Ronald Reagan was elected president, and the class had far more Republicans than Democrats. Students were engaged in a discussion about the role of business in society, and three or four in particular were discussing the value of more limited government.

When one of the students suggested getting rid of certain government agencies such as the Department of Health and Human Services, Dimon spoke up. "He said, 'I completely disagree with you.' At first I thought it was a courageous thing to stand up for his Democratic principles in that room. Then I realized he had these thoughts about things like the Department of Health and Human Services. There is a real human side to Jamie that you don't always see when he's in his business role. He really cares about people and he cares about inequities in society at large," Burke recalled.

Dimon puts his country near the top of his list of priorities, right up there with his family and humanity. In fact, "humanity" and "country" are so close on his list they are almost on the same line. "I would put my country in there, too, because I think this country is an unbelievable country. Both humanity and country are pretty close, because in spite of what's said about the United States, this is still the beacon of hope for the free world—for the whole world," said Dimon, whose grandfather emigrated to the United States from Greece and worked as a dishwasher before becoming a stockbroker.

Although he does not express any political ambitions, Dimon will not hesitate to voice his opinions on just about any topic related to public policy and the economy. In an interview in July 2008 on the *Charlie Rose* show, Dimon talked about the need for a "very serious plan to attack deficit spending going forward," as well as addressing the trade imbalance.[2] In a speech at a Federal Deposit Insurance Corporation (FDIC) forum—amidst remarks that were largely about the credit crisis and mortgage lending—Dimon also spoke about the need for "good long-term policies" for energy, Social Security, medical coverage, education, and infrastructure.

"We knew 40 years ago we had an oil problem. We have done nothing. We don't allow refineries to be built; we don't allow drilling to be done. We killed wind farms around this country. We don't allow LNG [liquefied natural gas] ports to be built. . . . And even the National Institute of Petroleum has made it clear that to solve this problem we need to do all of it. . . . And this is the thing we need to give the fortitude to our politicians to fix as long-term policies that transcend two-year Congresses. This is going to be a 10- or 20-year policy," Dimon told his FDIC audience.[3]

Loyal Friend, Family Man

What of the personal side of the man who gets up at five o'clock in the morning or half past three if he can't sleep; who reads several newspapers every day, and countless other publications and reports; who took up boxing during a career hiatus and tries to exercise at least two or three times a week?

Close associates described Dimon as being accessible and down-to-earth. Lipp, who back in the mid-1980s was part of the Commercial Credit team, considers Dimon to be a good friend. "He's loyal. I've spent a lot of time with him over the years. He's very busy, so there's not so much time now. But it's always quality time," he added fondly.

His wife, Judy, who met Dimon when they were both at Harvard Business School, is described as a warm and genuine person. "She is one of the most transparent and authentic people I have ever met in my life— and I have really met a lot of people, so in that she is really a remarkable person," commented Andrea Redmond, the executive recruiter who worked with the board at Bank One to recruit Dimon. "She is also highly intelligent, extremely sensitive, very giving, and very gracious." Active in charity work, Judy Dimon serves on the boards of several organizations.

In speeches that he's given over the years, Dimon has revealed a bit of his personal and family life. For example, he doesn't watch much television, although he once admitted to getting a kick out of the comedy *Everybody Loves Raymond*. As much as possible, he has tried to separate work and family life, especially when his daughters were younger.

Speaking to graduate students at Northwestern University's Kellogg School of Management in 2002, Dimon described learning the hard way

just how difficult that balance was to maintain. He told of a family vacation at Bethany Beach, Delaware, when his daughters were about seven,
five, and three years of age. Early each morning he went for a run, and
then tried to work and take phone calls; he played with the kids for a bit,
and in the evening went out to dinner with his wife and friends. "I was
so exhausted from all the exercise and the work and the phone calls; the
kids wanting to do something with me [and telling them] . . . 'Okay, fine,
let's go to the ocean; I only have 30 minutes,'" Dimon recalled.

The next summer, he completely changed the vacation routine. He
did not work, nor did he see friends for dinner every night. After getting up, he went for a run and read the paper, and then told his children, "I'm yours all day, whatever you want." The vacation experience
was totally different. "Well, I started having a great time in the pool . . .
doing stuff with them. They usually ditched me anyway about two or
three o'clock, at which point I might go take a nap or go do something
different, but I made it invisible to them. It wasn't my time and theirs,
and I think it made a tremendous difference."[4]

The story showed another side of the capable executive who takes
command of any situation, whom *Fortune* magazine once called "the
toughest guy on Wall Street." When it came time to play in the pool
with the kids, the world had to wait. It's the type of life lesson that
Dimon shares with students when he speaks with surprising candor and
a great deal of humor. "I do think that the hardest things to do in life
are marriage and kids. They are like complete secrets until you do it,"
Dimon told the Kellogg graduate students. "We teach you everything,
but we don't teach you that. . . . You've got to work [at] those things."[5]

While Dimon may have learned to balance his priorities better,
don't think for a moment that he ever really stops working—even on
vacation. "He'll still call in and say get this done and that done," Lipp,
who recently retired as a special adviser to JPMorgan Chase, said with
a laugh. "We joke about it a little bit, but no one complains. Everybody
respects Jamie. We are so blessed by him."

Outside of work and family, Dimon's hobby is music. He has taken
guitar lessons and even practiced chords on a flight to China. At home,
his habit is to blast music—he is especially fond of Frank Sinatra—to the
point that the interior walls of Dimon's Park Avenue apartment were lined
with lead soundproofing to keep from disturbing the neighbors.[6]

Such details of Dimon's life soften the image of the man who has been hailed as a shrewd deal maker and takes a no-nonsense approach when he communicates, whether in letters to shareholders or in testimony before Congress. Through it all, though, what comes across is his energy and passion, from the music blaring at full volume to taking the tough stance on turning a business around. There are few half measures where Jamie Dimon is concerned.

Loyal—to the End

If there is one word that close associates use to describe Dimon, it's *loyal*. Further, his loyalty and trust, once earned, are rock solid. Board member David Novak shared a personal story that showed this side of Dimon, involving a friend the two men had in common: Andrall "Andy" Pearson. A former president of PepsiCo, Pearson was the founding chairman of Yum! Brands, of which Novak is now chairman and CEO, as well as a Harvard professor. At Pearson's suggestion, Dimon joined the board of Yum! Brands, where he and Novak forged their friendship.

In 2006, at the age of 80, Pearson died of a heart attack. As soon as Novak found out that Pearson, whom he considered to be a friend and a mentor, had died, he went to the family home. When he arrived, Dimon, who by this point was CEO of JPMorgan Chase, was already there. "Now, Andy Pearson was one of my best friends, but Jamie was already there," Novak said. "Jamie is a fiercely loyal person and extremely passionate. And the thing about Jamie Dimon is he'll be there."

People who work for and with Dimon hope he'll be there, at JPMorgan Chase, for a good long time. Given the strength of his performance, his laudable leadership, and the fact he is only 52, Dimon could presumably stay in the CEO position for many more years if he so desires. But what if something else comes along, another opportunity where Dimon could apply his intelligence and his experience? When asked in July 2008 if he had ever given thought to going to Washington one day, Dimon shrugged it off. "I'm still happy to show up as chairman of JPMorgan. I have a very short-term focus these days."

The interviewer Charlie Rose observed in response, "Survival is to be admired in the financial services industry in 2008."

"It is these days," Dimon agreed.[7]

A similar question came up in another discussion in early October 2008. What about the legacy that Dimon wants to leave behind? One might think that the man who can so easily launch into a discussion on any number of topics, from fiscal policy to energy, to education, could paint a picture of how he might change the world. Instead, Dimon paused and gave a much different answer.

"Honestly, the only legacy we leave is that when people walk by your grave they say, 'You know, he was a good son of a bitch. The world is better off for him having been here.' And they miss you because they liked having you there."

Notes

Chapter 1   The Dimon Way

1. CNBC.com, "CNBC Exclusive: CNBC Transcript: CNBC'S Erin Burnett Interviews JPMorgan Chase Chairman & CEO Jamie Dimon on 'Street Signs' Today at 2:00 PM," December 11, 2008, www.cnbc.com/id/28182805/print/1/displaymode/1098.

2. Ibid.

3. Yale School of Management, "JPMorgan's Jamie Dimon and Verizon's Ivan Seidenberg, Recognized as Legends of Leadership at Yale CEO Summit," December 10, 2008, http://mba.yale.edu/news_events/CMS/Articles/6733.shtml.

4. CNBC Exclusive.

5. Yale School of Management.

6. Paul R. LaMonica, "Jamie Dimon's Shopping List," *CNNMoney.com*, April 9, 2008, http://money.cnn.com/2008/04/09/markets/thebuzz/index.htm?postversion=2008040911.

7. Shawn Tully, "How J.P. Morgan's CEO and His Crew Are Helping the Big Bank Beat the Credit Crunch," *Fortune*, September 15, 2008.

8. Ibid.

9. Jamie Dimon, presentation at Kellogg School of Management, Northwestern University, October 4, 2002, www.kellogg.northwestern.edu/news/whatsnew/dimon.htm (accessed May 14, 2008).

Chapter 2 Taking a Bear-Sized Bite

1. "Game Changers," *Condé Nast Portfolio.com*, April 14, 2008, www.portfolio.com/executives/features/2008/04/14/Brilliant-Issue-Game-Changers (accessed July 21, 2008).

2. "A Perfect Chance to Take a Bow," *Newsweek.com*, July 28, 2003, www.newsweek.com/id/57985.

3. Christopher Dodd, United States Senator for Connecticut, "Opening Statement: Turmoil in U.S. Credit Markets: Examining the Recent Actions of Federal Financial Regulators, April 3, 2008, http://dodd.senate.gov/index.php?q=node/4352.

4. Stephen LaBaton, "Testimony Offers Details of Bear Stearns Deal," *New York Times*, April 4, 2008, www.nytimes.com/2008/04/04/business/04fed.html?sq=Dimon%20and%20Dodd%20and%20Geithner&st=cse&adxnnl=1&scp=1&pagewanted=1&adxnnlx=1218049327-G+2jQJ/4NNhrrEFSArwyLg.

5. Glenn Schorr, "JPMorgan Chase & Co.: Good Things Come to Those Who Wait," UBS Investment Research, March 17, 2008.

6. Yale School of Management, "JPMorgan's Jamie Dimon and Verizon's Ivan Seidenberg, Recognized as Legends of Leadership at Yale CEO Summit," December 10, 2008, http://mba.yale.edu/news_events/CMS/Articles/6733.shtml.

7. Jamie Dimon, interview by Charlie Rose, *Charlie Rose*, PBS, July 13, 2008.

8. Kate Kelly, "Fear, Rumors Touched Off Fatal Run on Bear Stearns," *Wall Street Journal*, May 28, 2008.

9. "Bear Stearns Agrees to Secured Loan Facility with JPMorgan Chase," *BusinessWire*, March 14, 2008.

10. "Bear Gets Temporary Funding as Liquidity Erodes," DealBook, *New York Times*, March 14, 2008, http://dealbook.blogs.nytimes.com/2008/03/14/bear-to-receive-emergency-funding-from-jp-morgan/?scp=3&sq=Bear%20Stearns%20Schwarz%20liquidity&st=cse.

11. "Bear Stearns Agrees."

12. "Bear Stearns, on Upswing, Sees No Need to Seek Cash," *Bloomberg News*, October 5, 2007, www.nytimes.com/2007/10/05/business/05wall.html?scp=26&sq=Bear%20Stearns%20liquidity&st=cse.

13. Kate Kelly, "Lost Opportunities Haunt Final Days of Bear Stearns," *Wall Street Journal*, May 27, 2008.

14. "Bear Stearns' Greenberg: Liquidity Talk Is 'Ridiculous.'" *CNBC.com*, March 10, 2008, www.cnbc.com/id/23559810.

15. Securities and Exchange Commission, Chairman Christopher Cox, "Testimony Concerning Recent Events in the Credit Markets," April 3, 2008, www.sec.gov/news/testimony/2008/ts040308cc.htm.

16. Dimon, interview by Charlie Rose.

17. Kate Kelly, "Bear Stearns Neared Collapse Twice in Frenzied Last Days," *Wall Street Journal*, May 29, 2008.

18. "JPMorgan Chase to Acquire Bear Stearns," JPMorgan.com, March 16, 2008, www.jpmorgan.com/cm/Satellite?c=JPM_Content_C&cid=115933855760 4&pagename=JPM_redesign%2FJPM_Content_C%2FGeneric_Detail_Page_ Template.

19. Thomson StreetEvents, Final Transcript, "JPM—JPMorgan Chase to Acquire Bear Stearns—Conference Call," March 16, 2008.

20. Ibid.

21. Dimon, interview by Charlie Rose.

22. "JPMorgan Chase and Bear Stearns Announce Amended Merger Agreement," JPMorgan.com, March 24, 2008, www.jpmorgan.com/cm/Satellite?c=JPM_ Content_C&cid=1159339104093&pagename=JPM_redesign%2FJPM_ Content_C%2FGeneric_Detail_Page_Template.

23. Ibid.

24. Dimon, interview by Charlie Rose.

25. Robin Sidel, "How J.P. Morgan Does 'Merger in Reverse,'" *Wall Street Journal*, May 24, 2008.

26. Federal Deposit Insurance Corporation, Forum on Mortgage Lending, July 8, 2008, www.vodium.com/MediapodLibrary/index.asp?library=pn100472_ fdic_advisorycommittee&SessionArgs=0A1U0100000100000101.

27. Ibid.

Chapter 3   The Weill Years: In the Trenches

1. Harvey Mackay, *Fired Up: How the Best of the Best Survived and Thrived after Getting the Boot* (New York: Ballantine Books, 2005).

2. Michael Bloomberg, "Jamie Dimon," The 2008 *Time* 100: Builders & Titans, *Time*, www.time.com/time/specials/2007/time100/article/0,28804,1733748_ 1733758_1736192,00.html (accessed August 7, 2008).

3. Peter Truell, "Becoming His Own Man," *New York Times*, July 13, 1995.

4. "Ticker Tape in the Genes," *BusinessWeek.com*, October 21, 1996, www .businessweek.com/1996/43/b3498157.htm.

5. Patrick McGeehan, "Openers: Suits; Like Son, Like Father," *New York Times*, August 27, 2006, http://query.nytimes.com/gst/fullpage .html?res=9B07E2DC103EF934A1575BC0A9609C8B63.

6. Sandy Weill and Judah S. Kraushaar, *The Real Deal: My Life in Business and Philanthropy* (New York: Warner Business Books, 2006).

7. Ibid.

8. Jamie Dimon, presentation at Kellogg School of Management, Northwestern University, October 4, 2002, www.kellogg.northwestern.edu/news/whatsnew/dimon.htm (accessed May 14, 2008).

9. Philip M. Rosenzweig and Andrall E. Pearson, "Primerica: Sandy Weill and His Corporate Entrepreneurs," Boston: Harvard Business School, November 30, 1992.

10. Weill and Kraushaar, *Real Deal.*

11. Rosenzweig and Pearson, "Primerica."

12. Carol J. Loomis and Nancy J. Perry, "Sanford Weill, 53, Exp'd Mgr, Gd Refs," *Fortune*, May 12, 1986.

13. Weill and Kraushaar, *Real Deal.*

14. Dimon, Kellogg School of Management, 2002.

15. Ibid.

16. Weill and Kraushaar, *Real Deal.*

17. Julie Connelly and Reed Abelson, "The Return of Second-Hand Rose," *Fortune*, October 24, 1986.

18. Ibid.

19. Rosenzweig and Pearson, "Primerica."

20. Dimon, Kellogg School of Management, 2002.

21. Kurt Eichenwald, "Company Earnings; Gains on Wall St. Swell Primerica's Profit," *New York Times*, October 15, 1991, http://query.nytimes.com/gst/fullpage.html?res=9D0CE4D81238F936A25753C1A967958260.

Chapter 4   A Force on Wall Street

1. Kurt Eichenwald, "Business People: President of Primerica Surprised by Promotion," *New York Times*, September 26, 1991, http://query.nytimes.com/gst/fullpage.html?res=9D0CEFDE1239F935A1575AC0A967958260&scp=3&sq=Zarb%20and%20Dimon&st=cse.

2. Ibid.

3. Ibid.

4. Jamie Dimon, presentation at Kellogg School of Management, Northwestern University, October 4, 2002, www.kellogg.northwestern.edu/news/whatsnew/dimon.htm (accessed May 14, 2008).

5. Monica Langley, *Tearing Down the Walls: How Sandy Weill Fought His Way to the Top of the Financial World . . . and Then Nearly Lost It All* (New York: Wall Street Journal Books/Simon & Schuster, 2003).

6. Leah Nathans Spiro, "Smith Barney's Whiz Kid: Can Jamie Dimon Turn Smith Barney into a Wall Street Dynamo?" *BusinessWeek*, October 21, 1996, www.businessweek.com/1996/43/b3498153.htm.

7. Sarah Bartlett, "Company News: Smith Barney to Get 16 of Drexel's Offices," *New York Times*, April 26, 1989, http://query.nytimes.com/gst/fullpage.html?res=950DE6D81338F935A15757C0A96F948260&sec=&spon=&&scp=2&sq=Primerica%20and%20Drexel%20&st=cse.

8. Stephen LaBaton, "American Express in Reversal," *New York Times*, March 5, 1990, http://query.nytimes.com/gst/fullpage.html?res=9C0CE1D81039F936A35750C0A966958260&sec=&spon=&&scp=5&sq=Primerica%20and%20American%20Express%20&st=cse.

9. Sandy Weill and Judah S. Kraushaar, *The Real Deal: My Life in Business and Philanthropy* (New York: Warner Business Books, 2006).

10. Ibid.

11. Adam Bryant, "Primerica to Invest $722 Million in Travelers," *New York Times*, September 21, 1992, http://query.nytimes.com/gst/fullpage.html?res=9E0CE2DB143CF932A1575AC0A964958260&scp=1&sq=Primerica%20and%20Travelers%20and%2027%20percent&st=cse.

12. Langley, *Tearing Down the Walls*.

13. Michael Quint, "Primerica Will Buy Shearson for $1 Billion," *New York Times*, March 13, 1993, http://query.nytimes.com/gst/fullpage.html?res=9F0CE0D8143AF930A25750C0A965958260&sec=&spon=&pagewanted=2.

14. Allen Myerson, "Deal Maker Picked to Run Smith Barney Shearson," *New York Times*, June 25, 1993, http://query.nytimes.com/gst/fullpage.html?res=9F0CEFDF173BF936A15755C0A965958260&scp=1&sq=Deal%20Maker%20and%20Smith%20Barney%20Shearson%20&st=cse.

15. Stephanie Strom, "Smith Barney Unit Is Shaken by Infighting," *New York Times*, March 23, 1995, http://query.nytimes.com/gst/fullpage.html?res=990CE7DA1739F930A15750C0A963958260&scp=1&sq=Smith%20Barney%20Unit%20Shaken%20by%20Infighting&st=cse.

16. Peter Truell, "Becoming His Own Man," *New York Times*, July 13, 1995, http://query.nytimes.com/gst/fullpage.html?res=990CE5D81431F930A25754C0A963958260.

17. Ibid.

18. Stephanie Strom, "Smith Barney Reassigns Its Research Chief," *New York Times*, October 21, 1995, http://query.nytimes.com/gst/fullpage.html?res=990CE0DF113CF932A15753C1A963958260&scp=1&sq=Smith%20Barney%20Reassigns&st=cse.

19. Dimon, Kellogg School of Management, 2002.

20. Langley, *Tearing Down the Walls*.

21. Spiro, "Smith Barney's Whiz Kid."

22. Langley, *Tearing Down the Walls*.

23. Weill and Kraushaar, *Real Deal*.

24. Langley, *Tearing Down the Walls*.

25. Edward Wyatt, "Smith Barney's Chief of Funds Quits for Post at Small Firm," *New York Times*, June 14, 1997, http://query.nytimes.com/gst/fullpage .html?res=9D03E6D7153FF937A25755C0A961958260.

26. Jonathan Fuerbringer, "Upheaval at Salomon: Suddenly, an Outsider Becomes 'Mr. Inside,'" *New York Times*, August 19, 1991, http://query.nytimes.com/gst/ fullpage.html?res=9D0CE2DC143CF93AA2575BC0A967958260&sec=&sp on=&pagewanted=1.

27. Peter Truell, "A Wall Street Behemoth: The Deal; Travelers to Buy Salomon, Making a Wall St. Giant," September 25, 1997, http://query.nytimes.com/ gst/fullpage.html?res=9803E6D81E3BF936A1575AC0A961958260.

28. Jeffrey Laderman, "Dimon and Maughan: How Long Can These Two Tango?" *BusinessWeek*, October 6, 1997, www.businessweek.com/1997/40/b3547006 .htm.

29. Jamie Dimon, Kellogg School of Management, Northwestern University, Speaker Video Archive, January 9, 2006, www.kellogg.northwestern.edu/ news/video/archive.htm (accessed September 13, 2008).

30. Langley, *Tearing Down the Walls*.

31. Timothy O'Brien and Joseph Treaster, "Shaping a Colossus: The Overview; In Largest Deal Ever, Citicorp Plans Merger with Travelers Group," *New York Times*, April 7, 1998, http://query.nytimes.com/gst/fullpage.html?res=9800E 1DA1E3AF934A35757C0A96E958260&sec=&spon=&pagewanted=3.

32. Quoted in speech by SEC Chairman Christopher Cox, "Gramm-Leach-Bliley Seven Years Later," Securities and Exchange Commission, September 21, 2006, www.sec.gov/news/speech/2006/spch092106cc.htm.

33. Richard Bookstaber, *A Demon of Our Own Design: Markets, Hedge Funds, and the Perils of Financial Innovation* (Hoboken, NJ: John Wiley & Sons, 2007).

34. Peter Truell, "Salomon Set to End Group on Arbitrage," The Markets, *New York Times*, July 7, 1998, http://query.nytimes.com/gst/fullpage .html?res=9A07EED8133EF934A35754C0A96E958260.

35. Ibid.

36. Bookstaber, *Demon*.

37. Timothy O'Brien and Peter Truell, "Downfall of a Peacemaker: Heir Apparent's Departure May Signal Strain at Citigroup," *New York Times*, November 3, 1998, http://query.nytimes.com/gst/fullpage.html?res=9807E2 D7103FF930A35752C1A96E958260&scp=1&sq=Downfall%20of%20a%20p eacemaker&st=cse.

38. Ibid.

Chapter 5   The Recruitment of Jamie Dimon

1. Michael Bloomberg, "Jamie Dimon," The 2008 *Time* 100: Builders & Titans, *Time*, www.time.com/time/specials/2007/time100/article/0,28804,1733748_ 1733758_1736192,00.html (accessed August 7, 2008).

2. Jamie Dimon, presentation at Kellogg School of Management, Northwestern University, October 4, 2002, www.kellogg.northwestern.edu/news/whatsnew/ dimon.htm (accessed May 14, 2008).

3. Paul W. Marshall and Todd Thedinga, "Jamie Dimon and Bank One (A)," Boston: Harvard Business School, 2003 (revised February 27, 2006).

4. David Barboza, "Bank One Again Warns about Profits," *New York Times*, November 11, 1999, http://query.nytimes.com/gst/fullpage.html?res=9C03 E4DA1E3AF932A25752C1A96F958260&scp=6&sq=%22Bank%20One%22 %20and%201999%20earnings%20&st=cse.

5. Marshall and Thedinga, "Dimon and Bank One."

6. Rakesh Khurana, *Searching for a Corporate Savior: The Irrational Quest for Charismatic CEOs* (Princeton, NJ: Princeton University Press, 2002).

7. Dimon, Kellogg School of Management, 2002.

8. Ibid.

9. Ibid.

10. Peter Eavis, "Bank One Bounces on News of Dimon's Appointment," *TheStreet.com*, March 27, 2009, www.thestreet.com/p/stocks/banking/ 907750.html.

11. "News Analysis: Can Jamie Dimon Make Bank One Welcome Again on Wall Street?" *BusinessWeek.com*, March 28, 2000, www.businessweek.com/bwdaily/ dnflash/mar2000/nf00328f.htm.

12. Carol J. Loomis, "Dimon Finds His 'Fat Pitch,' One Bank That Needs Saving," *Fortune*, April 17, 2000, http://money.cnn.com/magazines/fortune/fortune_ archive/2000/04/17/278065/index.htm.

13. Dimon, Kellogg School of Management, 2002.

14. Daniel Eisenberg, "Dimon Polishes Bank One," *Time*, November 3, 2002.

15. Jamie Dimon, Kellogg School of Management, Northwestern University, Speaker Video Archive, January 9, 2006, www.kellogg.northwestern.edu/ news/video/archive.htm (accessed September 13, 2008).

16. Dimon, Kellogg School of Management, 2002.

17. Ibid.

18. Ibid.

19. Ibid.

Chapter 6 The Turnaround of Bank One

1. Jamie Dimon, presentation at Kellogg School of Management, Northwestern University, October 4, 2002, www.kellogg.northwestern.edu/news/whatsnew/dimon.html (accessed May 14, 2008).

2. Ibid.

3. Shawn Tully, "The Jamie Dimon Show," *Fortune*, July 22, 2002, www2.una.edu/sborah/Prinman/bone702.htm.

4. Angela Key, "Dimon in the Rough, the Problem Solver," *Fortune*, June 26, 2000, http://money.cnn.com/magazines/fortune/fortune_archive/2000/06/26/282996/index.htm.

5. Paul W. Marshall and Todd Thedinga, "Jamie Dimon and Bank One (A)," Boston: Harvard Business School, 2003 (revised February 27, 2006).

6. Ibid.

7. Dimon, Kellogg School of Management, 2002.

8. Key, "Dimon in the Rough."

9. Bank One Annual Report, 2000.

10. Marshall and Thedinga, "Dimon and Bank One."

11. Dimon, Kellogg School of Management, 2002.

12. McGeehan, Patrick, "Market Place: Bank One Loss Fails to Scare Investors Away," The Markets, *New York Times*, July 20, 2000, http://query.nytimes.com/gst/fullpage.html?res=9D03E1DF1F3BF933A15754C0A9669C8B63&scp=1&sq=Bank%20One%202000%20loss&st=cse.

13. Ibid.

14. Bank One Annual Report, 2000.

15. Ibid.

16. Ibid.

17. Ibid.

18. Dimon, Kellogg School of Management, 2002.

19. Bank One Annual Report, 2000.

20. Dimon, Kellogg School of Management, 2002.

21. Bank One Annual Report, 2000.

22. Dimon, Kellogg School of Management, 2002.

23. Bank One Annual Report, 2000.

24. Joseph Weber, "Bank One, Take Two," *BusinessWeek*, October 29, 2001, www.businessweek.com/magazine/content/01_44/b3755091.htm.

25. Bank One Annual Report, 2001.

26. Ibid.

27. "Morningstar Names Bank One's Dimon as 2002 CEO of the Year," Morningstar, Inc., http://corporate.morningstar.com/us/asp/subject.aspx? xmlfile=426.xml&filter=PR4043.

28. Bank One Annual Report, 2003.

Chapter 7   Back on Wall Street

1. Jamie Dimon, Kellogg School of Management, Northwestern University, Speaker Video Archive, January 9, 2006, www.kellogg.northwestern.edu/ news/video/archive.htm (accessed September 13, 2008).

2. "J.P. Morgan Chase CEO Jamie Dimon Lists Chicago Mansion for $13.5 Million, Pays $17.05 Million for House in Bedford Corners, NY," BergProperties.com, May 4, 2007, www.bergproperties.com/blog/jp-morgan-chase-ceo-jamie-dimon-lists-chicago-mansion-for-135-million-pays-1705-million-for-house-in-bedford-corners-ny/601/chicago.

3. Shawn Tully, "The Deal Maker and the Dynamo," *Fortune*, February 9, 2004, http://money.cnn.com/magazines/fortune/fortune_archive/2004/02/09/36 0092/index.htm.

4. Ibid.

5. "History of JPMorgan Chase, 1799 to Present," JPMorgan.com, www.jpmorgan .com/cm/BlobServer?blobtable=Document&blobcol=urlblob&blobkey= name&blobheader=application/pdf&blobwhere=jpmc/about/history/ shorthistory.pdf.

6. Ron Chernow, *The House of Morgan: An American Banking Dynasty and the Rise of Modern Finance* (New York: Grove Press, 1990).

7. "J.P. Morgan Chairman Warner to Retire," Reuters, September 26, 2001, www.usatoday.com/money/finance/2001-09-26-morgan-retirement.htm.

8. Riva D. Atlas, "Chase and J.P. Morgan's Paper Anniversary: A Year after the Merger, Rosy Plans Meet Reality," *New York Times*, November 23, 2001, http://query.nytimes.com/gst/fullpage.html?res=9D02EFD7143AF930A15752 C1A9679C8B63&scp=1&sq=Chase%20and%20J.P.%20Morgan's% 20Paper%20Anniversary&st=cse.

9. "SEC Settles Enforcement Proceedings against J.P. Morgan Chase and Citigroup," Securities and Exchange Commission, July 28, 2003, www.sec .gov/news/press/2003-87.htm.

10. JPMorgan Chase & Co. Annual Report, 2003.

11. Tully, "Deal Maker."

12. Ibid.

13. Landon Thomas Jr., "The Yin, the Yang, and the Deal," *New York Times*, June 27, 2004, www.nytimes.com/2004/06/27/business/yourmoney/27dimon.html.

14. JPMorgan Chase Annual Report, 2004.

15. Greg Farrell, "Dimon Adds Sparkle to JPMorgan Chase," *USA Today*, November 28, 2005, www.usatoday.com/money/companies/management/2005-11-28-dimon_x.htm.

16. Dimon, Kellogg School of Management, 2006.

17. Shawn Tully, "In This Corner! The Contender," *Fortune*, March 29, 2006, http://money.cnn.com/magazines/fortune/fortune_archive/2006/04/03/8373068/index.htm.

18. Dimon, Kellogg School of Management, 2006.

19. Eric Dash, "Who Runs J.P. Morgan?" *New York Times*, October 20, 2005, www.nytimes.com/2005/10/20/business/20bank.html.

20. JPMorgan Chase Annual Report, 2005.

21. JPMorgan Chase Annual Report, 2006.

22. Shawn Tully, "How J.P. Morgan's CEO and His Crew Are Helping the Big Bank Beat the Credit Crunch," *Fortune*, September 15, 2008.

23. JPMorgan Chase Annual Report, 2006.

24. Michiyo Nakamoto and David Wighton, "Citigroup Chief Stays Bullish on Buy-Outs," *Financial Times*, July 9, 2007, www.ft.com/cms/s/0/80e2987a-2e50-11dc-821c-0000779fd2ac.html.

25. Louise Story, "Merrill's Chief Defends Recent Sale," *New York Times*, August 5, 2008, www.nytimes.com/2008/08/05/business/05merrill.html?_r=1&scp=2&sq=Merrill%20Lynch%20and%20CDO&st=cse.

Chapter 8 The Dimon Fortress

1. Maria Der Hovanesian, "The World's Most Influential Companies: JPMorgan Chase," *BusinessWeek.com*, December 12, 2008, http://images.businessweek.com/ss/08/12/1211_most_influential/4.htm.

2. Peter Nulty, "Shopping for Regional Banks," *Fortune*, August 5, 1985, http://money.cnn.com/magazines/fortune/fortune_archive/1985/08/05/66221/index.htm.

3. Wachovia Corporation Annual Report, 2003. www.wachoviasec.com/pdfs/WB2003annualreport.pdf.

4. "Citi Concedes Wachovia to Wells Fargo," DealBook, *New York Times*, October 9, 2008, http://dealbook.blogs.nytimes.com/2008/10/09/citi-withdraws-from-wells-fargo-talks/?scp=3&sq=Wachovia%20and%20bankrupt&st=cse.

5. Colin Barr, "AIG Chief under Siege," *Fortune*, May 9, 2008, http://money .cnn.com/2008/05/09/news/newsmakers/aig.under.pressure.fortune/index .htm?postversion=2008050914.

6. Mary Sue Penn, "Jamie Dimon's Advice on Freak Economic Storms," *University of Chicago GSB News*, January 24, 2006, www.chicagogsb.edu/ news/2006-01-24_dimon_fireside.aspx.

7. Jamie Dimon, Kellogg School of Management, Northwestern University, Speaker Video Archive, January 9, 2006, www.kellogg.northwestern.edu/ news/video/archive.htm (accessed September 13, 2008).

8. Penn, "Dimon's Advice."

9. Jamie Dimon, interview by Charlie Rose, *Charlie Rose*, PBS, July 13, 2008.

10. JPMorgan Chase Annual Report, 2007.

11. Dimon, interview by Charlie Rose.

12. JPMorgan Chase, Perspective, "Building a Fortress Balance Sheet: Protect Your Bank's Financial Health While Positioning It for Growth," September 2008, www.chase.com/ccp/index.jsp?pg_name=ccpmapp/commercial/resource_ center/page/perspective_fortressbalance.

13. "Marshal Sebastien le Prestre de Vauban," Answers.com, www.answers.com/ topic/vauban (accessed October 4, 2008).

14. JPMorgan Chase, Perspective.

15. Dimon, interview by Charlie Rose.

16. JPMorgan Chase Annual Report, 2007.

17. Ibid.

18. Liz Moyer, "Dimon's Banking Magic," *Forbes*, October 17, 2007, www.forbes .com/home/wallstreet/2007/10/17/banking-jpmorgan-citigroup-biz-wallst- cx_lm_1017banks.html.

19. Grace Wong, "J.P. Morgan Profit Rises Despite Markdown," *CNNMoney.com*, October 17, 2007, http://money.cnn.com/2007/10/17/news/companies/ jpm_earnings/index.htm.

20. "JPMorgan Chase Reports Third-Quarter 2008 Net Income of $527 Million, or $0.11 per Share, Including Estimated Losses of $640 Million (After- Tax) or $0.18 per Share for Washington Mutual Merger-Related Items," JPMorganChase.com, October 15, 2008, http://investor.shareholder.com/ jpmorganchase/press/releases.cfm.

Chapter 9 Taking Over WaMu: A Sign of the Times

1. Madlen Read, "WaMu Becomes Biggest Bank to Fail in US History," Associated Press, September 26, 2008, http://news.yahoo.com/s/ap/20080926/ ap_on_bi_ge/washington_mutual_future.

2. Robin Sidel and Dan Fitzpatrick, "J.P. Morgan Bets on the Consumer," *Wall Street Journal*, September 27, 2008, http://online.wsj.com/article/ SB122243718542978849.html.

3. Alistair Barr, "Dimon Steers J.P. Morgan through Financial Storm," *MarketWatch.com*, December 4, 2008, www.marketwatch.com/news/story/ dimons-tactics-help-jp-morgan/story.aspx?guid=%7B7D289B2E%2D8623% 2D4050%2DA926%2D7F35C04D586B%7D&dist=msr_5.

4. Ibid.

5. Robin Sidel, David Enrich, and Dan Fitzpatrick, "WaMu Is Seized, Sold Off to J.P. Morgan, in Largest Failure in U.S. Banking History," *Wall Street Journal*, September 26, 2008, http://online.wsj.com/article/SB122238415586576687 .html.

6. Sandra Goldschneider, "Corporate Update: A Sweet Deal for JP Morgan; Hold," UBS Securities, September 26, 2008.

7. Washington Mutual Annual Report, 2007.

8. Eric Dash, "Washington Mutual Acts to Shore Up Stock," *New York Times*, September 11, 2008, www.nytimes.com/2008/09/12/business/12bank .html?scp=50&sq=Washington%20Mutual&st=cse.

9. Office of Thrift Supervision, "Washington Mutual Acquired by JPMorgan Chase," September 25, 2008, www.ots.treas.gov/?p=PressReleases&ContentRecord_id= 9c306c81-1e0b-8562-eb0c-fed5429a3a56.

10. Federal Deposit Insurance Corporation, Forum on Mortgage Lending, July 8, 2008, www.vodium.com/MediapodLibrary/index.asp?library=pn100472_ fdic_advisorycommittee&SessionArgs=0A1U0100000100000101.

11. Peter S. Goodman and Gretchen Morgenson, "By Saying Yes, WaMu Built Empire on Shaky Loans," *New York Times*, December 27, 2008, http://www .nytimes.com/2008/12/28/business/28wamu.html?hp.

12. Ibid.

13. Jamie Dimon, Kellogg School of Management, Northwestern University, Speaker Video Archive, January 9, 2006, www.kellogg.northwestern.edu/ news/video/archive.htm (accessed September 13, 2008).

14. CNBC.com, "CNBC Exclusive: CNBC Transcript: CNBC'S Erin Burnett Interviews JP Morgan Chase Chairman & CEO Jamie Dimon on 'Street Signs' Today at 2:00 PM," December 11, 2008, www.cnbc .com/id/28182805/print/1/displaymode/1098.

15. Jon Hilsenrath, Damian Paletta, and Aaron Lucchetti, "Goldman, Morgan Scrap Wall Street Model, Become Banks in Bid to Ride Out Crisis," *Wall Street Journal*, September 22, 2008, http://online.wsj.com/article/ SB122202739111460721.html?mod=crnews.

16. Henry M. Paulson, interview by Charlie Rose, CharlieRose.com, October 21, 2008, www.charlierose.com/guests/henry-paulson.

17. Paulson, interview by Charlie Rose.

18. CNBC exclusive.

19. Yale School of Management, "JPMorgan's Jamie Dimon and Verizon's Ivan Seidenberg, Recognized as Legends of Leadership at Yale CEO Summit," December 10, 2008, http://mba.yale.edu/news_events/CMS/Articles/6733.shtml.

20. David Enrich and Dan Fitzpatrick, "Parsons Named Citi Chairman," *Wall Street Journal*, January 22, 2009, http://online.wsj.com/article/SB123257364537303599 .html.

21. Ron Chernow, *The House of Morgan: An American Banking Dynasty and the Rise of Modern Finance* (New York: Grove Press, 1990).

Chapter 10 Navigating Financial Storms

1. Richard Bookstaber, *A Demon of Our Own Design: Markets, Hedge Funds, and the Perils of Financial Innovation* (Hoboken, NJ: John Wiley & Sons, 2007).

2. Michiyo Nakamoto and David Wighton, "Citigroup Chief Stays Bullish on Buy-Outs," *Financial Times*, July 9, 2007, www.ft.com/cms/s/0/80e2987a-2e50-11dc-821c-0000779fd2ac.html.

3. Markus K. Brunnermeier, "Deciphering the Liquidity and Credit Crunch 2007–08," *Journal of Economic Perspectives* 23, no. 1 (2009).

4. Federal Reserve Board, Testimony of Chairman Alan Greenspan, "Monetary Policy and the Economic Outlook," before the Joint Economic Committee, U.S. Congress, April 17, 2002, www.federalreserve.gov/boarddocs/testimony/ 2002/20020417/default.htm.

5. Brunnermeier, "Deciphering."

6. Ibid.

7. Carrick Mollenkamp, Serena Ng, Liam Pleven, and Randall Smith, "Behind AIG's Fall, Risk Models Failed to Pass Real-World Test," *Wall Street Journal*, October 31, 2008, http://online.wsj.com/article/SB122538449722784635.html.

8. JPMorgan Chase Annual Report, 2007.

9. FDIC.gov, Remarks by Sheila C. Bair, Chairman, Federal Deposit Insurance Corporation, on "The Future of Mortgage Finance," at the 2008 Annual Meeting, National Association for Business Economics, Washington, D.C., October 6, 2008, www.fdic.gov/news/news/speeches/chairman/spoct0608.html.

10. Federal Deposit Insurance Corporation, Forum on Mortgage Lending, July 8, 2008, www.vodium.com/MediapodLibrary/index.asp?library=pn100472_ fdic_advisorycommittee&SessionArgs=0A1U0100000100000101.

11. Ibid.

12. Charles R. Morris, *Money, Greed, and Risk: Why Financial Crises and Crashes Happen* (New York: Crown Business, 1999).

13. Federal Reserve Board, Chairman Ben S. Bernanke, "Developments in the Financial Markets," Testimony before the Committee on Banking, Housing, and Urban Affairs, U.S. Senate, April 3, 2008, www.federalreserve.gov/newsevents/testimony/bernanke20080403a.htm.

14. Tobias Adrian and Markus K. Brunnermeier, "CoVaR," www.princeton.edu/~markus/research/papers/CoVaR.

15. Christopher Cox, "Swapping Secrecy for Transparency," Op-Ed, *New York Times*, October 18, 2008, www.nytimes.com/2008/10/19/opinion/19cox.html?_r=1&scp=1&sq=%22Credit%20Default%20Swaps%22%20and%20Christopher-Cox&st=cse&oref=slogin.

16. Financial Services Roundtable, "The Blueprint for U.S. Financial Competitiveness," www.fsround.org/cec/pdfs/FINALExecutiveSummaryCompetitivenessReport.pdf (accessed November 5, 2008).

17. FDIC Forum.

18. Joseph A. Giannone, "Lazard CEO Says Wall St Leverage Fueled Bubble," Reuters, June 4, 2008, www.reuters.com/articlePrint?articleID= USN0441657420080604.

19. Eric Dash, "Dennis Weatherstone, Banking Sage, Dies at 77," *New York Times*, June 18, 2008, www.nytimes.com/2008/06/18/business/18weatherstone.html?scp=1&sq=%22Dennis%20Weatherstone,%20Banking%20Sage%22&st=cse.

Chapter 11 A Wall Street Statesman

1. "Wall Street Mogul, Jamie Dimon, A78, Awarded Light on the Hill," Tufts University, April 14, 2006, www.tufts.edu/alumni/06-n-archive/n-dimond.htm.

2. Jamie Dimon, interview by Charlie Rose, *Charlie Rose*, PBS, July 13, 2008.

3. Federal Deposit Insurance Corporation, Forum on Mortgage Lending, July 8, 2008, www.vodium.com/MediapodLibrary/index.asp?library=pn100472_fdic_advisorycommittee&SessionArgs=0A1U0100000100000101.

4. Jamie Dimon, presentation at Kellogg School of Management, Northwestern University, October 4, 2002, www.kellogg.northwestern.edu/news/whatsnew/dimon.htm (accessed May 14, 2008).

5. Ibid.

6. Shawn Tully, "In This Corner! The Contender," *Fortune*, March 29, 2006, http://money.cnn.com/magazines/fortune/fortune_archive/2006/04/03/8373068/index.htm.

7. Dimon, interview by Charlie Rose.

About the Author

Patricia Crisafulli is an accomplished writer and author who has written or ghostwritten more than 15 books, including one previous nonfiction book of her own. A former business journalist, Ms. Crisafulli was a correspondent and deputy equities editor in the Chicago bureau of Reuters America. Her articles appeared in the *New York Times*, *Chicago Tribune*, *Boston Globe*, and other prestigious national newspapers. Her previously published works include creative essays on Africa, Berlin, and Switzerland published in the *Christian Science Monitor*. In addition, she has written articles for the Leisure & Arts page of the *Wall Street Journal*. To learn more about Ms. Crisafulli, see her web site at www.PatriciaCrisafulli.com.

Index